Building AI Applications with ChatGPT APIs

Master ChatGPT, Whisper, and DALL-E APIs by building ten innovative AI projects

Martin Yanev

BIRMINGHAM—MUMBAI

Building AI Applications with ChatGPT APIs

Copyright © 2023 Packt Publishing

All rights reserved. No part of this book may be reproduced, stored in a retrieval system, or transmitted in any form or by any means, without the prior written permission of the publisher, except in the case of brief quotations embedded in critical articles or reviews.

Every effort has been made in the preparation of this book to ensure the accuracy of the information presented. However, the information contained in this book is sold without warranty, either express or implied. Neither the author, nor Packt Publishing or its dealers and distributors, will be held liable for any damages caused or alleged to have been caused directly or indirectly by this book.

Packt Publishing has endeavored to provide trademark information about all of the companies and products mentioned in this book by the appropriate use of capitals. However, Packt Publishing cannot guarantee the accuracy of this information.

Group Product Manager: Niranjan Naikwadi
Publishing Product Manager: Tejashwini R
Book Project Manager: Sonam Pandey
Senior Editor: Aamir Ahmed
Technical Editor: Simran Ali
Copy Editor: Safis Editing
Proofreader: Safis Editing
Indexer: Manju Arasan
Production Designer: Shyam Sundar Korumilli
DevRel Marketing Coordinator: Vinishka Kalra

First published: September 2023

Production reference: 1010923

Published by Packt Publishing Ltd.
Grosvenor House
11 St Paul's Square
Birmingham
B3 1RB, UK.

ISBN 978-1-80512-756-7

www.packtpub.com

To my girlfriend, Xhulja Kola, for being my loving partner throughout our joint life journey. To my grandma, Maria, whose unwavering support and boundless love have shaped me into the person I am today. To my parents, Plamen and Zhana, who have been my pillars of strength.

– Martin Yanev

Contributors

About the Author

Martin Yanev is a highly accomplished software engineer with a wealth of expertise spanning diverse industries, including aerospace and medical technology. With an illustrious career of over 8 years, Martin has carved a niche for himself in developing and seamlessly integrating cutting-edge software solutions for critical domains such as air traffic control and chromatography systems.

Renowned as an esteemed instructor, Martin has empowered an impressive global community of over 280,000 students. His instructional prowess shines through as he imparts knowledge and guidance, leveraging his extensive proficiency in frameworks such as Flask, Django, Pytest, and TensorFlow. Possessing a deep understanding of the complete spectrum of OpenAI APIs, Martin exhibits mastery in constructing, training, and fine-tuning AI systems.

Martin's commitment to excellence is exemplified by his dual master's degrees in aerospace systems and software engineering. This remarkable academic achievement underscores his unwavering dedication to both the practical and theoretical facets of the industry. With his exceptional track record and multifaceted skill set, Martin continues to propel innovation and drive transformative advancements in the ever-evolving landscape of software engineering.

About the Reviewers

Sourabh Sharma has been working at Oracle as a lead technical member where he is responsible for developing and designing the key components of the blueprint solutions. He was the key member of the team and designed architecture that is being used by various Oracle products. He has over 20 years of experience delivering enterprise products and applications for leading companies. His expertise lies in conceptualizing, modeling, designing, and developing N-tier and cloud-based applications, as well as leading teams. He has vast experience in developing microservice-based solutions and implementing various types of workflow and orchestration engines. He also believes in continuous learning and sharing knowledge through his books and training.

Sourabh has also worked on two other books: *Mastering Microservices with Java, Third Edition*, and *Modern API Development with Spring and Spring Boot, Second Edition*.

Arindam Ganguly is an experienced data scientist who has worked in the software development industry for more than 7 years. He has proven skill sets in developing and managing a number of software products, mainly in the field of data science and artificial intelligence. He is also a published author and has written a book, *Build and Deploy Machine Learning Solutions using IBM Watson*, which teaches how to build artificial intelligence applications using the popular IBM Watson toolkit.

Ashutosh Vishwakarma is the co-founder of a conversational AI company called *Verifast.tech*. He has developed multiple high-scale and ML-based systems over the past 8 years as a backend engineer and is currently working with the LLM ecosystem to build next-gen UX.

Table of Contents

Preface — xiii

Part 1: Getting Started with OpenAI APIs

1

Beginning with the ChatGPT API for NLP Tasks — 3

Technical Requirements	4	Setting Up Your Python Development Environment	12
The ChatGPT Revolution	4	Installing Python and the PyCharm IDE	12
Using ChatGPT from the Web	5	Setting Up a Python Virtual Environment	13
Creating an OpenAI Account	5	The pip Package Installer	15
ChatGPT Web Interface	7	Building a Python Virtual Environment from the Terminal	16
Getting Started with the ChatGPT API	8	A Simple ChatGPT API Response	16
Obtaining an API Key	8	Summary	21
API Tokens and Pricing	10		

2

Building a ChatGPT Clone — 23

Technical Requirements	24	Enhancing the ChatGPT Clone Design	31
Creating a ChatGPT Clone with Flask	24	Intercepting ChatGPT API Endpoints	33
Frontend HTML Generation	28	Summary	36

Part 2: Building Web Applications with the ChatGPT API

3

Creating and Deploying an AI Code Bug Fixing SaaS Application Using Flask 39

Technical Requirements	40	Using Text Areas and Containers	46
Performing Multiple ChatGPT API Requests	40	Testing the Code Bug Fixer App	51
Setting Up the Code Bug Fixer Project	41	Deploying the ChatGPT App to the Azure Cloud	54
Implementing the Code Bug Fixer Backend	44	Summary	59

4

Integrating the Code Bug Fixer Application with a Payment Service 61

Technical Requirements	62	Implementing the Usage Counters	71
Integrating Payments with Stripe	62	Adding Payments to a ChatGPT Application	74
Setting Up a SQL User Database	65	Building the Payments Page	74
Initializing a SQL Database	66	Confirming User Payments	80
Getting a Browser Fingerprint ID	68	Summary	83
Tracking Application Users	69		

5

Quiz Generation App with ChatGPT and Django 85

Technical Requirements	86	Running Your Django Application	98
Building a Django Project	86	Integrating ChatGPT and Django for Quiz Generation	100
Creating the Exam App Frame and Views	91	Building the Quiz Generation Text Area and Submit Button	100
Connecting Django Views and URLs	91	Creating ChatGPT API Views with Django	102
Developing Django Templates	93		

Storing and Downloading Generated Quizzes	107	Building the Download Quiz View	110
Saving the Quizzes in an SQLite Database	107	Designing the Download Template	112
		Summary	116

Part 3: The ChatGPT, DALL-E, and Whisper APIs for Desktop Apps Development

6

Language Translation Desktop App with the ChatGPT API and Microsoft Word — 121

Technical Requirements	122	Integrating Microsoft Word Text with the ChatGPT API	128
Integrating ChatGPT API with Microsoft Office	122	Translating a Word Text with ChatGPT 3.5 Turbo	129
Building a User Interface with Tkinter	125	Summary	134

7

Building an Outlook Email Reply Generator — 135

Technical Requirements	136	Accessing Email Data with the win32com Client	139
Passing Outlook Data to the ChatGPT API	136	Generating automatic email replies	143
Setting Up the Outlook Email	137	Summary	148

8

Essay Generation Tool with PyQt and the ChatGPT API — 151

Technical Requirements	152	Creating Essay Generation Methods with the ChatGPT API	159
Building a Desktop Application with PyQT	152	Controlling the ChatGPT API Tokens	162
Setting Up the Essay Generation Tool Project	153	Summary	165
Building the Application GUI with PyQt	154		

9

Integrating ChatGPT and DALL-E API: Build End-to-End PowerPoint Presentation Generator   167

Technical Requirements	168	Generating Art with the DALL-E API	175
Using DALL-E and the DALL-E API	168	Finalizing and Testing the AI Presentation Generator	177
Building PowerPoint Apps with the PPTX Python Framework	170	Summary	182

10

Speech Recognition and Text-to-Speech with the Whisper API   183

Technical Requirements	184	Application	188
Implementing Text Translation and Transcription with the Whisper API	184	Using PyDub for Longer Audio Inputs	191
Building a Voice Transcriber		Summary	193

Part 4: Advanced Concepts for Powering ChatGPT Apps

11

Choosing the Right ChatGPT API Model   197

Technical Requirements	198	Using Chat Completion Parameters	203
ChatGPT API Models – GPT-3, GPT-4, and Beyond	198	ChatGPT API Rate Limits	209
		Summary	211

12

Fine-Tuning ChatGPT to Create Unique API Models 213

Technical Requirements	214	Building and Using the Fine-Tuned Model	220
Fine-Tuning ChatGPT	214		
Fine-Tuned Model Dataset Preparation	216	Summary	225

Index 227

Other Books You May Enjoy 234

Preface

Hello there! The ChatGPT API is a powerful tool provided by OpenAI that enables developers to integrate the state-of-the-art ChatGPT language model into their own applications, allowing for interactive and dynamic conversational experiences through API calls. As the field of AI rapidly evolves, so does the demand for intelligent and interactive systems that can understand and respond to human language and generate creative visual content.

There are three main OpenAI APIs that can enable developers to harness the power of the Artificial Intelligence:

- **ChatGPT API**: Unleash human-like text generation capabilities
- **Whisper API**: Enhance speech recognition and text-to-speech capabilities
- **DALL-E API**: Dive into the world of AI-generated art

The aim of this book is to empower you, the reader, with the knowledge and skills required to leverage these powerful APIs effectively. Through a series of nine innovative AI projects, we will take you on a step-by-step journey toward becoming a proficient developer, capable of creating, deploying, and monetizing your own intelligent applications.

Throughout this book, you will gain practical experience in integrating ChatGPT with popular frameworks and tools, such as Flask, Django, Microsoft Office APIs, and PyQt. We will cover a wide range of NLP tasks, and you will learn how to build your very own ChatGPT clone and create an AI-powered code-bug-fixing SaaS application. Additionally, we will explore speech recognition, text-to-speech capabilities, language translation, and generating email replies and PowerPoint presentations.

Furthermore, I will teach you how to fine-tune your own ChatGPT model. ChatGPT API fine-tuning opens possibilities to create highly tailored and specialized AI applications. By fine-tuning the ChatGPT model, we can train it on specific datasets, allowing the AI to learn and adapt to specific domains, industries, or user requirements. This fine-tuning process enables the creation of AI applications with enhanced accuracy, improved relevance, and a deeper understanding of specific contexts.

In this era of the AI revolution, an abundance of opportunities awaits those with the skills to develop AI applications.

Who this book is for

This book is aimed at a diverse range of professionals, including programmers, entrepreneurs, students, and software enthusiasts, with the goal of providing best practices, tips, and tricks to build applications using the ChatGPT API. It's especially beneficial for beginner programmers, software developers who want to integrate AI technology, and web developers looking to create AI-powered web applications with ChatGPT.

This book is intended for three main target audience personas:

- **AI enthusiasts**: These individuals have a passion for AI and are eager to explore its practical applications. They may be hobbyists, students, or professionals from various backgrounds who want to gain a deeper understanding of AI technologies and leverage them to build innovative applications. This book will provide them with the necessary knowledge and hands-on experience to start their AI journey with the ChatGPT API.

- **Software developers**: Software developers, including both beginners and experienced professionals, who are interested in integrating AI capabilities into their applications will find this book valuable. They may be seeking to enhance their existing projects with AI-powered features, such as chatbots, sentiment analysis, or natural language understanding. By mastering the ChatGPT API, they can elevate their software development skills and deliver intelligent and conversational experiences to their users.

- **AI entrepreneurs**: Entrepreneurs looking to leverage the potential of AI and build AI-powered applications for business purposes will benefit from this book. Whether they want to create chat-based customer support systems, virtual assistants, or other AI-driven solutions, this book will guide them through the process of building self-sustaining applications. They will learn how to monetize their AI applications, integrate payment platforms, and deploy scalable SaaS solutions, enabling them to capitalize on the opportunities presented by the ChatGPT API.

Regardless of their background or expertise, these three target audiences will find practical guidance, real-world examples, and comprehensive instructions in this book to master the ChatGPT API and develop their own AI applications successfully.

What this book covers

Chapter 1, Beginning with the ChatGPT API for NLP Tasks, introduces ChatGPT and the ChatGPT API, guides you in setting up your Python environment and necessary downloads, and explores OpenAI account registration, API token usage, and the pricing model to utilize OpenAI APIs.

Chapter 2, Building a ChatGPT Clone, provides a step-by-step guide on designing a ChatGPT clone, covering backend development using the ChatGPT API, deploying the project locally, and designing the frontend using HTML, CSS, and basic JavaScript, offering a hands-on project to prepare you for the more advanced SaaS app development covered in subsequent chapters.

Chapter 3, Creating and Deploying an AI Code Bug Fixing SaaS Application Using Flask, guides you through building and deploying a robust SaaS app using the ChatGPT API. It shows you how to build a complete development cycle, from deployment to web hosting, enabling global usage. The app, leveraging ChatGPT, offers code debugging and error description, introducing a unique and valuable project.

Chapter 4, Integrating the Code Bug Fixer Application with a Payment Service, provides insights into integrating a payment service into a ChatGPT application, utilizing visitor tracking to implement a Stripe API-based payment mechanism. Readers will also gain knowledge on incorporating a basic database into their projects.

Chapter 5, Quiz Generation App with ChatGPT and Django, provides a comprehensive guide on integrating the ChatGPT API into Django, teaching you how to create Django pages and views with AI capabilities. You will learn how to build a Django project generating exam questions from study material and run it locally as a SaaS application.

Chapter 6, Language Translation Desktop App with ChatGPT API and Microsoft Word, guides you through utilizing the ChatGPT API for Microsoft Word text translation, while also teaching you how to package your Python script into a functional desktop application using Tkinter. It introduces the integration of the ChatGPT API with Microsoft Office automation tools, empowering you to create a custom text translation application.

Chapter 7, Building an Outlook Email Reply Generator, provides a practical guide to building an app that utilizes Outlook email data to generate personalized replies and prompt design.

Chapter 8, Essay Generation Tool with PyQt and ChatGPT API, provides you with a step-by-step guide on how to integrate the ChatGPT API with PyQt for desktop app development, and how to control API tokens from the app frontend.

Chapter 9, Integrating ChatGPT and DALL-E API: Build End-to-End PowerPoint Presentation Generator, provides a hands-on approach to integrating two AI APIs, ChatGPT and DALL-E, and creating an AI-generated PowerPoint presentation.

Chapter 10, Speech Recognition and Text-to-Speech with Whisper API, provides you with an overview of the Whisper API and guides you through a practical project to generate subtitles and translations using audio files.

Chapter 11, Choosing the Right ChatGPT API Model, provides an overview of ChatGPT API models and parameters, helping you to choose the best model for your project and understand the limitations of the models.

Chapter 12, Fine-Tuning ChatGPT to Create Unique API Models, provides an overview of fine-tuning the ChatGPT API model, along with a case study to illustrate how to use this process in a real-world application to reduce the cost of building AI applications.

To get the most out of this book

Before embarking on this book, it is important for you to have a fundamental understanding of Python programming and API concepts. Additionally, familiarity with the basics of frontend and backend technologies used in application development is highly recommended. This prerequisite knowledge will enhance your comprehension and enable you to fully grasp the concepts and examples presented throughout the book.

Software/hardware covered in the book	Operating system requirements
Python	Windows, macOS, or Linux
Django	Windows, macOS, or Linux
Flask	Windows, macOS, or Linux
PyQt	Windows, macOS, or Linux
OpenAI library	Windows, macOS, or Linux
Stripe	Windows, macOS, or Linux
Azure CLI	Windows, macOS, or Linux

Rest assured, this book provides comprehensive coverage of all the necessary installations, including Python and the PyCharm IDE. You will find step-by-step instructions and detailed explanations within the book to guide you through the installation process. By following the instructions provided, you will be able to set up your Python environment and PyCharm IDE with ease, ensuring a smooth journey through the book's content.

If you are using the digital version of this book, we advise you to type the code yourself or access the code from the book's GitHub repository (a link is available in the next section). Doing so will help you avoid any potential errors related to the copying and pasting of code.

I highly encourage you to actively engage with the applications being built in this book by experimenting with variable changes and observing the resulting impact on the app. This hands-on approach will provide a deeper understanding of how different variables affect the application's behavior. Furthermore, I urge you to leverage the knowledge gained from the book to embark on your own application-building journey. By using the applications from the book as a foundation, you can apply your newfound skills and creativity to develop your own unique applications, fostering a deeper mastery of the concepts covered.

Download the example code files

You can download the example code files for this book from GitHub at `https://github.com/PacktPublishing/Building-AI-Applications-with-ChatGPT-APIs`. If there's an update to the code, it will be updated in the GitHub repository.

We also have other code bundles from our rich catalog of books and videos available at `https://github.com/PacktPublishing/`. Check them out!

Conventions used

There are a number of text conventions used throughout this book.

`Code in text`: Indicates code words in text, database table names, folder names, filenames, file extensions, pathnames and user input. Here is an example: "Create a new file called `app.py`."

A block of code is set as follows:

```
response = openai.Completion.create(
    engine="text-davinci-003",
    prompt=question,
    max_tokens=1024,
    n=1,
    stop=None,
    temperature=0.8,
)
```

When we wish to draw your attention to a particular part of a code block, the relevant lines or items are set in bold:

```
answer = response["choices"][0]["text"]
print(answer)
```

Any command-line input or output is written as follows:

```
$ pip install openai
"What would you like to ask ChatGPT?
```

Bold: Indicates a new term, an important word, or words that you see on screen. For instance, words in menus or dialog boxes appear in **bold**. Here is an example: "Select the **Terminal** button from the **View** menu."

> Tips or important notes
> Appear like this.

Get in touch

Feedback from our readers is always welcome.

General feedback: If you have questions about any aspect of this book, email us at customercare@packtpub.com and mention the book title in the subject of your message.

Errata: Although we have taken every care to ensure the accuracy of our content, mistakes do happen. If you have found a mistake in this book, we would be grateful if you would report this to us. Please visit www.packtpub.com/support/errata and fill in the form.

Piracy: If you come across any illegal copies of our works in any form on the internet, we would be grateful if you would provide us with the location address or website name. Please contact us at copyright@packt.com with a link to the material.

If you are interested in becoming an author: If there is a topic that you have expertise in and you are interested in either writing or contributing to a book, please visit authors.packtpub.com.

Share Your Thoughts

Once you've read *Building AI Applications with ChatGPT APIs*, we'd love to hear your thoughts! Scan the QR code below to go straight to the Amazon review page for this book and share your feedback.

https://packt.link/r/180512756X

Your review is important to us and the tech community and will help us make sure we're delivering excellent quality content.

Download a free PDF copy of this book

Thanks for purchasing this book!

Do you like to read on the go but are unable to carry your print books everywhere? Is your eBook purchase not compatible with the device of your choice?

Don't worry, now with every Packt book you get a DRM-free PDF version of that book at no cost.

Read anywhere, any place, on any device. Search, copy, and paste code from your favorite technical books directly into your application.

The perks don't stop there, you can get exclusive access to discounts, newsletters, and great free content in your inbox daily

Follow these simple steps to get the benefits:

1. Scan the QR code or visit the link below

```
https://packt.link/free-ebook/9781805127567
```

2. Submit your proof of purchase
3. That's it! We'll send your free PDF and other benefits to your email directly

Part 1: Getting Started with OpenAI APIs

In the first part, encompassing two chapters, the focus is on providing a comprehensive overview of ChatGPT and its significance for **natural language processing** (NLP). We will discuss the fundamentals of ChatGPT, exploring its impact and usage in web applications, as well as introducing readers to the ChatGPT API. This part demonstrates the process of building a ChatGPT clone, which is a chatbot that utilizes OpenAI's language model to generate human-like responses to user input. The application will be built using Flask, a lightweight web framework for Python.

This part has the following chapters:

- *Chapter 1, Beginning with the ChatGPT API for NLP Tasks*
- *Chapter 2, Building a ChatGPT Clone*

1
Beginning with the ChatGPT API for NLP Tasks

Natural Language Processing (**NLP**) is an area of artificial intelligence that focuses on the interaction between computers and humans through natural language. Over the years, NLP has made remarkable progress in the field of language processing, and **ChatGPT** is one such revolutionary NLP tool that has gained significant popularity in recent years.

ChatGPT is an advanced AI language model developed by **OpenAI**, and it has been trained on a massive dataset of diverse texts, including books, articles, and web pages. With its ability to generate human-like text, ChatGPT has become a go-to tool for many NLP applications, including chatbots, language translation, and content generation.

In this chapter, we will explore the basics of ChatGPT and how you can use it for your NLP tasks. We will start with an introduction to ChatGPT and its impact on the field of NLP. Then we will explore how to use ChatGPT from the web and its benefits. Next, we will learn how to get started with the ChatGPT API, including creating an account and generating API keys. After that, we will take a walkthrough of setting up your development environment to work with the ChatGPT API. Finally, we will see an example of a simple ChatGPT API response to understand the basic functionalities of the tool.

In this chapter, we will cover the following topics:

- The ChatGPT Revolution.
- Using ChatGPT from the Web.
- Getting Started with the ChatGPT API.
- Setting Up Your Python Development Environment.
- A simple ChatGPT API Response.

By the end of this chapter, you will have a solid experience with ChatGPT and you will learn how to use it to perform NLP tasks efficiently.

Technical Requirements

To get the most out of this chapter, you will need some basic tools to work with the Python code and the ChatGPT APIs. This chapter will guide you through all software installations and registrations.

You will require the following:

- Python 3.7 or later installed on your computer
- An OpenAI API key, which can be obtained by signing up for an OpenAI account
- A code editor, such as **PyCharm** (recommended), to write and run Python code

The code examples from this chapter can be found on GitHub at https://github.com/PacktPublishing/Building-AI-Applications-with-ChatGPT-APIs/tree/main/Chapter01%20ChatGPTResponse.

The ChatGPT Revolution

ChatGPT is an advanced AI language model developed by OpenAI, and it has made a significant impact on the field of **natural language processing** (**NLP**). The model is based on the transformer architecture, and it has been trained on a massive dataset of diverse texts, including books, articles, and web pages.

One of the key features of ChatGPT is its ability to generate text that is coherent and contextually appropriate. In contrast to earlier NLP models, ChatGPT possesses a more extensive comprehension of language, and it can generate text that is similar in style and structure to human-generated text. This feature has made ChatGPT a valuable tool for various applications, including conversational AI and content creation.

ChatGPT has also made significant progress in the field of conversational AI, where it has been used to develop chatbots that can interact with humans naturally. With its ability to understand context and generate text that is similar in style to human-generated text, ChatGPT has become a go-to tool for developing conversational AI.

The emergence of **large language models** (**LLMs**) such as GPT-3 has revolutionized the landscape of chatbots. Prior to LLMs, chatbots were limited in their capabilities, relying on rule-based systems with predefined responses. These chatbots lacked contextual understanding and struggled to engage in meaningful conversations. However, with LLM-based chatbots, there has been a significant transformation. These models comprehend complex queries, generate coherent and nuanced responses, and possess a broader knowledge base. They exhibit improved contextual understanding, learn from user interactions, and continually enhance their performance. LLM-based chatbots have elevated the user experience by providing more natural and personalized interactions, showcasing the remarkable advancements in chatbot technology.

ChatGPT has a long and successful history in the field of NLP. The model has undergone several advancements over the years, including the following:

- GPT-1 (2018): Had 117 million parameters and was trained on a diverse set of web pages. It demonstrated impressive results in various NLP tasks, including question-answering, sentiment analysis, and language translation.
- GPT-2 (2019): Had 1.5 billion parameters and was trained on over 8 million web pages. It showed remarkable progress in language understanding and generation and became a widely used tool for various NLP applications.
- GPT-3 (2020): Had a record-breaking 175 billion parameters and set a new benchmark for language understanding and generation. It was used for various applications, including chatbots, language translation, and content creation.
- GPT-3.5: The latest version of the model, released after continued refinement and improvement by OpenAI.

GPT-4 can solve difficult problems with greater accuracy, thanks to its broader general knowledge and problem-solving abilities. Developers can harness the power of GPT models without requiring them to train their own models from scratch. This can save a lot of time and resources, especially for smaller teams or individual developers.

In the next section, you will learn how to use ChatGPT from the web. You will learn how to create an OpenAI account and explore the ChatGPT web interface.

Using ChatGPT from the Web

Interacting with ChatGPT via the OpenAI website is incredibly straightforward. OpenAI provides a web-based interface that can be found at `https://chat.openai.com`, enabling users to engage with the model without any prior coding knowledge or setup required. Once you visit the website, you can begin entering your questions or prompts, and the model will produce its best possible answer or generated text. Notably, ChatGPT Web also provides users with various settings and options that allow them to track the conversation's context and save the history of all interactions with the AI. This feature-rich approach to web-based AI interactions allows users to effortlessly experiment with the model's capabilities and gain insight into its vast potential applications. To get started with the web-based interface, you'll need to register for an account with OpenAI, which we will cover in detail in the next section. Once you've created an account, you can access the web interface and begin exploring the model's capabilities, including various settings and options to enhance your AI interactions.

Creating an OpenAI Account

Before using ChatGPT or the ChatGPT API, you must create an account on the OpenAI website, which will give you access to all the tools that the company has developed. To do that, you can visit `https://chat.openai.com`, where you will be asked to either log in or sign up for a new account, as shown in *Figure 1.1*:

Welcome to ChatGPT

Log in with your OpenAI account to continue

Log in   Sign up

Figure 1.1: OpenAI Welcome Window

Simply click the **Sign up** button and follow the prompts to access the registration window (see *Figure 1.2*). From there, you have the option to enter your email address and click **Continue**, or you can opt to register using your Google or Microsoft account. Once this step is complete, you can select a password and validate your email, just like with any other website registration process.

After completing the registration process, you can begin exploring ChatGPT's full range of features. Simply click the **Log in** button depicted in *Figure 1.1* and enter your credentials into the **Log In** window. Upon successfully logging in, you'll gain full access to ChatGPT and all other OpenAI products. With this straightforward approach to access, you can seamlessly explore the full capabilities of ChatGPT and see firsthand why it's become such a powerful tool for natural language processing tasks.

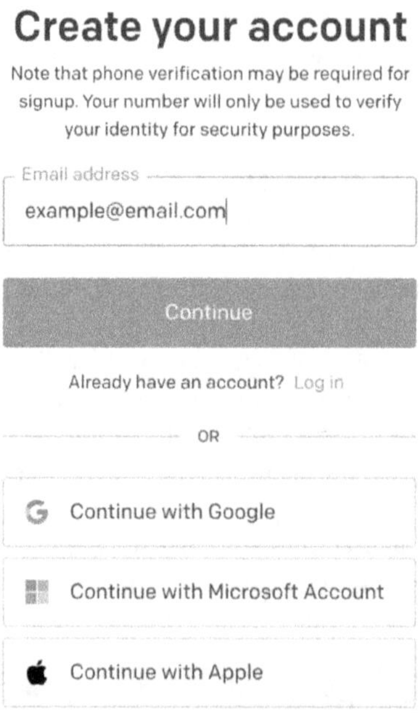

Figure 1.2: OpenAI Registration Window

Now we can explore the features and functionality of the ChatGPT web interface in greater detail. We'll show you how to navigate the interface and make the most of its various options to get the best possible results from the AI model.

ChatGPT Web Interface

The ChatGPT web interface allows users to interact with the AI model. Once a user registers for the service and logs in, they can enter text prompts or questions into a chat window and receive responses from the model. You can ask ChatGPT anything using the **Send a message…** text field. The chat window also displays previous messages and prompts, allowing users to keep track of the conversation's context, as shown in *Figure 1.3*:

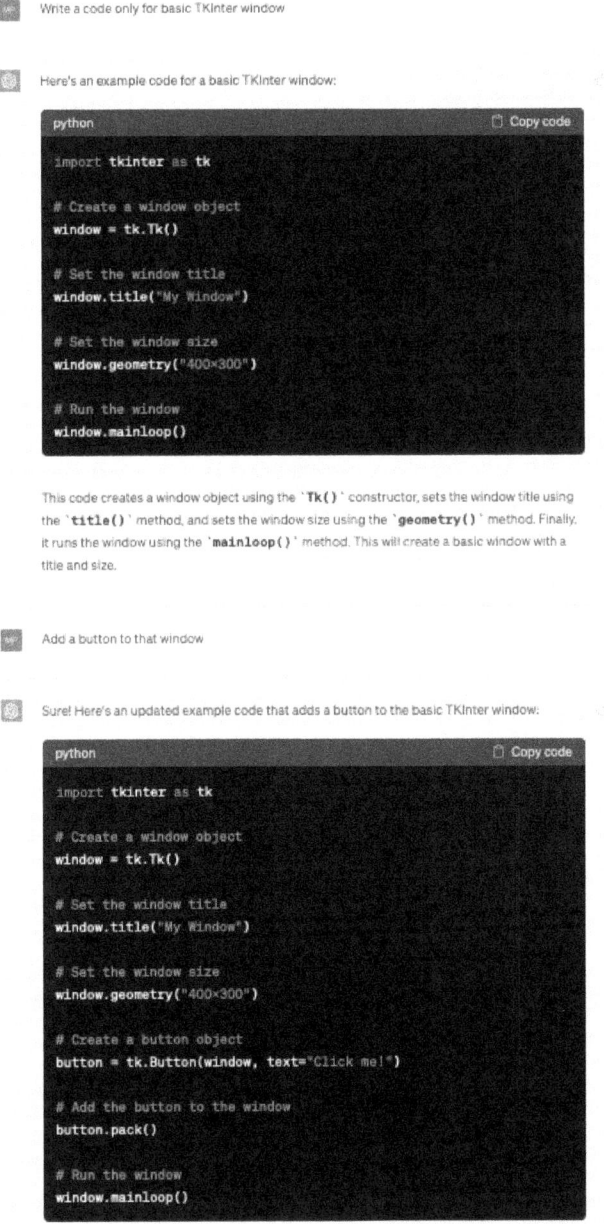

Figure 1.3: ChatGPT Following Conversational Context

In addition to that, ChatGPT allows users to easily record the history of their interactions with the model. Users' chat logs are automatically saved, which can later be accessed from the left sidebar for reference or analysis. This feature is especially useful for researchers or individuals who want to keep track of their conversations with the model and evaluate its performance over time. The chat logs can also be used to train other models or compare the performance of different models. You are now able to distinguish and use the advancements of different ChatGPT models. You can also use ChatGPT from the web, including creating an account and generating API keys. The ChatGPT API is flexible, customizable, and can save developers time and resources, making it an ideal choice for chatbots, virtual assistants, and automated content generation. In the next section, you will learn how to access the ChatGPT API easily using Python.

Getting Started with the ChatGPT API

The **ChatGPT API** is an application programming interface developed by OpenAI that allows developers to interact with **Generative Pre-trained Transformer** (**GPT**) models for natural language processing (NLP) tasks. This API provides an easy-to-use interface for generating text, completing prompts, answering questions, and carrying out other NLP tasks using state-of-the-art machine learning models.

The ChatGPT API is used for chatbots, virtual assistants, and automated content generation. It can also be used for language translation, sentiment analysis, and content classification. The API is flexible and customizable, allowing developers to fine-tune the model's performance for their specific use case. Let's now discover the process of obtaining an API key. This is the first step to accessing the ChatGPT API from your own applications.

Obtaining an API Key

To use the ChatGPT API, you will need to obtain an API key. This can be obtained from OpenAI. This key will allow you to authenticate your requests to the API and ensure that only authorized users can access your account.

To obtain an API key, you must access the OpenAI Platform at `https://platform.openai.com` using your ChatGPT credentials. The OpenAI Platform page provides a central hub for managing your OpenAI resources. Once you have signed up, you can navigate to the API access page: `https://platform.openai.com/account/api-keys`. On the API access page, you can manage your API keys for the ChatGPT API and other OpenAI services. You can generate new API keys, view and edit the permissions associated with each key, and monitor your usage of the APIs. The page provides a clear overview of your API keys, including their names, types, and creation dates, and allows you to easily revoke or regenerate keys as needed.

Click on the **+Create new secret key** button and your API key will be created:

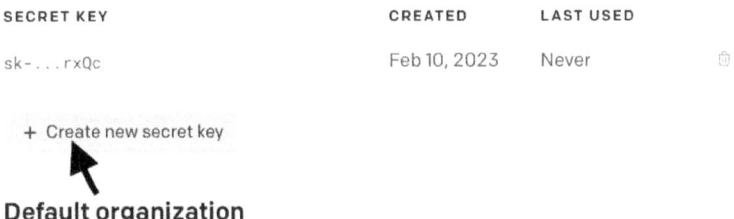

Figure 1.4: Creating an API Key

After creating your API key, you will only have one chance to copy it (see *Figure 1.5*). It's important to keep your API key secure and confidential, as anyone who has access to your key could potentially access your account and use your resources. You should also be careful not to share your key with unauthorized users and avoid committing your key to public repositories or sharing it in plain text over insecure channels.

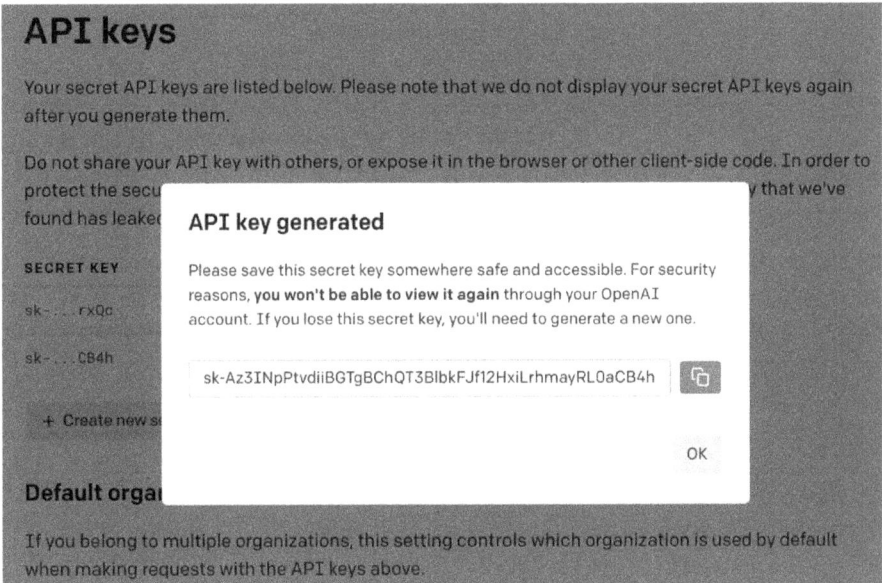

Figure 1.5: Saving an API Key

Copying and pasting the API key in our applications and scripts allows us to use the ChatGPT API. Now, let's examine the ChatGPT tokens and their involvement in the OpenAI pricing model.

API Tokens and Pricing

When working with ChatGPT APIs, it's important to understand the concept of tokens. Tokens are the basic units of text used by models to process and understand the input and output text.

Tokens can be words or chunks of characters and are created by breaking down the text into smaller pieces. For instance, the word *"hamburger"* can be broken down into *"ham,"* *"bur,"* and *"ger,"* while a shorter word such as *"pear"* is a single token. Tokens can also start with whitespace, such as *" hello"* or *" bye"*.

The number of tokens used in an API request depends on the length of both the input and output text. As a rule of thumb, one token corresponds to approximately 4 characters or 0.75 words in English text. It's important to note that the combined length of the text prompt and generated response must not exceed the maximum context length of the model. *Table 1.1* shows the token limits of some of the popular ChatGPT models.

MODEL	MAX TOKENS
gpt-4	8,192 tokens
gpt-4-32k	32,768 tokens
gpt-3.5-turbo	4,096 tokens
text-davinci-003	4,096 tokens

Table 1.1: API model token limits

To learn more about how text is translated into tokens, you can check out OpenAI's **Tokenizer** tool. The tokenizer tool is a helpful resource provided by OpenAI for understanding how text is translated into tokens. This tool breaks down text into individual tokens and displays their corresponding byte offsets, which can be useful for analyzing and understanding the structure of your text.

You can find the tokenizer tool at `https://platform.openai.com/tokenizer`. To use the tokenizer tool, simply enter the text you want to analyze and select the appropriate model and settings. The tool will then generate a list of tokens, along with their corresponding byte offsets (*see Figure 1.6*).

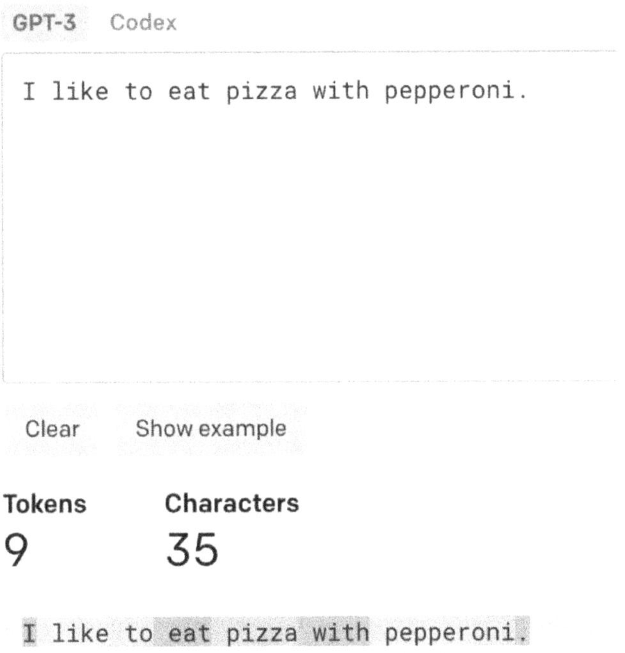

Figure 1.6: The Tokenizer Tool

The ChatGPT API pricing is structured such that you are charged per 1,000 tokens processed, with a minimum charge per API request. This means that the longer your input and output texts are, the more tokens will be processed and the higher the cost will be. *Table 1.2* displays the cost of processing 1,000 tokens for several commonly used ChatGPT models.

MODEL	PROMPT	COMPLETION
gpt-4	$0.03 / 1K tokens	$0.06 / 1K tokens
gpt-4-32k	$0.06 / 1K tokens	$0.12 / 1K tokens
gpt-3.5-turbo	$0.002 / 1K tokens	$0.002 / 1K tokens
text-davinci-003	$0.0200 / 1K tokens	$0.0200 / 1K tokens

Table 1.2: ChatGPT API Model Pricing

> **Important note**
> It is important to keep an eye on your token usage to avoid unexpected charges. You can track your usage and monitor your billing information through the **Usage** dashboard at `https://platform.openai.com/account/usage`.

As you can see, ChatGPT is has easy-to-use interface that allows developers to interact with GPT models for natural language processing tasks. Tokens are the basic units of text used by the models to process and understand the input and output text. The pricing structure for the ChatGPT API is based on the number of tokens processed, with a minimum charge per API request.

In the next section, we will cover how to set up the Python development environment for working with the ChatGPT API. This involves installing Python and the PyCharm IDE, setting up a virtual environment, and installing the necessary Python packages. Additionally, we will give you instructions on how to create a Python virtual environment using the built-in **venv** module and how to access the **Terminal** tab within PyCharm.

Setting Up Your Python Development Environment

Before we start writing our first code, it's important to create an environment to work in and install any necessary dependencies. Fortunately, Python has an excellent tooling system for managing virtual environments. Virtual environments in Python are a complex topic, but for the purposes of this book, it's enough to know that they are isolated Python environments that are separate from your global Python installation. This isolation allows developers to work with different Python versions, install packages within the environment, and manage project dependencies without interfering with Python's global installation.

In order to utilize the ChatGPT API in your NLP projects, you will need to set up your Python development environment. This section will guide you through the necessary steps to get started, including the following:

- Installing Python
- Installing the PyCharm IDE
- Installing pip
- Setting up a virtual environment
- Installing the required Python packages

A properly configured development environment will allow you to make API requests to ChatGPT and process the resulting responses in your Python code.

Installing Python and the PyCharm IDE

Python is a popular programming language that is widely used for various purposes, including machine learning and data analysis. You can download and install the latest version of Python from the official website, `https://www.python.org/downloads/`. Once you have downloaded the Python installer, simply follow the instructions to install Python on your computer. The next step is to choose an **Integrated Development Environment** (IDE) to work with (see *Figure 1.7*).

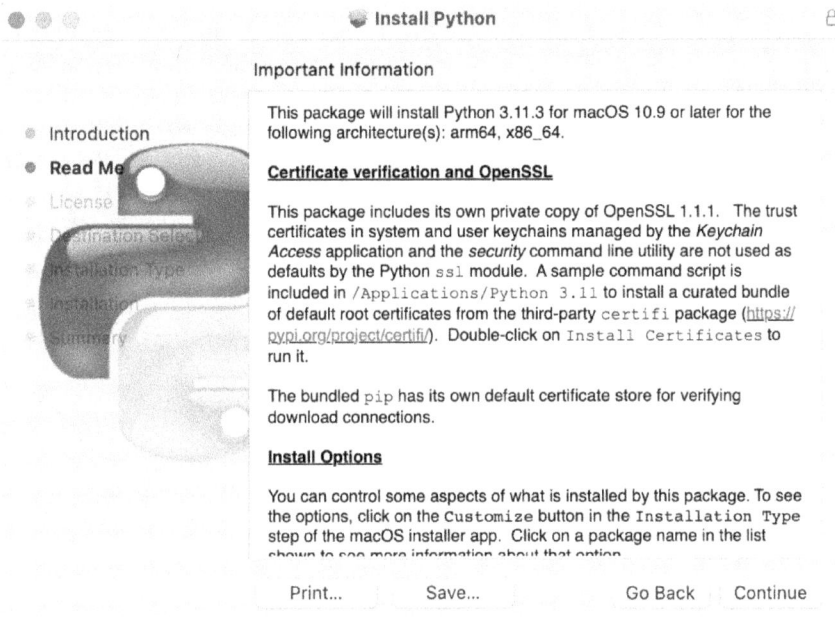

Figure 1.7: Python Installation

One popular choice among Python developers is PyCharm, a powerful and user-friendly IDE developed by JetBrains. PyCharm provides a wide range of features that make it easy to develop Python applications, including code completion, debugging tools, and project management capabilities.

To install PyCharm, you can download the Community Edition for free from the JetBrains website, `https://www.jetbrains.com/pycharm/download/`. Once you have downloaded the installer, simply follow the instructions to install PyCharm on your computer.

Setting Up a Python Virtual Environment

Setting up a Python virtual environment is a crucial step in creating an isolated development environment for your project. By creating a virtual environment, you can install specific versions of Python packages and dependencies without interfering with other projects on your system.

Creating a Python virtual environment specific to your ChatGPT application project is a recommended best practice. By doing so, you can ensure that all the packages and dependencies are saved inside your project folder rather than cluttering up your computer's global Python installation. This approach provides a more organized and isolated environment for your project's development and execution.

PyCharm allows you to set up the Python virtual environment directly during the project creation process. Once installed, you can launch PyCharm and start working with Python. Upon launching PyCharm, you will see the **Welcome Window**, and from there, you can create a new project. By doing so, you will be directed to the **New Project** window, where you can specify your desired project name

14   Beginning with the ChatGPT API for NLP Tasks

and, more importantly, set up your Python virtual environment. To do this, you need to ensure that **New environment using** is selected. This option will create a copy of the Python version installed on your device and save it to your local project.

As you can see from *Figure 1.8*, the **Location** field displays the directory path of your local Python virtual environment situated within your project directory. Beneath it, **Base interpreter** displays the installed Python version on your system. Clicking the **Create** button will initiate the creation of your new project.

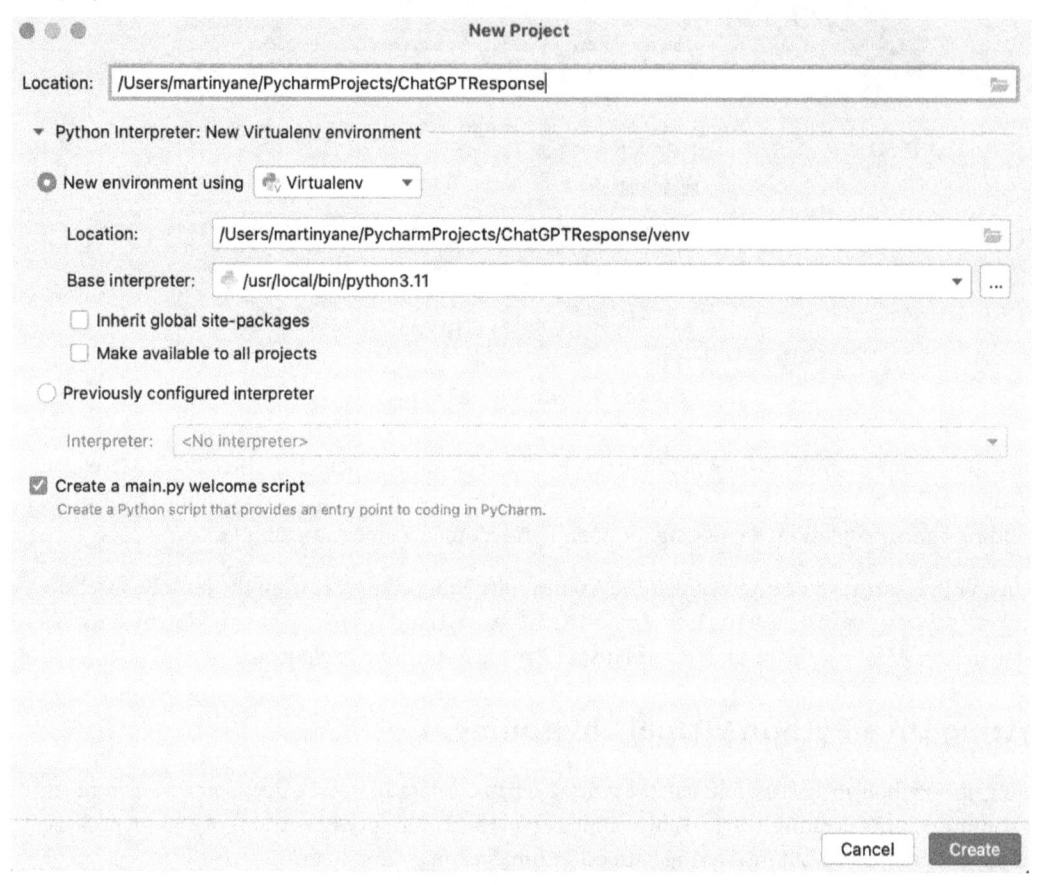

Figure 1.8: PyCharm Project Setup

Figure 1.9 displays the two main indicators showing that the Python virtual environment is correctly installed and activated. One of these indications is the presence of a venv folder within your PyCharm project, which proves that the environment is installed. Additionally, you should observe **Python 3.11 (ChatGPTResponse)** in the lower-right corner, confirming that your virtual environment has been activated successfully.

Setting Up Your Python Development Environment   15

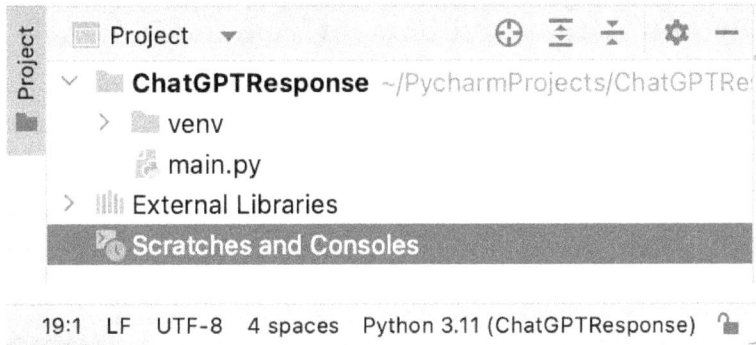

Figure 1.9: Python Virtual Environment Indications

A key component needed to install any package in Python is **pip**. Lets's see how to check whether pip is already installed on your system, and how to install it if necessary.

The pip Package Installer

pip is a package installer for Python. It allows you to easily install and manage third-party Python libraries and packages such as **openai**. If you are using a recent version of Python, **pip** should already be installed. You can check whether pip is installed on your system by opening a command prompt or terminal and typing `pip` followed by the *Enter* key. If **pip** is installed, you should see some output describing its usage and commands.

If **pip** is not installed on your system, you can install it by following these steps:

1. First, download the `get-pip.py` script from the official Python website: https://bootstrap.pypa.io/get-pip.py.
2. Save the file to a location on your computer that you can easily access, such as your desktop or downloads folder.
3. Open a command prompt or terminal and navigate to the directory where you saved the `get-pip.py` file.
4. Run the following command to install pip: `python get-pip.py`
5. Once the installation is complete, you can verify that pip is installed by typing `pip` into the command prompt or terminal and pressing *Enter*.

You should now have pip installed on your system and be able to use it to install packages and libraries for Python.

Building a Python Virtual Environment from the Terminal

Alternatively, to create a Python virtual environment, you can use the built-in `venv` module that comes with Python. Once you create your project in PyCharm, click on the **Terminal** tab located at the bottom of the screen. If you don't see the **Terminal** tab, you can open it by going to **View | Tool Windows | Terminal** in the menu bar. Then, run this command:

```
$ python3 -m venv myenv
```

This will create a new directory named `myenv` that contains the virtual environment. You can replace `myenv` with any name you want.

To activate the virtual environment, run the following command:

- On Windows:

  ```
  $ myenv\Scripts\activate.bat
  ```

- On macOS or Linux:

  ```
  $ source myenv/bin/activate
  ```

Once activated, you should see the name of the virtual environment in the command prompt or terminal. From here, you can install any packages or dependencies you need for your project without interfering with other Python installations on your system.

This was a complete guide on how to set up a Python development environment for using the ChatGPT API in NLP projects. The steps included installing Python, the PyCharm IDE, and `pip`, and setting up a virtual environment. Setting up a virtual environment was a crucial step in creating an isolated development environment for your project. You are now ready to complete your first practice exercise on using the ChatGPT API with Python to interact with the OpenAI library.

A Simple ChatGPT API Response

Using the ChatGPT API with Python is a relatively simple process. You'll first need to make sure you create a new PyCharm project called **ChatGPTResponse** (see *Figure 1.8*). Once you have that set up, you can use the OpenAI Python library to interact with the ChatGPT API. Open a new Terminal in PyCharm, make sure that you are in your project folder, and install the `openai` package:

```
$ pip install openai
```

Next, you need to create a new Python file in your PyCharm project. In the top-left corner, right-click on **ChatGPTResponse | New | Python File**. Name the file `app.py` and hit *Enter*. You should now have a new Python file in your project directory.

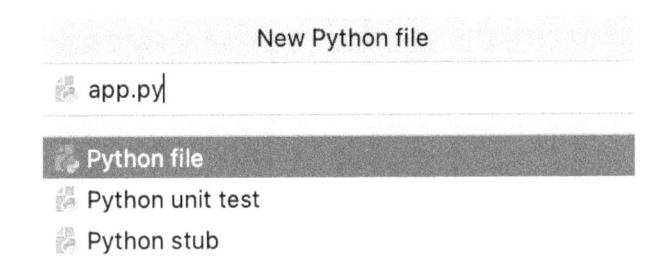

Figure 1.10: Create a Python File

To get started, you'll need to import the **openai** library into your Python file. Also, you'll need to provide your OpenAI API key. You can obtain an API key from the OpenAI website by following the steps outlined in the previous sections of this book. Then you'll need to set it as a parameter in your Python code. Once your API key is set up, you can start interacting with the ChatGPT API:

```
import openai
openai.api_key = "YOUR_API_KEY"
```

Replace YOUR_API_KEY with the API key you obtained from the OpenAI platform page. Now, you can ask the user for a question using the input() function:

```
question = input("What would you like to ask ChatGPT? ")
```

The input() function is used to prompt the user to input a question they would like to ask the ChatGPT API. The function takes a string as an argument, which is displayed to the user when the program is run. In this case, the question string is "What would you like to ask ChatGPT?". When the user types their question and presses *Enter*, the input() function will return the string that the user typed. This string is then assigned to the question variable.

To pass the user question from your Python script to ChatGPT, you will need to use the ChatGPT API Completion function:

```
response = openai.Completion.create(
    engine="text-davinci-003",
    prompt=question,
    max_tokens=1024,
    n=1,
    stop=None,
    temperature=0.8,
)
```

The openai.Completion.create() function in the code is used to send a request to the ChatGPT API to generate the completion of the user's input prompt. The engine parameter allows us to specify the specific variant or version of the GPT model we want to utilize for the request, and in this case, it is set to "text-davinci-003". The prompt parameter specifies the text prompt for the API to complete, which is the user's input question in this case.

The `max_tokens` parameter specifies the maximum number of tokens the request and the response should contain together. The `n` parameter specifies the number of completions to generate for the prompt. The `stop` parameter specifies the sequence where the API should stop generating the response.

The `temperature` parameter controls the creativity of the generated response. It ranges from 0 to 1. Higher values will result in more creative but potentially less coherent responses, while lower values will result in more predictable but potentially less interesting responses. Later in the book, we will delve into how these parameters impact the responses received from ChatGPT.

The function returns a **JSON object** containing the generated response from the ChatGPT API, which then can be accessed and printed to the console in the next line of code:

```
print(response)
```

In the project pane on the left-hand side of the screen, locate the Python file you want to run. Right-click on the `app.py` file and select **Run app.py** from the context menu. You should receive a message in the **Run** window that asks you to write a question to ChatGPT (see *Figure 1.11*).

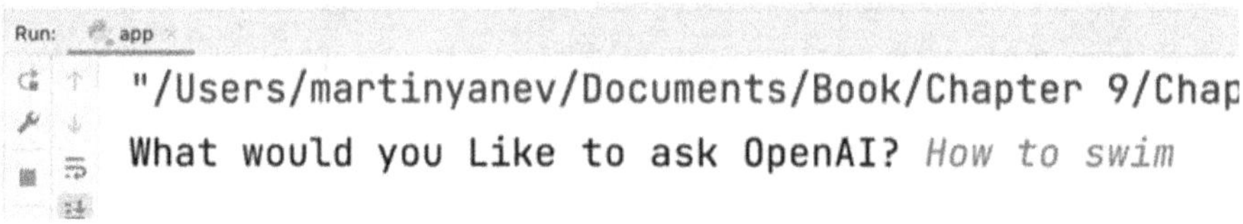

Figure 1.11: Asking ChatGPT a Question

Once you have entered your question, press the *Enter* key to submit your request to the ChatGPT API. The response generated by the ChatGPT API model will be displayed in the **Run** window as a complete JSON object:

```
{
  "choices": [
    {
      "finish_reason": "stop",
      "index": 0,
      "logprobs": null,
      "text": "\n\n1. Start by getting in the water. If you're swimming in a pool, you can enter the water from the side, ............ "
    }
  ],
  "created": 1681010983,
  "id": "cmpl-73G2JJCyBTfwCdIyZ7v5CTjxMiS6W",
  "model": "text-davinci-003",
  "object": "text_completion",
  "usage": {
```

```
      "completion_tokens": 415,
      "prompt_tokens": 4,
      "total_tokens": 419
   }
}
```

This JSON response produced by the OpenAI API contains information about the response generated by the GPT-3 model. This response consists of the following fields:

- The `choices` field contains an array of objects with the generated responses, which in this case only contains one response object as the parameter `n=1`.
- The `text` field within the response object contains the actual response generated by the GPT-3 model.
- The `finish_reason` field indicates the reason why the response was generated; in this case, it was because the model reached the **stop** condition provided in the request. Since in our case `stop=None`, the full response from the ChatGPT API was returned.
- The `created` field specifies the Unix timestamp of when the response was created.
- The `id` field is a unique identifier for the API request that generated this response.
- The `model` field specifies the GPT-3 model that was used to generate the response.
- The `object` field specifies the type of object that was returned, which in this case is `text_completion`.
- The `usage` field provides information about the resource usage of the API request. It contains information about the number of tokens used for the completion, the number of tokens in the prompt, and the total number of tokens used.

The most important parameter from the response is the `text` field, which contains the answer to the question asked to the ChatGPT API. This is why most API users would like to access only that parameter from the JSON object. You can easily separate the text from the main body as follows:

```
answer = response["choices"][0]["text"]
print(answer)
```

By following this approach, you can guarantee that the `answer` variable will hold the complete ChatGPT API text response, which you can then print to verify. Keep in mind that ChatGPT responses can significantly differ depending on the input, making each response unique.

OpenAI:

```
1. Start by getting in the water. If you're swimming in a pool, you
can enter the water from the side, ladder, or diving board. If you are
swimming in the ocean or lake, you can enter the water from the shore
or a dock.
```

```
2. Take a deep breath in and then exhale slowly. This will help you
relax and prepare for swimming.
```

ChatGPT can be employed for a multitude of NLP tasks across a wide array of topics accessible in the vast expanse of available data. We can utilize our script to inquire about diverse areas of expertise and receive advanced responses from the ChatGPT API, as demonstrated here:

1. Mathematics:

    - User: What is the square root of 256?

    - ChatGPT: The square root of 256 is 16.

2. Sentiment analysis:

    - User: Analyze the sentiment of the sentence "I had a great day today!"

    - ChatGPT: The sentiment of the sentence "I had a great day today!" is positive.

3. Programming:

    - User: How do you declare a variable in Python?

    - ChatGPT: To declare a variable in Python, you can use the following syntax: `variable_name = value`.

4. Science:

    - User: What is the process of photosynthesis in plants?

    - ChatGPT: The process of photosynthesis in plants is the fundamental mechanism by which they convert light energy into chemical energy.

5. Literature:

    - User: What are the major themes in Shakespeare's play "Hamlet"?

    - ChatGPT: "Hamlet," one of Shakespeare's most renowned tragedies, explores several major themes that continue to captivate audiences and provoke thought.

In this section, you learned how to use the OpenAI Python library to interact with the ChatGPT API by sending a request to generate the completion of a user's input prompt/question. You also learned how to set up your API key and how to prompt the user to input a question, and finally, how to access the generated response from ChatGPT in the form of a JSON object containing information about the response. You are now ready to build more complex projects and integrate the ChatGPT API with other frameworks.

Summary

In this chapter, you learned the basics of getting started with the ChatGPT API. We covered the concept of natural language processing and how ChatGPT has revolutionized the field. You also learned how to access the ChatGPT API through the web interface and how to create an OpenAI account.

We dived into the technical details of using the ChatGPT API, including obtaining an API key, API tokens, and pricing. We covered how to set up a Python development environment, specifically using the PyCharm IDE, and creating a virtual environment. To help you get started with using the ChatGPT API, we walked through a simple example of obtaining a ChatGPT API response.

Chapter 2, Building a ChatGPT Clone, builds upon the foundational knowledge gained in the previous chapter by guiding you through the process of creating your own ChatGPT clone using the Flask framework. This chapter will provide you with a comprehensive overview of how to seamlessly integrate the ChatGPT API with Flask to develop your first end-to-end AI application.

2
Building a ChatGPT Clone

The first application in this chapter and in this book is going to be a ChatGPT clone that utilizes OpenAI's powerful language model to generate human-like responses to user input. The application will be built using **Flask**, a lightweight web framework for Python, and will feature a simple and elegant frontend interface for users to interact with. With just a few lines of code, users will be able to input their text and receive a response generated by the OpenAI language model. Specifically, the application will be able to do the following:

- Render a simple browser chat interface to interact with a chatbot.
- The chatbot will accept user input and send it to the ChatGPT API.
- Display the response from the ChatGPT API to the user.
- Show chat history.

The clone app will be able to take in a user's input, send it to OpenAI's API, and receive a response, which will be displayed to the user in real time. The app will be customizable to allow for the use of different OpenAI models and other options such as the length of the generated text.

To keep our project simple, our chatbot will lack the ability to maintain a contextual conversation. While it will generate responses based on individual queries, it will not possess the memory to retain information from previous interactions. We will explore the ChatGPT API conversational context in *Chapter 6*, *Language Translation Desktop App with the ChatGPT API and Microsoft Word*, where we will use the GPT-3.5 turbo language model. There, we will explore techniques and tools that enable our chatbot to understand and respond coherently within the context of an ongoing dialogue.

In this chapter, we will cover the following topics:

- Creating a ChatGPT Clone using **Flask**.
- Generating frontend **HTML** for the ChatGPT clone.
- Intercepting ChatGPT API endpoints.
- OpenAI's ChatGPT API for text generation.

- Passing user input from the frontend to the backend using AJAX.
- Displaying the generated text in the frontend.

When building a ChatGPT clone with **Flask**, there are a few things to keep in mind. It's important to set up a Python virtual environment to keep your dependencies separate from other projects on your machine. This ensures that your project has all the necessary dependencies and won't conflict with other projects. Additionally, make sure to securely store your ChatGPT API key to avoid unauthorized access. It's also important to carefully manage your API requests, as the pricing is based on the number of tokens processed. Finally, Flask offers flexibility in terms of how you structure your application, but it's important to keep your code organized and maintainable as your project grows.

Technical Requirements

In order to fully benefit from this chapter, you will require some fundamental tools. In-depth explanations of all installations not covered in the preceding chapter will be provided.

You will require the following:

- Python 3.7 or later installed on your computer.
- An OpenAI API key, obtained from your OpenAI account
- A code editor, such as PyCharm (recommended)
- The Flask framework installed in your Python virtual environment

The code examples from this chapter can be found on GitHub at `https://github.com/PacktPublishing/Building-AI-Applications-with-ChatGPT-APIs/tree/main/Chapter02%20ChatGPTClone`.

In the next section, we will start building the ChatGPT clone with Flask by setting up a backend that communicates with the ChatGPT API to generate responses to user input. You will create a simple Flask application and gradually enhance it by incorporating the ChatGPT API. We will also structure the code and store the ChatGPT API key as an environment variable to improve its security.

Creating a ChatGPT Clone with Flask

To create a ChatGPT clone with Flask, you will need to set up a backend that communicates with the ChatGPT API to generate responses to user input. Flask is a popular Python web framework that can be used to create web applications, including ChatGPT clones. We will begin our project by creating a simple Flask application and gradually enhance it by incorporating the ChatGPT API, additional web pages, and the frontend.

To get started, initiate a new PyCharm project and give it the name `ChatGPT_Clone`. Create a new file named `app.py` to serve as the backend of your application, where you'll define your Flask application and interact with the ChatGPT API. Once you have created the project, you will need to install the Flask package using **pip**. You can do this by running the following command in your project's terminal:

```
$ pip install flask
```

After installing Flask, you can start building your Flask application. To do this, you need to create a new Python file and import the Flask module. Then, you should create a new instance of the `Flask` class and pass your application's name as an argument. Here's how you can create a new Flask app in your `app.py` file:

```
from flask import Flask
app = Flask(__name__)
```

In Flask, a route is a URL path that a user can visit in your application. You can define routes using the `@app.route` decorator and a Python function. Let's create a route that displays `Hello, World!` as follows:

```
@app.route("/")
def index():
    return "Hello, World!"
```

Finally, you can run your Flask app using the `app.run()` method. This will allow you to start a development server that you can access in your web browser:

```
if __name__ == "__main__":
    app.run()
```

Once you have created the run configuration, you can run your Flask application by clicking the **Run** button in PyCharm's toolbar or by right-clicking on `app.py` and selecting the **Run** option. You will then see the URL to your **Flask** application in the **Run** window, as shown in *Figure 2.1*:

```
  app
/Users/martinyanev/Documents/Book/Reso
 * Serving Flask app 'app'
 * Debug mode: off
WARNING: This is a development server.
 * Running on http://127.0.0.1:5000
Press CTRL+C to quit
```

Figure 2.1: Flask Application URL

With these steps, you can build a basic Flask application that displays `Hello, World!` when a user visits the root URL of the application. From here, you can add more routes, templates, and functionality to your Flask app to build more complex web applications with the ChatGPT API (see *Figure 2.2*).

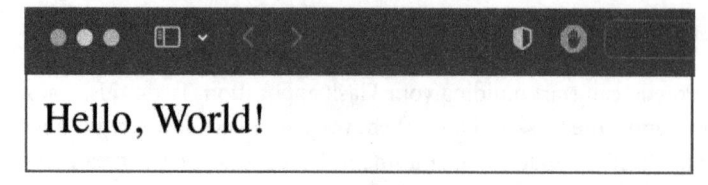

Figure 2.2: Flask Application Page

Every ChatGPT application starts with setting up your API key. When using ChatGPT API keys in a Python file, you would typically hardcode the keys directly into the file, just like you did when building *a simple ChatGPT API response*, which means the key is visible in the code itself. This can be a security risk if someone gains access to the code or if you accidentally push your code to a public repository.

On the other hand, adding the ChatGPT API key as an environment variable means that the key is stored outside the code base and can be accessed by the code at runtime. This makes it more secure because the key is not visible in the code itself and can be changed easily without modifying the code.

Another way to store your API key securely is by adding it to a separate file that is kept outside your Git repository. To follow that approach, let's create the `config.py` and then use the `config` package to access it from the `app.py`. The following code is an example of how to structure both files accordingly:

config.py

```python
API_KEY = "YOUR_API_KEY"
```

app.py

```python
from flask import Flask
import config

openai.api_key = config.API_KEY

app = Flask(__name__)

@app.route("/")
def index():
    return "Hello, World!"

if __name__ == "__main__":
    app.run()
```

> **Important note**
>
> If you want to push your project to a **Git** repository, it is important to add the `config.py` file to your project's `.gitignore` file to prevent accidentally committing your API key to version control.

Let's modify the functionality of your `index()` function by configuring it to return an HTML template from the frontend:

```
@app.route("/")
def index():
    return render_template("index.html")
```

This code defines a Flask route for the root URL of the application, (`"/"`). When a user navigates to the root URL, Flask will call the function decorated with `@app.route("/")`.

The function returns the result of `render_template("index.html")`. The `render_template` function is a Flask method that renders an HTML template. In this case, it renders the `index.html` template that will be created in the text section. You can also modify your imports to incorporate the `render` function:

```
from flask import Flask, render_template
```

The purpose of this code is to serve the initial web page when a user navigates to the application. The `index.html` file is typically the first page that a user will see when they load a web application. This is where the user will enter their initial input to start the chat with the ChatGPT API.

The next step is to build a function that will get the response from the ChatGPT API, so you can use that response in your chat clone. You can do that easily, by building the `get_bot_response()` function, just under the `index()` function:

```
@app.route("/get")
def get_bot_response():
    userText = request.args.get('msg')
    response = openai.Completion.create(
        engine="text-davinci-003",
        prompt=userText,
        max_tokens=1024,
        n=1,
        stop=None,
        temperature=1,
    )
    answer = response["choices"][0]["text"]
    return str(answer)
```

This code sets up a `/get` route for the Flask app. When a user makes a request to this route, the `get_bot_response()` is called.

The `request.args.get()` method is used to retrieve the value of the `msg` parameter from the URL query string. This parameter is used as the input for the ChatGPT API. Later, we will create a button on our frontend that will activate the `/get` upon selection.

The `openai.Completion.create()` method is used to generate a response from the ChatGPT API. It takes in several parameters, such as the engine to use, the prompt to provide to the API, and the number of tokens to generate in the response.

After generating the response, the function extracts the response text from the API's JSON response using dictionary keys. Finally, the response is returned as a string.

When a user types a message and hits send, the JavaScript code will make an HTTP request to this route to get the AI response and then display it on the web page.

To finalize the backend of your chatbot application, it's important to update your imports and add any necessary packages for the `get_bot_response()`:

```
from flask import Flask, request, render_template
import openai
import config
```

This is how you can efficiently create a Flask application by installing Flask, defining routes, setting up the API key, creating an HTML template, and building a function to get the response from the ChatGPT API. You also learned how to structure the configuration files and we emphasized the importance of securing the API key.

In the next section, you will learn how to connect the backend endpoints to the frontend of the chat application. We will also use jQuery to handle communication between the frontend and the backend, allowing for real-time messaging in the chat application.

Frontend HTML Generation

Let's start creating the HTML and **CSS** necessary to generate the frontend of our chat application. We will be using HTML, CSS, and **Bootstrap** to create the user interface and **jQuery** to handle the communication between the frontend and the backend. The HTML and CSS will be responsible for creating the structure and style of the user interface.

When creating a Flask web application, it is recommended to keep your HTML files in a separate folder called `templates`. This is because Flask uses the **Jinja2** template engine, which allows you to write reusable HTML code in a more modular way by separating it into smaller, reusable pieces called templates.

To create the `templates` folder, simply create a new directory in your project directory and name it `templates`. Inside the `templates` folder, you can create your HTML file, called `index.html` in this case. To do that, right-click on the `templates` folder and select **New** | **HTML file**. Here is what the project directory should look like:

```
ChatGPTChatBot/
├── config.py
├── app.py
├── templates/
│   └── index.html
```

Creating a `templates` folder is important because it allows you to organize your HTML files separately from your Python code, which makes it easier to manage and modify your web application. Additionally, the Flask framework is specifically designed to look for the templates folder in order to render HTML templates, so creating this folder is necessary for the proper functioning of your Flask application.

We can now create the frontend of our chat application using HTML and **Bootstrap**. Initially, our frontend code will contain a basic layout with a chat window, an input field, and a submit button. You can include the following code in your `index.html` file:

```html
<!DOCTYPE html>
<html>
<head>
    <title>OpenAI GPT Chat</title>
</head>
<body>
    <div class="container">
        <h2>OpenAI GPT Chat</h2>
        <hr>
        <div class="panel panel-default">
            <div class="panel-heading">Chat Messages</div>
            <div class="panel-body" id="chat">
                <ul class="list-group">
                </ul>
            </div>
        </div>
        <div class="input-group">
            <input type="text" id="userInput" class="form-control">
            <span class="input-group-btn">
                <button class="btn btn-default" id="submit">Submit
                </button>
            </span>
        </div>
```

```
        </div>
    </body>
</html>
```

The `<!DOCTYPE html>` declaration at the beginning of the code indicates the document type and version. The `<html>` tag indicates the start of the HTML document, and the `<head>` tag contains information about the document, such as the title of the document, which is specified in the `<title>` tag. The `<body>` tag contains the visible content of the document that is displayed in the browser, which includes the chat history and user messages.

In HTML, the `div` element is a container that is used to group other HTML elements together and apply styles to them as a group. It does not have any inherent semantic meaning, but its flexibility allows web developers to create layouts and organize content in a structured manner.

The first `<div>` element has a class attribute of container. The entire chat application will be contained within this container. We also have an `<h2>` element with the text `"OpenAI GPT Chat"`. This is the title of the chat application.

Next, we have an `<hr>` element, which is used to create a horizontal line to separate the title from the rest of the chat interface. Following that, we have another `<div>` element with a class attribute of `panel panel-default`. The `panel` will construct a bordered container that encompasses the content within and provides additional space around it through padding. This class is used to create a panel that will contain the chat message history. In the chat history window, there are two more elements.

The first `<div>` element has a class attribute of `panel-heading` and contains the text `"Chat Messages"`. This is the heading for the panel that will contain the chat messages.

The second `<div>` element has a class attribute of `panel-body` and an `id` attribute of `chat`. This element will be used to display the chat messages. Inside this `<div>` element, we have an unordered list `<ul>` element with a class attribute of `list-group`, which will contain the individual chat messages.

Next, we will build the input box where users can enter their messages and a submit button to send the message to the server for processing. The input box is created using the `<input>` tag with `type="text"`. The input box has a class of `"form-control"`, which is a Bootstrap class for styling the form control elements.

The submit button is created using the `<button>` tag with an ID of `submit`. The `input-group` class is a Bootstrap class used to group the input box and the submit button together.

Once the basic HTML file is created, you can activate your application by running the `app.py` file (see *Figure 2.3*).

Figure 2.3: Initial ChatGPT Clone Frontend

The interface will have a heading that says **OpenAI GPT Chat**, a chat panel where messages will be displayed, and an input box at the bottom where the user can type their message. There will also be a **Submit** button next to the input box. However, the chat functionality will not be working yet as the backend endpoints are not connected to the frontend of the application.

In this section, we discussed how to create the frontend of a chat application using HTML. We created the `templates` folder in Flask for reusable HTML templates for a basic chat interface with a chat window, input field, and a submit button. We can now explore different ways to customize the application's appearance, such as changing fonts and adding icons, to make it even more visually appealing.

Enhancing the ChatGPT Clone Design

In order to enhance the design and aesthetics of the ChatGPT Clone, we will be applying some CSS code. By applying CSS modifications, we can improve the overall visual appeal of the chat application and create a more user-friendly interface.

Let's first add an external style sheet provided by the Bootstrap framework. To do that, under the page title, you can add the following:

```
<link rel="stylesheet" href="https://maxcdn.bootstrapcdn.com/
bootstrap/3.3.7/css/bootstrap.min.css">
```

When added to the HTML code, it allows the use of the various classes provided by Bootstrap to style the web page. This link points to version 3.3.7 of the Bootstrap framework, and it includes various CSS rules for styling common HTML elements such as headings, paragraphs, forms, and buttons, among others. Using Bootstrap can help to ensure consistency in the design of the web page while also simplifying the task of styling and making the page responsive to different screen sizes.

Next, under the Bootstrap link, we can include the CSS code that includes customizing the background color and text color of the body element, setting the `margin-top` property of the `container` class, adjusting the height and overflow properties of the chat messages area, and styling the submit button and input field:

```
<style>
    body {
        background-color: #35372D;
        color: #ededf2;
    }
    .container {
        margin-top: 20px;
    }
    #chat {
        height: 400px;
        overflow-y: scroll;
        background-color: #444654;
    }
    .list-group-item {
        border-radius: 5px;
        background-color: #444654;
    }
    .submit {
        background-color:#21232e;
        color: white;
        border-radius: 5px;
    }
    .input-group input {
        background-color: #444654;
        color: #ededf2;
        border: none;
    }
}
</style>
```

The `body` rule sets the background color of the page to a dark greenish-gray color and the text color to a light gray color. The `.container` rule applies a 20-pixel margin on top of the container element, which will push the chat interface down a bit from the top of the page. The `#chat` rule sets the height of the chat message display area to 400 pixels and applies a vertical scrollbar to the area when the content exceeds the height limit.

The `.list-group-item` block sets the border radius and background color of the list items displayed in the chat panel. The `.submit` block sets the background color, text color, and border radius of the submit button. The `.input-group input` block styles the input field within the input group, setting the background color and text color and removing the border.

Those styles contribute to a cohesive and visually appealing design. You can now rerun the application to see the finalized style of the ChatGPT clone application.

In this section, we improved the design of the ChatGPT clone using CSS code, including an external style sheet from Bootstrap and custom CSS modifications. In the next section, you will learn how to intercept ChatGPT API endpoints using Flask. This will allow you to create custom routes to send and receive HTTP requests between the frontend of the ChatGPT clone application and the backend server.

Intercepting ChatGPT API Endpoints

Our ChatGPT clone needs to use JavaScript to handle user interactions with the chat application in real time. To do that, we can use a jQuery script that listens for a click on the submit button, gets the user input from the input field, sends a **GET** request to the server with the user input as a query parameter, and then receives a response from ChatGPT. The use of JavaScript in this way will enable the chat application to update and display new chat messages without the need for a page refresh, making for a more seamless and user-friendly experience.

We can write the JavaScript code just under the `input-group` class, as shown here:

```
        <div class="input-group">
            <input type="text" id="userInput" class="form-control">
            <span class="input-group-btn">
                <button class="btn btn-default" id="submit">Submit
                    </button>
            </span>
        </div>
    </div>
    <script src="https://ajax.googleapis.com/ajax/libs/
        jquery/3.2.1/jquery.min.js"></script>
    <script>
        $("#submit").click(function(){
            var userInput = $("#userInput").val();
            $.get("/get?msg=" + userInput, function(data){
                $("#chat").append("<li class='list-group-item'><b>You:
                    </b> " + userInput + "</li>");
                $("#chat").append("<li class='list-group-item'><b>
                    OpenAI:</b> " + data + "</li>");
            });
        });
    </script>
</body>
</html>
```

Firstly, we included the jQuery library from the Google **Content Delivery Network** (**CDN**). The jQuery library is used to add an event listener to the submit button. The `$("#submit")` selector is used to select the HTML element with the ID of `submit`, which is the submit button in the chat application. The `.click()` method is then used to attach a click event listener to this element. Every time the user clicks the submit button, the rest of the code in the JavaScript function will take action.

The `function()` code block that follows is the event handler function that is executed when the submit button is clicked. Within this function, the `var userInput` variable is used to retrieve the value entered by the user in the chat input field. This value is obtained using the jQuery selector `$("#userInput")` to select the HTML element with the ID of `userInput`, which is the chat input field. The `.val()` method is then used to get the value entered by the user in this field and store it in the `userInput` variable.

Then a **GET** request is sent to the server with the user input message as a parameter using the jQuery library's `$.get()` method. The response from the server is received as the data parameter in the anonymous function.

Once the response is received, the code appends two new list items to the chat area, (`#chat`), in the HTML document using the jQuery library's `append()` method. The first list item shows the user's input message as `"You: <message>"` in bold. This item will record and show the user input in the chat history. The second list item shows the response from the ChatGPT API as `"OpenAI: <response>"` in the chat history.

Once this step is done, you'll be all set to utilize the ChatGPT clone application and easily exchange responses with the ChatGPT API through a user-friendly interface. To get started, simply run the `app.py` file and begin chatting. Feel free to ask any question, and the answer will be saved in the chat history window. Here are a few examples (see *Figure 2.4*):

- Who invented the light bulb?
- Is the Panda a type of bear?
- Is it possible to divide a number by zero?
- If I have two apples and I eat a half apple, how many apples will I have left?

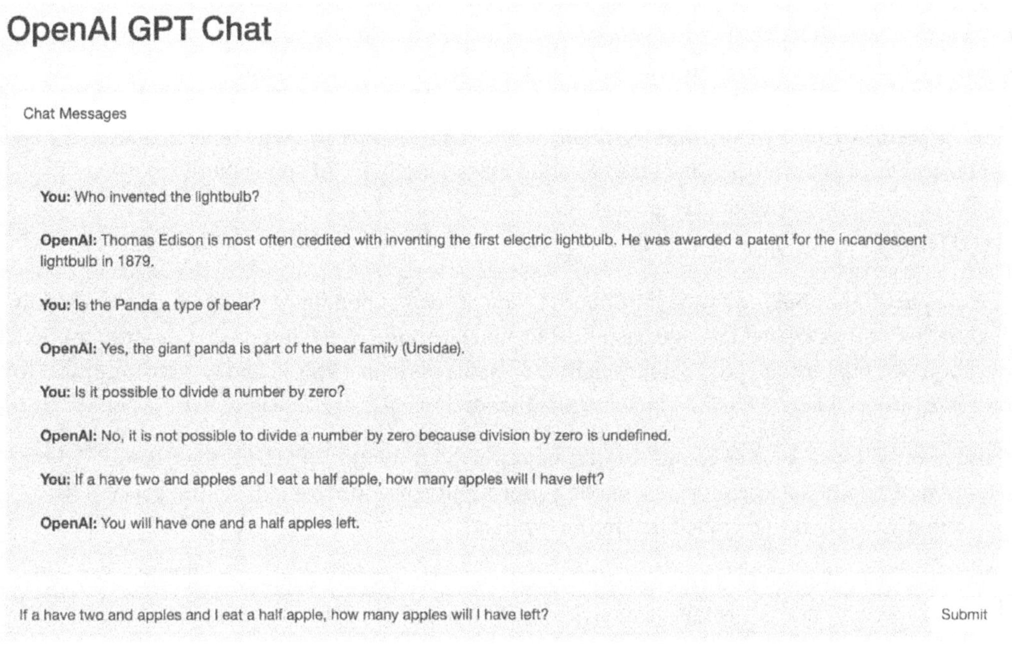

OpenAI GPT Chat

Chat Messages

You: Who invented the lightbulb?

OpenAI: Thomas Edison is most often credited with inventing the first electric lightbulb. He was awarded a patent for the incandescent lightbulb in 1879.

You: Is the Panda a type of bear?

OpenAI: Yes, the giant panda is part of the bear family (Ursidae).

You: Is it possible to divide a number by zero?

OpenAI: No, it is not possible to divide a number by zero because division by zero is undefined.

You: If a have two and apples and I eat a half apple, how many apples will I have left?

OpenAI: You will have one and a half apples left.

If a have two and apples and I eat a half apple, how many apples will I have left?   Submit

Figure 2.4: ChatGPT Clone Responses

> **Important note**
> The screenshot displayed here shows the application in the light color mode for clarity and visibility purposes. Please note that the actual application will be in dark mode, as per its default settings.

Going back to the PyCharm **Run** window, you can verify that all get requests were properly sent to ChatGPT. As you can see, we have received a response with a code 200, which means that the HTTP request was successful, and the server has returned the requested data. The server sends this code as a part of the HTTP response when it can process the client's request and deliver the requested data:

```
127.0.0.1 - - [11/Apr/2023 14:37:04] "GET / HTTP/1.1" 200 -
127.0.0.1 - - [11/Apr/2023 14:37:26] "GET /get?msg=Who%20invented%20
the%20lightbulb? HTTP/1.1" 200 -
127.0.0.1 - - [11/Apr/2023 14:37:53] "GET /get?msg=Is%20the%20Panda%20
a%20type%20of%20bear? HTTP/1.1" 200 -
127.0.0.1 - - [11/Apr/2023 14:38:24] "GET /get?msg=Is%20it%20
possible%20to%20divide%20a%20number%20by%20zero? HTTP/1.1" 200 -
127.0.0.1 - - [11/Apr/2023 14:44:39] "GET /get?msg=If%20I%20have%20
two%20apples%20and%20I%20eat%20a%20half%20apple,%20how%20many%20
apples%20will%20I%20have%20lest? HTTP/1.1" 200 -
```

Those are the instructions on how to use JavaScript to handle user interactions with a chat application. We used a jQuery script to listen to user inputs and send GET requests to the server with user input as a query parameter, then receive a response from the ChatGPT API. We also completed a few examples of how to use the ChatGPT clone and verify that all get requests were properly sent to ChatGPT, with a response code of 200. You are now ready to build more functional AI applications.

Summary

In this chapter of the book, you were introduced to the process of building a ChatGPT clone, which is a chatbot that utilizes OpenAI's language model to generate human-like responses to user input. The application was built using Flask, a lightweight web framework for Python, and was customizable to allow for the use of different OpenAI models and other options such as the length of the generated text.

We also covered topics such as creating and generating the frontend HTML for the ChatGPT clone, intercepting ChatGPT API endpoints, passing user input from the frontend to the backend using AJAX, and displaying the generated text in the frontend.

In *Chapter 3*, you will learn how to create and deploy an AI-powered code bug fixing SaaS application using Flask and the ChatGPT language model. You will become proficient in using the ChatGPT API. You will learn how to create a web form that accepts user inputs, deploy the application to the Azure cloud platform, and integrate it with a WordPress website. After completing the chapter, you will have the necessary skills to make a ChatGPT application accessible to individuals worldwide.

Part 2: Building Web Applications with the ChatGPT API

In this part, you will master web application development through the seamless integration of ChatGPT with renowned Python web frameworks such as Django and Stripe. You will embark on the journey of creating two cutting-edge applications from the ground up: a dynamic code-fixing tool and an innovative quiz generation application, harnessing the immense potential of the ChatGPT API. Additionally, you will acquire valuable insights on deploying your web application to the Azure cloud, uploading it to your website, and implementing user payment functionalities with the Stripe API.

This part has the following chapters:

- *Chapter 3, Creating and Deploying an AI Code Bug Fixing SaaS Application Using Flask*
- *Chapter 4, Integrating the Code Bug Fixer Application with a Payment Service*
- *Chapter 5, Quiz Generation App with ChatGPT and Django*

3
Creating and Deploying an AI Code Bug Fixing SaaS Application Using Flask

In this chapter, we will dive into the creation and deployment of an AI-powered code bug-fixing SaaS application using **Flask**. This application will leverage OpenAI's GPT-3 language model to provide code error explanations and fixes to users. With the rapid growth of software development, the need for effective and efficient error-debugging solutions has become more important than ever. By building this SaaS application, we aim to provide developers with a powerful tool to speed up their debugging process and improve the quality of their code.

To develop this SaaS application, we will be utilizing a tool that you may already be well acquainted with, namely, the Flask framework for building web applications in Python. Our aim is to become proficient in utilizing this framework to build an effective and scalable web application that can deliver efficient code error solutions to its users. Furthermore, we will be utilizing OpenAI's GPT-3 language model to provide natural language explanations and code fixes.

In this chapter, we will learn about the following:

- Building a code bug-fixing SaaS application using Flask.
- Using the ChatGPT API to generate explanations and solutions to code errors.
- Creating a web form that accepts user input for code and error messages
- Designing a web interface to display the generated explanations and solutions.
- Deploying an application to the Azure cloud platform.
- Integrating an application with a WordPress website.

Upon completing this chapter, you will have the necessary skills to make your ChatGPT application accessible to individuals worldwide.

Technical Requirements

The technical requirements for this project are as follows:

- Python 3.7 or later installed on your machine.
- A code editor, such as PyCharm (recommended).
- A Python virtual environment.
- The Flask web framework installed in the virtual environment
- An OpenAI API key.
- Access to Microsoft Azure.

The code examples from this chapter can be found on GitHub at `https://github.com/PacktPublishing/Building-AI-Applications-with-ChatGPT-APIs/tree/main/Chapter03%20CodeBugFixer`.

Performing Multiple ChatGPT API Requests

Let's first dive into the ChatGPT API requests and learn how to build your project and the `app.py` file. In this project, we will explore how to make multiple ChatGPT API requests to get the explanations and fixed code for our input queries. We will go through each step of the process and provide clear examples, so you can follow along with ease.

To fix users' code, ChatGPT needs two key components: some buggy code and the error provided by the system. The idea behind the Code Bug-Fixing application is that you provide ChatGPT with two separate requests simultaneously (see *Figure 3.1*):

- **Request 1**: ChatGPT uses the buggy code and the error to fix the code.
- **Request 2**: ChatGPT uses the buggy code and the error to explain the error to the user in plain English.

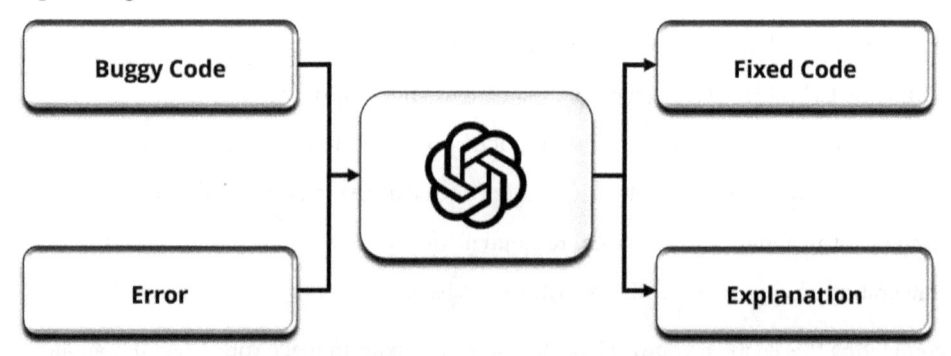

Figure 3.1: Code Bug Fixer Request/Response Map

As shown in *Figure 3.2*, the design of the code bug-fixing app is a web application with a clean and modern interface. It contains a form that allows the user to enter the code and the associated error. Upon submission of the form, the app sends the code and error to the server and displays the resulting explanation and fixed code in two separate text areas.

The design of the user interface is simple and intuitive, with two text areas for code and error input, and two read-only text areas for displaying the generated explanation and fixed code. The app's layout is clean, with a blue and white color scheme and a centered header that displays the app's name. The app is designed to provide a seamless user experience for identifying and fixing code errors.

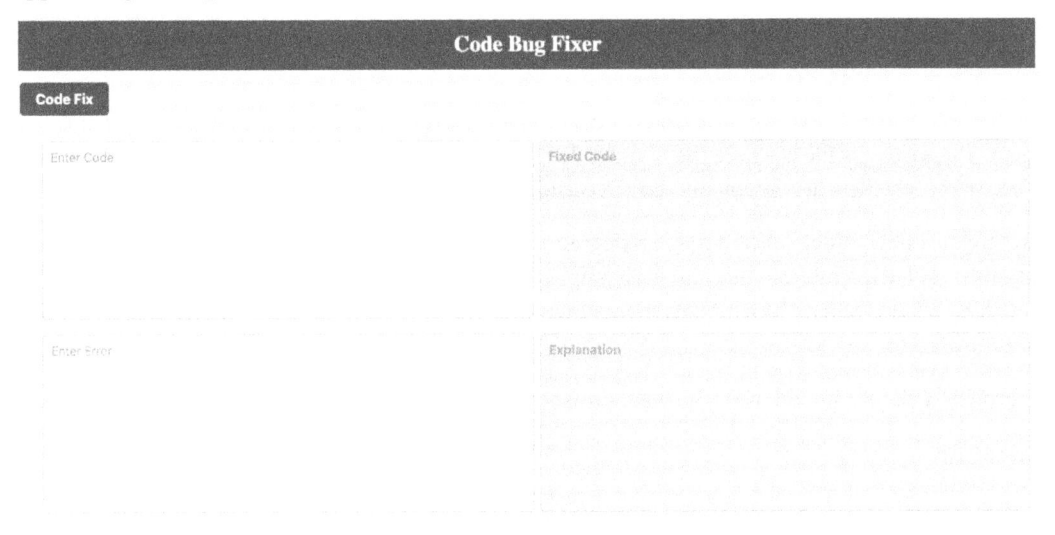

Figure 3.2: Code Bug Fixer App User Interface

Our application will take buggy code and an error and provide two requests simultaneously: one to fix the code and the other to explain the error to the user. The app will have an efficient interface with a simple layout, allowing for a seamless user experience. Now, we can go over creating the necessary files and folders for the `CodeBugFixer` project in PyCharm, including the `templates` folder, which will hold the HTML templates for the Flask app, and the `config.py` and `app.py` files to establish the foundation for utilizing the ChatGPT API in the `CodeBugFixer` app.

Setting Up the Code Bug Fixer Project

Creating a PyCharm project is an essential first step in any Python development process. By following a few simple steps, you can create a new PyCharm project in just a few minutes. Once you've set up your project, you'll be ready to start building and testing your code:

1. Open PyCharm: Double-click on the **PyCharm** icon on your desktop or search for it in your applications folder to open it.

2. On the PyCharm welcome screen, click on **Create New Project** or go to **File | New Project**.
3. Choose the directory where you want to save your project. You can either create a new directory or select an existing one.
4. Select the Python interpreter: Choose the version of Python you want to use for your project.
5. Configure project settings: Give your project the name `CodeBugFixer`, and choose a project location.
6. Once you've configured all the settings, click **Create** to create your new PyCharm project.

After creating a new PyCharm project, the next step is to create the necessary files and folders for the `CodeBugFixer` project.

Firstly, create two new Python files, called `app.py` and `config.py`, in the root directory of the project. The `app.py` file is where the main code for the `CodeBugFixer` app will be written, and the `config.py` file will contain any sensitive information such as API keys and passwords.

Next, create a new folder called `templates` in the root directory of the project. This folder will contain the HTML templates that the Flask app will render. Inside the `templates` folder, create a new file called `index.html`. This file will contain the HTML code for the home page of the `CodeBugFixer` app.

The project structure should look like the following:

```
CodeBugFixer/
├── config.py
├── app.py
├── templates/
│   └── index.html
```

By following these steps, you have created the necessary files and folders for your `CodeBugFixer` project in your PyCharm project. You can now start writing the code for your Flask app in the `app.py` file and the HTML code in the `index.html` file.

Once you have the correct interpreter, you can open the terminal within PyCharm by going to **View | Tool Windows | Terminal**. Check your terminal and ensure that you can see the (venv) indicator to confirm that you are working within your virtual environment. This is an essential step to prevent conflicting package installations between projects and guarantee that you are using the correct set of dependencies.

In the terminal window, you can install any necessary libraries as follows:

```
(venv)$ pip install flask
(venv)$ pip install openai
```

Finally, in order to establish the foundation for utilizing the ChatGPT API in your `CodeBugFixer` app, you'll need to add the following code to `config.py` and `app.py`:

config.py

```
API_KEY = <Your API Key>
```

app.py

```
from flask import Flask, request, render_template
import openai
import config

app = Flask(__name__)

# API Token
openai.api_key = config.API_KEY


@app.route("/")
def index():
    return render_template("index.html")


if __name__ == "__main__":
    app.run()
```

The `config.py` file will securely hold your OpenAI API key. Make sure to replace `<Your API Key>` with the actual API key that you obtained from OpenAI.

The `app.py` file is a Python script that defines a Flask application. It imports the `Flask` module and the necessary libraries for the `CodeBugFixer` project. It takes the API key provided in the `config.py` file. The script defines a route for the home page and renders the `index.html` template using Flask's `render_template` function.

To set up the `CodeBugFixer` project, you had to create a new PyCharm project, configure project settings, create necessary files and folders for the project, install Flask and OpenAI libraries, and add code to the `config.py` and `app.py` files. The `config.py` file securely holds the OpenAI API key, while the `app.py` file defines a Flask application and renders the `index.html` template.

In the next section, we will modify the `index()` function in the backend of the Code Bug-Fixing application to ensure that it can distinguish between `GET` and `POST` requests. We will also use the OpenAI GPT-3 API to generate explanations and fixed code for the user's input, which we will then pass to the `index.html` template using the `render_template` function.

Implementing the Code Bug Fixer Backend

The backend of the Code Bug-Fixing application should ensure that we properly send our buggy code to ChatGPT and, on the other side, receive the correct response. For this reason, you need to make sure that the `index()` function is able to clearly distinguish between GET and POST requests. You can add the following modification to the `index()` function to achieve that:

```python
@app.route("/", methods=["GET", "POST"])
def index():
    if request.method == "POST":
        # Code Errr
        code = request.form["code"]
        error = request.form["error"]

        prompt = (f"Explain the error in this code without fixing it:"
                  f"\n\n{code}\n\nError:\n\n{error}")
        model_engine = "text-davinci-003"
```

This function checks the HTTP request method – whether it is a GET or POST request. If the request method is POST, it means that the user has submitted a form from the `index.html` template. In that way, you can make sure that the ChatGPT API is invoked only after the user has submitted the form and clicked on the **Code Fix** button, which we will construct in the upcoming section.

The function then retrieves the user's input in the **Error Code** and **Enter Error** fields from the form and stores them in the `code` and `error` variables, respectively. Those variables will hold the code that the user wants to fix and the error code received. The extracted `code` and `error` variables are then used to create a prompt that is passed to the OpenAI GPT-3 API. Those variables are formatted using **f-strings** in Python.

For instance, let's say the `code` and `error` variables take the following values:

```
code = print(1
error = SyntaxError: '(' was never closed
```

In this case, our prompt will be displayed as follows:

```
Explain the error in this code without fixing it:
print(1
Error:
SyntaxError: '(' was never closed
The API is instructed to generate an explanation for the error in the
code.
```

The `prompt` variable provides a clear and specific task for the ChatGPT model to perform and ensures that the output generated by the model will be relevant to the user's input.

You can set the `text-davinci-003` string value to the `model_engine` variable. This variable is later used to specify the OpenAI language model to be used for both text completions. In this case, `text-davinci-003` is one of the most capable and versatile models provided by OpenAI.

Inside the `if` statement, you can now call the ChatGPT API to construct both `explanation_completion` and `fixed_code_completion` for the user:

```python
explanation_completions = openai.Completion.create(
    engine=model_engine,
    prompt=prompt,
    max_tokens=1024,
    n=1,
    stop=None,
    temperature=0.2,
)

explanation = explanation_completions.choices[0].text
fixed_code_prompt = (
    f"Fix this code: \n\n{code}\n\nError:\n\n{error}."
    f" \n Respond only with the fixed code."
)
fixed_code_completions = openai.Completion.create(
    engine=model_engine,
    prompt=fixed_code_prompt,
    max_tokens=1024,
    n=1,
    stop=None,
    temperature=0.2,
)
fixed_code = fixed_code_completions.choices[0].text
```

The preceding code makes use of the ChatGPT API to generate completions based on a given prompt. The `openai.Completion.create()` function is called twice in this code snippet to generate two different completions: `explanation_completions` and `fixed_code_completions`.

After the `openai.Completion.create()` function is called twice, the `explanation` and `fixed_code` variables are assigned the generated text from the choices attribute of the two objects, respectively. These generated texts will be used in the next steps of the code to display the explanations and fixed code to the user.

Finally, you can use the `render_template` function to update an HTML template with the ChatGPT response:

```python
return render_template("index.html",
                       explanation=explanation,
                       fixed_code=fixed_code)
```

The function takes two parameters: the first is the name of the template to render, and the second is a dictionary of variables that will be used in the template. The variables passed to the template are `explanation` and `fixed_code`. Now, `explanation` is the text generated by the ChatGPT API that explains the error in the user's code, and `fixed_code` is the text generated by the ChatGPT API that represents the fixed version of the user's code.

The variables are passed to the `index.html` template so that they can be displayed to the user. The template will use these variables to dynamically update the page content with the explanation and fixed code generated by the API.

After executing your Flask application, no error should be displayed. Nevertheless, your browser will show a completely blank screen since our `index.html` file is empty. Our next task is to create that file, and this will be discussed in the following section.

That is how you can modify the `index()` function to ensure that the ChatGPT API is only invoked after the user has submitted the form and clicked on the **Code Fix** button. We also saw how to generate explanations and fixed code using the ChatGPT API based on user input and how to update an HTML template with the ChatGPT response using the `render_template` function.

In the next section, you will learn how to create an `index.html` file and construct the **Code Fix** button, which allows users to submit their code for debugging. You will also learn how to use JavaScript and AJAX to handle the form submission and display the response from the Flask application without reloading the page.

Using Text Areas and Containers

In this section, you will learn how to create a simple user interface for your `CodeBugFixer` application using HTML and CSS. We will walk through the process of designing a simple form for users to input their code and error message and display the results of the ChatGPT API call. By the end of this section, you will have a fully functional web application that can help users fix errors in their code.

To modify the `index.html` file, first, you need to open the file located in the `templates` folder of your project. You can open this file in any text editor, or you can use the built-in HTML editor in PyCharm. Once you have the file open, you add the basic HTML structure:

```
<!DOCTYPE html>
<html>
<head>
    <meta charset="UTF-8">
    <title>Code Bug Fixer</title>
</head>
<body>
<div class="header">
    <h1>Code Bug Fixer</h1>
</div>
```

```
    </body>
</html>
```

The `<title>` tag sets the title of the HTML page to `Code Bug Fixer`. This is the text that will appear on the browser tab when the page is loaded. It is also used by search engines to display the title of the page in search results.

Then, you can use the `<h1>` tag to create a header on the web page with the text **Code Bug Fixer** in large font.

Next, we will add an input form to our `index.html` file. This form will allow the user to input their code and the corresponding error message, and then hit the **Code Fix** button to trigger the ChatGPT API to fix their code and provide an explanation. You can place the form just under the header `<div>` tag:

```
<div class="header">
    <h1>Code Bug Fixer</h1>
</div>
<form action="/" method="post">
    <button class="submit-button" type="submit">Code Fix</button>
    <div class="container">
        <div class="left-column">
            <textarea name="code" placeholder="Enter Code"></textarea>
            <textarea name="error" placeholder="Enter Error">
                </textarea>
        </div>
        <div class="right-column">
            <textarea class="fixed-code" name="fixed-code"
                placeholder="Fixed Code" readonly>{{ fixed_code }}
                </textarea>
            <textarea class="explanation" name="explanation"
                placeholder="Explanation" readonly>{{ explanation }}
                </textarea>
        </div>
    </div>
</form>
```

The form is enclosed in HTML `<form>` tags, with the `action` attribute set to `"/"` and the `method` attribute set to `post`. This means that when the user submits the form, the data will be sent to the server at the root URL (`"/"`) using the HTTP `POST` method. This refers to our `index()` function in the `app.py` file.

Inside the form, we have two text areas with the `name` attributes set to `code` and `error`, respectively. These will allow the user to input their code and error message.

The form also contains a `submit` button with the `submit-button` class. When the user clicks this button, the form will be submitted and the data will be sent to the backend server.

The form is divided into two columns using a `<div>` tag with the `container` class. The left column contains the code and error message text areas, while the right column contains the fixed code and explanation text areas.

The fixed code and explanation text areas have the `name` attributes set to `fixed-code` and `explanation`, respectively. They are also set to `readonly`, so the user cannot modify their content. These text areas will be updated with the fixed code and explanation generated by the ChatGPT API after the user submits the form.

Now that you have added the necessary HTML code for the `index` page, let's run the Flask app and see how it looks in the browser. When you run the Flask app, you should see a page with a header that says **Code Bug Fixer** and a form with two text areas to enter your code and the error message. There is also a submit button labeled **Code Fix**. On the right side of the form, you will see two more text areas that will display the fixed code and the explanation. However, these text areas will be initially empty until the user enters the code and error message and clicks the **Code Fix** button (see *Figure 3.3*).

Currently, the app's appearance might not be visually appealing since we have not incorporated any styling into the HTML.

Figure 3.3: HTML-based frontend of the Code Bug Fixer app

Finally, we will add some CSS to our application to style the HTML elements. The CSS code will define the fonts, colors, sizes, and positions of the elements on the page. We will add CSS code to our `index.html` file to enhance the look and feel of our application. With these styling improvements, our app will become more visually appealing and easier to use for our users.

You can add your CSS code under the `title` inside the `head` of the `index.html` file:

```
<title>Code Bug Fixer</title>
<style type="text/css">
    body {
        font-family: Arial sans-serif;
        background-color: #f6f7f9;
    }
```

Firstly, let's open the CSS style block. It indicates that the following code is CSS and will be applied to the HTML elements in the web page.

The CSS code targets a `<body>` element in the HTML. In CSS, you can target elements using their tag name, class name, or ID. Here, we are targeting the entire body of the web page.

Here, we can also set `font-family` to `Arial sans-serif`, which means that any text inside the `body` element will be displayed using the Arial font, or a similar sans-serif font if Arial is not available. We can also set the background color of the body to a light grayish-blue color:

```
.header {
    background-color: #3b5998;
    color: #ffffff;
    padding: 15px;
    text-align: center;
}
.header h1 {
    margin: 0;
    font-size: 28px;
    font-weight: bold;
}
.container {
    display: flex;
    justify-content: space-between;
    padding: 15px;
}
```

The `.header` class specifies the background color, text color, padding, and alignment for the header. Here, the text is centered using the `text-align` property.

The `.header h1` class `font-size` property is set to 28 pixels, `font-weight` is set to `bold`, and `margin` is set to 0, so there is no space between the top of the page and the header.

The `.container` class' `display` property is set to `flex` to allow us to use Flexbox for layout, and `justify-content` is set to `space-between` to evenly distribute the contents of the container across the horizontal axis:

```
.left-column, .right-column {
    width: 49%;
    padding: 15px;
}
textarea {
    width: 100%;
    height: 200px;
    font-size: 16px;
```

```css
        padding: 10px;
        margin-bottom: 15px;
        border: 1px solid #cccccc;
        border-radius: 5px;
        resize: none;
    }
    .fixed-code, .explanation {
        background-color: #e9ebee;
        color: #3b5998;
        font-weight: bold;
    }
}
```

Next, let's design the two-column layout, where the left column contains the input fields for the user to enter their code and error, while the right column displays the output of the program.

The `.left-column` and `.right-column` classes were given a width of `49%` so that they take up almost an equal amount of space on the page. The `textarea` elements were styled to have a fixed width of `100%` and a height of `200px` to create a clear input field. The `resize: none` property ensures that the user cannot resize the input fields.

The `.fixed-code` and `.explanation` classes were given `bold` for `font-weight` to make them stand out from the input fields. This helps the user to quickly identify the output fields:

```css
    .submit-button {
        background-color: #3b5998;
        color: #ffffff;
        font-size: 18px;
        font-weight: bold;
        padding: 10px 20px;
        border: none;
        border-radius: 5px;
        margin-top: 15px;
        cursor: pointer;
    }
    .submit-button:hover {
        background-color:  #4b76be;
    }
</style>
```

Our final goal is to make the `submit` button visually appealing and to give feedback to the user when they hover over it. We set the background color to a dark blue color (`#3b5998`) and the font color to white (`#ffffff`) to create contrast. We also added padding and a border radius to make the button more noticeable and attractive.

The `margin-top` property adds some space between the button and the text areas. Finally, we added the `:hover` pseudo-class to change the background color of the button when the user hovers over it, which provides visual feedback to the user that the button is interactive.

You have now completed the `index.html` file for the `CodeBugFixer` application. You can now run the `app.py` file and test the application to make sure everything is working correctly. In the next section, we will provide some examples of how to use the application to fix code bugs. Alternatively, you can try out your own code examples to see how the app performs.

That is how we can create a user interface for the `CodeBugFixer` application using HTML and CSS. We walked through designing a form for users to input their code and error message and display the results of the ChatGPT API call.

In the next section, you will learn how to test the `CodeBugFixer` application by writing test cases and verifying that it handles different scenarios correctly. You will also see examples of how the Code Bug Fixer app can fix code written in two different programming languages, Java and Python, and learn how to test the fixed code to confirm its accuracy.

Testing the Code Bug Fixer App

Now, we will learn how to test our Code Bug Fixer application. We will write some test cases to ensure that the application is functioning correctly and handling different scenarios appropriately. Testing is a critical part of software development, as it ensures that the application works as intended and meets the user's requirements.

The Code Bug Fixer app can fix any programming language, making it a versatile tool. Therefore, we will demonstrate its effectiveness by using examples written in two different programming languages: Java and Python.

The Python example has the following properties:

- Code:

    ```
    def factorial(n):
        if n == 0:
            return 1
        else:
            return n * factorial(n-1)
    print("The factorial of 5 is: " + factorial(5))
    ```

- Error: `Type Error:`

This code is returning an error because it is attempting to concatenate a string and an integer in the `print` statement. The `factorial` function returns an integer, but it is being concatenated to the string `"The factorial of 5 is: "`.

To fix this code in the Code Bug Fixer app, you can follow these steps:

1. Paste the code inside the **Enter Code** field.
2. Paste the error inside the **Enter Error** field.
3. Left-click on the **Code Fix** button.

Once you complete the steps listed, the fixed code and the explanation generated by ChatGPT API will be displayed in the corresponding field. As depicted in *Figure 3.4*, the response from ChatGPT appears in bold font and is not editable. You can also see that the explanation is accurate.

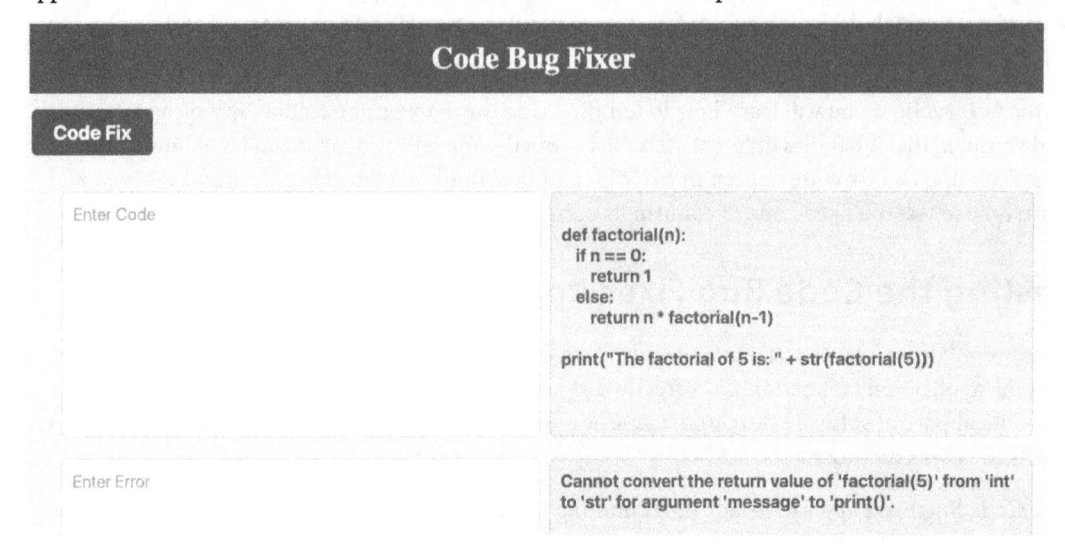

Figure 3.4: Code Bug Fixer processing some Python code

To ensure that the fixed code is functioning correctly, you can test it by running it in a Python IDE such as PyCharm or any other online Python compiler. By examining the explanation provided alongside the fixed code, you can confirm that it provides an accurate and detailed explanation of the error.

Finally, to verify that the Code Bug Fixer app works with any programming language, let's try to fix the following Java code:

1. Code:

    ```
    public class ComplexError {
        public static void main(String[] args) {
            String str = "Hello, World!";
            int length = str.length();
            for (int i = 0; i <= length; i++) {
                System.out.println(str.charAt(i));
            }
        }
    }
    ```

2. Error:

   ```
   Exception in thread "main" java.lang.
   StringIndexOutOfBoundsException
   ```

The code is returning an error because the `for` loop is iterating from 0 to `length`, which is the length of the string. However, the index of the last character in the string is length -1, so when i equals `length`, the program will try to access an index that is out of bounds and throw an `IndexOutOfBoundsException` message.

Once you run the code through the Code Bug Fixer, you will get a response similar to the one depicted in *Figure 3.5*. You can verify that the fixed code and the description are correct. ChatGPT fixed the error because it changed the condition in the `for` loop from `i <= length` to `i < length`. By changing the condition to `i < length`, the loop only iterates up to the last index of the string and avoids accessing an index that does not exist.

This confirms that your Code Bug Fixer has the ability to differentiate between two distinct programming languages and was able to repair the code within a matter of seconds.

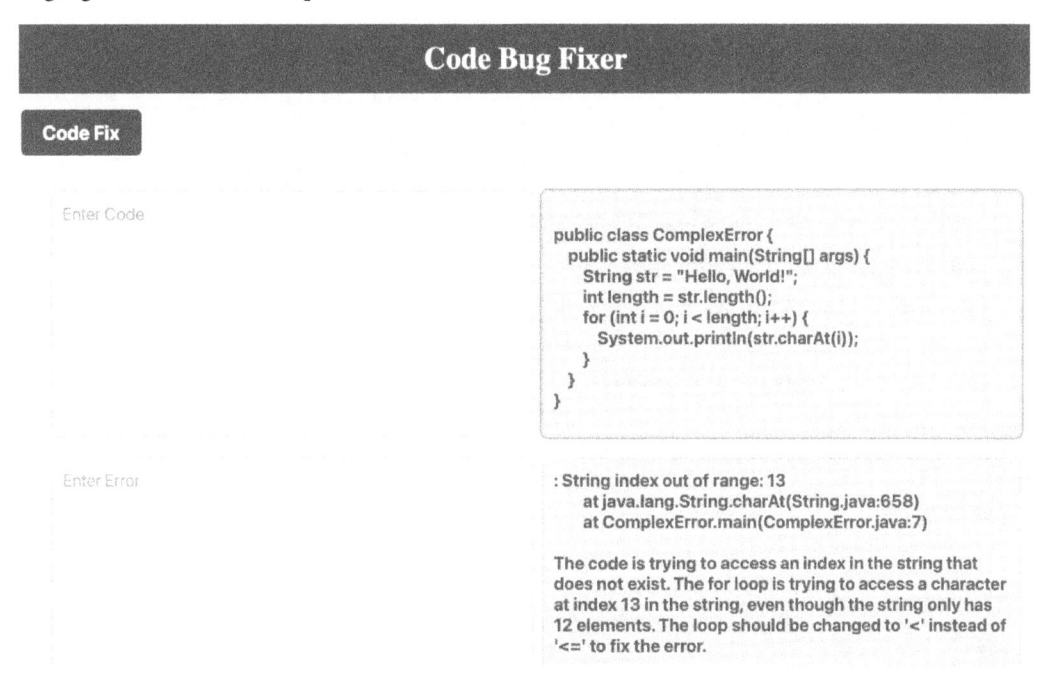

Figure 3.5: Code Bug Fixer processing some Java code

This section explained how to test the Code Bug Fixer application by providing examples in the Python and Java programming languages. The application can fix any programming language, and the fixed code can be verified by running it in a Python or Java IDE. We saw how the application can differentiate between two programming languages and fix code within seconds.

In the next section, you will learn how to set up an Azure account, install the Azure CLI, and deploy your application to the cloud using the CLI. You will also learn how to create a `requirements.txt` file in the root directory of your project, listing all the Python packages and their specific versions that your app needs to run.

Deploying the ChatGPT App to the Azure Cloud

Now let's upload our Code Bug Fixer application to the **Azure** cloud platform. Azure is a cloud computing service provided by Microsoft that allows developers to host, manage, and scale their applications in the cloud. By hosting our application on Azure, we can make our application accessible to a wider audience. We will go through the steps required to create an Azure account, set up our application for deployment, and deploy it to Azure using the Azure CLI.

You can create your Azure account by following these steps:

1. Go to the Azure website at `https://azure.microsoft.com/free/` and click on **Start free**.
2. Sign in with your Microsoft account or create one if you don't have one.
3. Enter your personal information and payment details. You won't be charged unless you upgrade to a paid plan.
4. Choose your subscription type and agree to the terms and conditions.
5. Verify your account by entering a phone number and entering the code you receive.
6. You can log in to your account at `https://signup.azure.com/`.
7. Once you log in, on the **Welcome** page, left-click on **Use an existing subscription in your account**. You will be automatically redirected to `portal.azure.com/#home`, where you can start using Azure services (see *Figure 3.6*).

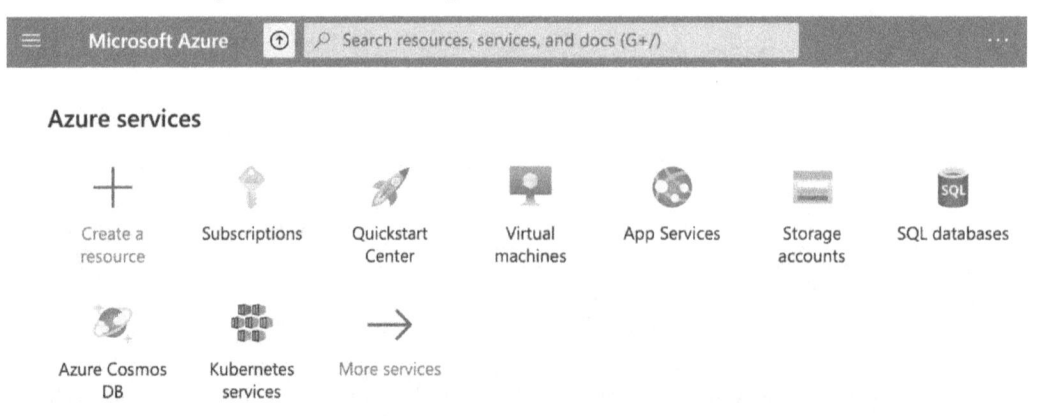

Figure 3.6: Azure home page

> **Important note**
>
> When deploying the Code Bug Fixer app to the Azure cloud, it is important to name the file containing the Flask app `app.py`. This is because Azure expects the main file to be named `app.py` for deployment to work properly.

To deploy our application on Azure, we need to install the Azure **command-line interface** (**CLI**). The CLI provides us with an efficient way to automate and manage our Azure resources. Next, you can find the steps to install the Azure CLI.

These are the steps for macOS users (https://learn.microsoft.com/en-us/cli/azure/install-azure-cli-macos):

1. Open your macOS Terminal.

2. Install `brew`. Homebrew is a popular package manager for macOS:

   ```
   $ /bin/bash -c "$(curl -fsSL https://raw.githubusercontent.com/Homebrew/install/HEAD/install.sh)"
   ```

3. Once Homebrew is installed, run the following command to install Azure CLI:

   ```
   $ brew update && brew install azure-cli
   ```

4. Verify that the installation was successful by running the following command:

   ```
   $ az --version
   ```

5. This should display the version number of the Azure CLI that you just installed:

   ```
   azure-cli                          2.47.0

   core                               2.47.0
   telemetry                          1.0.8

   Dependencies:
   msal                               1.20.0
   azure-mgmt-resource                22.0.0

   Python location '/opt/homebrew/Cellar/azure-cli/2.47.0/libexec/bin/python'
   Extensions directory '/Users/martinyanev/.azure/cliextensions'
   Python (Darwin) 3.10.11 (main, Apr  7 2023, 07:24:47) [Clang 14.0.0 (clang-1400.0.29.202)]
   Legal docs and information: aka.ms/AzureCliLegal
   Your CLI is up-to-date.
   ```

These are the steps for Windows users (`https://learn.microsoft.com/en-us/cli/azure/install-azure-cli-windows?tabs=azure-cli`):

1. Open a web browser and navigate to `https://docs.microsoft.com/en-us/cli/azure/install-azure-cli-windows`.
2. Scroll down to the section titled **Install or update** and click on the **Microsoft Installer (MSI)** tab.
3. Click on the **Latest release of the Azure CLI** button to start the MSI package download.
4. Once the MSI package has downloaded, double-click on the file to begin the installation process.
5. Follow the prompts in the installation wizard to complete the installation process.
6. Once the installation is complete, open a Command Prompt window or PowerShell window and type the following:

```
$ az -version
```

For Linux users (`https://learn.microsoft.com/en-us/cli/azure/install-azure-cli-linux?pivots=script`), you can type the following in the Terminal:

```
curl -L https://aka.ms/InstallAzureCli | bash
```

This line will automatically download the installation script and you can follow all steps for setting up your Azure CLI.

> **Important note**
> After installing the Azure CLI, you may need to close and re-open your Terminal window to ensure that the CLI is fully recognized and operational.

You should now be able to use the Azure CLI on your Linux machine.

Before deploying your app to Azure using the CLI, you'll need to log in to your Azure account from the CLI. This will enable you to manage your resources and perform other tasks related to your account.

To log in to your Azure account using the Azure CLI, you can type the following in the Terminal window:

```
$ az login
```

A pop-up window will appear asking you to enter your Azure account credentials. Enter your account email and password and click on the **Sign in** button. Once you are successfully logged in, you will see a message in the Command Prompt indicating that you are authenticated.

To prepare our app for deployment, we need to create a file called `requirements.txt` in the root directory of our `CodeBugFixer` project. This file will list all the Python packages and their specific versions that our app needs to run. Using a `requirements.txt` file is a common practice in Python projects to document and manage the project's dependencies. It lists all the external packages and their versions that are necessary for the application to function properly. Each line in the `requirements.txt` file typically represents a separate package and may include a specific version number or a version range. Azure will use this file to install the dependencies in the server where our app will be hosted.

The project structure should look like the following:

```
CodeBugFixer/
├── config.py
├── app.py
├── requirements.txt
├── templates/
│   └── index.html
```

To create a `requirements.txt` file in your PyCharm project, follow these steps:

1. Right-click on your `CodeBugFixer` project folder in the project explorer on the left-hand side of PyCharm.
2. Select **New** | **File** from the **Context** menu.
3. In the **New File** dialog box, type `requirements.txt` as the filename.
4. Click the **Create** button.

Once the file is created, you can add the necessary libraries to it. To include Flask and OpenAI libraries, add the following lines to your `requirements.txt` file:

```
Flask==2.2.3
openai==0.27.4
```

Now that we have everything set up, it's time to deploy the app to Azure. We'll be using the Azure CLI to accomplish this. First, navigate to the root directory of your project, where the `app.py` and `requirements.txt` files are located.

Next, run the following command in the CLI:

```
$ az webapp up --name <app_name>
```

In this command, `webapp up` deploys the web app to Azure. Replace `<app-name>` with a unique name of your choice.

After deploying the app, if everything is set up correctly, you should see a JSON output in the Azure CLI terminal. This output will contain information about the deployed app, such as the app name, URL, location, resource group, and other details. It will also include the status of the deployment, such as whether it was successful or whether there were any errors:

```
{
  "URL": "http://<app_name>.azurewebsites.net",
```

```
    "appserviceplan": "martinyanev94_asp_7277",
    "location": "location",
    "name": "Your App Name",
    "os": "Linux",
    "resourcegroup": "resourcegroup",
    "runtime_version": "python|3.10",
    "runtime_version_detected": "-",
    "sku": "PREMIUMV2",
    "src_path": "//Local/app/path"
}
```

After successfully deploying your app on Azure, you can access it from anywhere around the world using the URL provided in the JSON output. Simply copy the URL and paste it into your web browser's address bar to open the app. You can also share this URL with others to let them use your Code Bug Fixer app.

If you want to upload the Code Bug Fixer app to your WordPress website, you can easily do so by using an `iframe`. Simply copy and paste the following code into the text editor, replacing `<your_app_url>` with the URL of your deployed app:

```
<iframe src="<your_app_url> " width="100%" height="1000"></iframe>
```

This will embed the app into your website and allow your visitors to access it directly from your page.

Finally, you can access your deployed application from the Azure web portal. To access your app from your Azure web account, follow these steps:

1. Sign in to the Azure portal at `https://portal.azure.com/#home`.
2. In the left-hand menu, click on **App Services**.
3. From there, you will be able to manage the app that you deployed.

Here, you can modify or delete the deployment from your Azure web account (see *Figure 3.7*):

- To modify the deployment, you can upload a new version of your code using the Azure CLI or Azure portal.
- To delete the deployment, simply click on the **Delete** button on the **Overview** page of your app in the Azure portal.

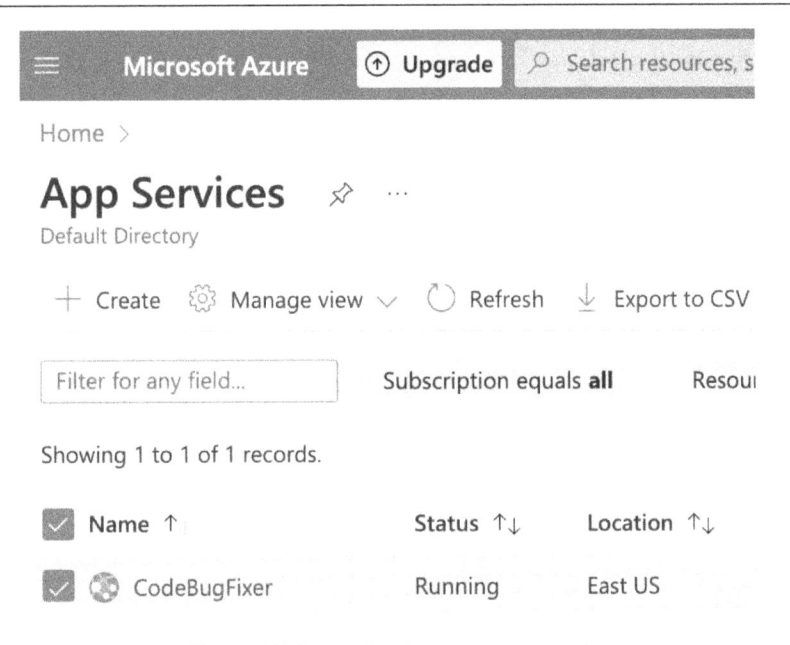

Figure 3.7: Azure cloud app management

That is how you can deploy your app on the Azure cloud using the Azure CLI. We listed all steps to create an Azure account, install the Azure CLI, and prepare the app for deployment. This section also emphasized that the main file of the app should be named app.py for proper deployment, and a requirements.txt file was needed to list all the Python packages required by the app to run. The steps to install the Azure CLI for macOS and Windows users were also listed.

Summary

This chapter described the creation and deployment of an AI-powered SaaS application, Code Bug Fixer, which uses OpenAI's GPT-3 language model to provide code error explanations and fixes to users. It covered building the application using Flask, creating a web form that accepts user input for code and error messages, and designing a web interface for displaying the generated explanations and solutions. The chapter also provided instructions on how to test and deploy the application to the Azure cloud platform, offering security and scalability features to the application.

Furthermore, you learned how to create a user interface for Code Bug Fixer using HTML and CSS, adding a basic HTML structure, a header, an input form, and two columns containing text areas for the user to enter their code and error message. The testing process involved running test cases for the application in two different programming languages, Python and Java. By following the given steps, users can check whether the application is repairing the code accurately or not. This chapter provided a comprehensive guide to building, testing, and deploying an AI-powered SaaS application that can help users fix errors in their code.

In *Chapter 4, Integrating the Code Bug Fixing Application with a Payment Service*, you will learn how to integrate the popular Stripe payment service into your web application using the Stripe API. The chapter will cover the step-by-step process of setting up a Stripe account, configuring the API keys, creating a form to collect user payment information, and processing payments securely through Stripe. Additionally, the chapter will explain how to track and store user data securely for future transactions and analysis.

4
Integrating the Code Bug Fixer Application with a Payment Service

In this chapter, we will explore how to integrate a payment service into your ChatGPT Code Bug Fixer application using the **Stripe** API. This will allow you to keep track of the number of visits a user performs on your ChatGPT application and implement a payment mechanism for premium features or content. You will also learn how to use a basic database in your ChatGPT project, which is necessary to track user data and transactions.

First, we will introduce Stripe and show you how to set up an account and API key. We will then go through the steps of creating a SQL user database that will be used to store user data and transaction histories. Finally, we will guide you through the process of adding payment functionality to your ChatGPT application using the Stripe API, including creating a checkout process, handling payment Webhooks, and updating a database.

In this chapter, we will learn how to do the following:

- Use Stripe to implement payments in a ChatGPT application.
- Set up a basic SQL database for user management.
- Integrate Stripe with the ChatGPT API to keep track of the number of app usages.
- Test the payment flow using Stripe's test mode.
- Monitor and analyze payment data using Stripe's dashboard and analytics features.

By the end of this chapter, you will have the necessary knowledge and tools to add payment services to your ChatGPT application and build a successful online business.

Technical Requirements

The technical requirements for this project are as follows:

- Python 3.7 or later installed on your machine.
- A code editor, such as PyCharm (recommended).
- A Python virtual environment.
- An OpenAI API key.
- A Stripe account and API key.

In the next section, you will learn how to integrate payments with Stripe. You will see how to create a Stripe account, obtain the necessary API keys, and set up the Stripe API for use in your application.

The code examples from this chapter can be found on GitHub at `https://github.com/PacktPublishing/Building-AI-Applications-with-ChatGPT-APIs/tree/main/Chapter04%20CodeBugFixer`.

Integrating Payments with Stripe

Stripe is a popular payment gateway that provides an easy way to accept payments online. It allows businesses and individuals to accept payments over the internet, manage subscriptions, and track revenue all in one place. Stripe has an easy-to-use API that allows developers to integrate payment functionality into their websites and applications. We will begin by creating a Stripe account and configuring the Stripe API keys that we will use to authenticate our requests to the Stripe API. Here, you will use the Stripe API to create a payment form and process payments securely in your Python code.

The first step toward accepting payments in your Code Big Fixer application is to create a Stripe account. Stripe is a popular payment processing platform that enables businesses to accept payments online. By setting up a Stripe account, you can integrate it with your ChatGPT application and start accepting payments from your users. Setting up a Stripe account is easy and straightforward, and we will guide you through all steps.

To get started with Stripe, you need to create an account. Follow these steps to create a new Stripe account:

1. Go to the Stripe website registration form: `https://dashboard.stripe.com/register` (see *Figure 4.1*).
2. Fill out the registration form with your personal or business information. You'll need to provide your name, email address, and password.
3. Confirm your email address by clicking the link in the verification email that Stripe sends you.
4. Provide your business details, such as your business name, address, and tax ID number (optional).
5. Set up your payment settings. You can choose to accept payments from all major credit cards and debit cards, as well as digital wallets such as Apple Pay and Google Pay (optional).

Integrating Payments with Stripe 63

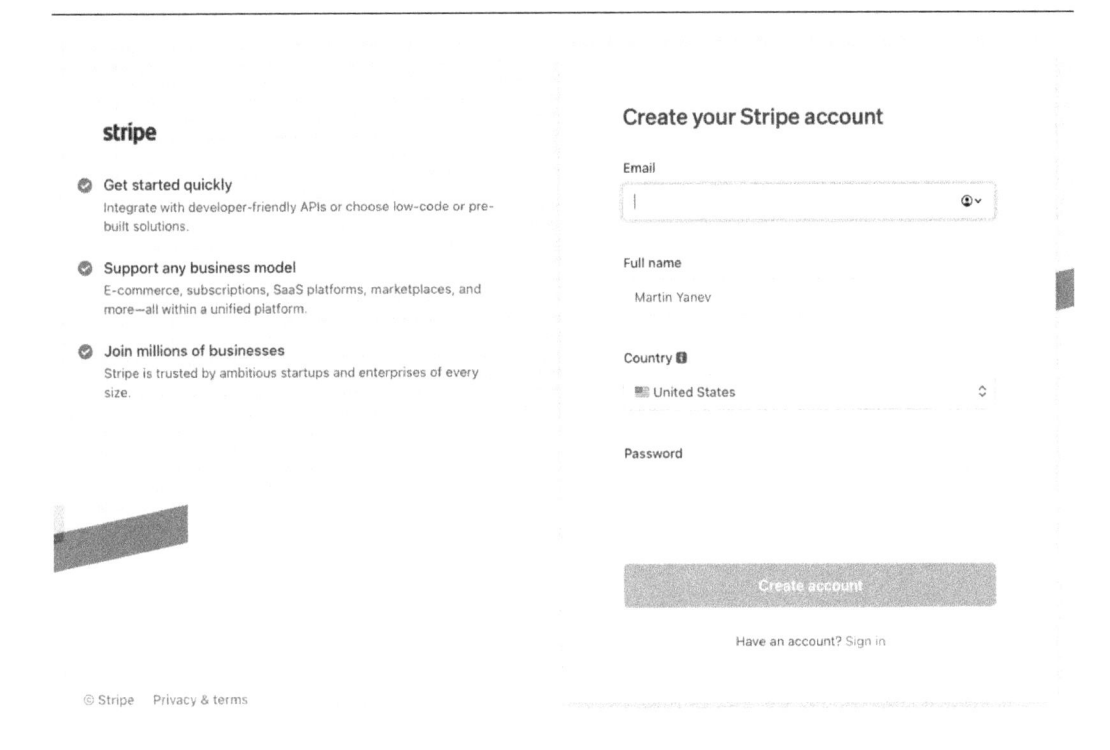

Figure 4.1: The Stripe Registration Form

Once you've created your Stripe account, you can start accepting payments from your customers. You can also use Stripe's dashboard, as shown in *Figure 4.2*, to manage your transactions, issue refunds, and view reports on your payment activity. Stripe charges a fee for each transaction processed through its platform, but the fees are competitive and transparent.

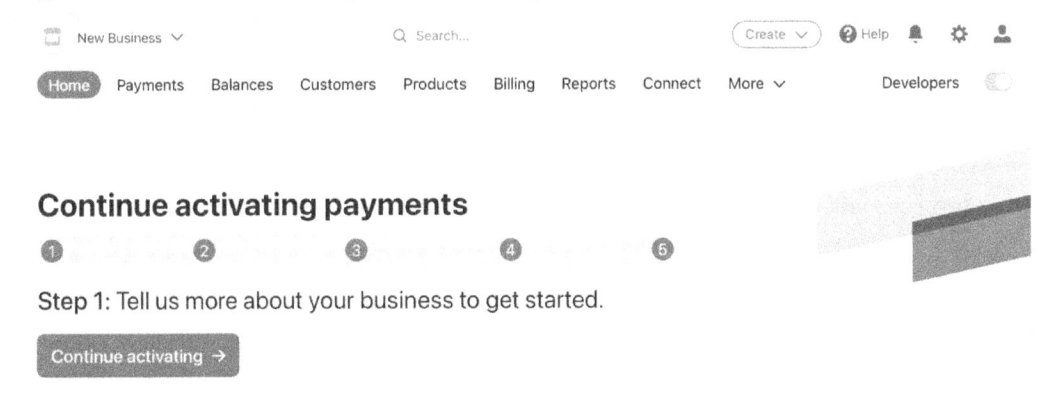

Figure 4.2: The Stripe Dashboard

Next, you need to obtain access to your Stripe API keys, which will be used later in your application to facilitate payment processing. From the dashboard, click on the **Developers** tab on the left-hand side of the screen, and then click on **API keys**. On this page, you will see your live and test API keys, along with the option to reveal each key's secret. Make sure to copy and securely store your keys, as you will need them to make API requests to Stripe from your ChatGPT application.

> **Important note**
> Your live API keys should be kept private and not shared publicly, as they provide access to your Stripe account's sensitive data and allow users to make changes. Instead, you can use your **test API keys** for development and testing purposes.

Stripe provides three types of API keys – publishable keys, secret keys, and test keys:

1. The **Publishable Key** is used on the client side to make requests to Stripe securely. It does not have any access to your account and can be shared publicly. This key is normally placed in the application frontend.

2. The **Secret Key** is used on the server side to make requests to Stripe and has full access to your account, including the ability to make charges. It should be kept secret and should never be shared publicly. This key is normally placed in the application backend.

3. The **Test Key** is used in testing environments to perform test transactions without charging any money. It works like the secret key but only affects test data, and it should not be used in production.

On the **API keys** page, you will see both the **Publishable** and **Test** API keys. We will use **Publishable** key to identify your account with Stripe in the frontend of your application, while the **Test** key is used for server-side communication with Stripe. You will need to add the **Publishable** key to the frontend code of your ChatGPT application, and the **Test** key to the backend code.

This is how you can integrate payments into a website or application using **Stripe**, a popular payment gateway that provides an easy way to accept payments online. In this section, to use Stripe, you created a Stripe account and obtained the API keys, including the publishable key and a secret key, which have different access levels and should be kept secure. You also saw a step-by-step guide on how to create a Stripe account and obtain the necessary API keys.

In the next section, you will learn about setting up a SQL user database for the Code Big Fixer application. We will explore the different payment models and understand how to design a subscription-based payment plan.

Setting Up a SQL User Database

Prior to implementing the payment infrastructure into your application, it's essential to determine your business strategy, which pertains to how you'll charge users of your web application. There are several ways to accomplish this:

- **Subscription plan**: This is a recurring payment model that allows users to pay for a service or product on a regular basis, such as monthly or yearly. It is a common payment option for **software-as-a-service** (**SaaS**) products and online publications, where users pay for access to the service or content.
- **One-time payment plan**: Customers make a single payment for a product or service.
- **Usage-based plan**: Customers are charged based on their usage of a product or service, such as pay-per-view or pay-per-click.

For our Code Big Fixer application, we will design a subscription model that provides users with three different plans to choose from. Furthermore, to make the user onboarding process smoother, we will include a **free trial** period that allows users to try out the application a certain number of times before committing to a payment plan.

The free trial period will provide users with the opportunity to explore the application's features and determine whether it meets their needs. During the trial period, users can use the application for a specific number of times without any charge. After the trial period, users will be prompted to select a payment plan to continue using the application. This subscription-based approach is beneficial to both the users and you as an application owner. The users can select the subscription plan that best fits their budget and usage, while you can generate a steady stream of revenue from the subscription fees.

In order to implement the payment mechanism for our application, we will need to set up a database to track user visits and usage. The database will need to record two types of information – the browser ID (see *Table 4.1*), which is unique to each user accessing the application, and the usage counter, which keeps track of how many times each user has accessed the application. By tracking this information, we can identify unique users and ensure that they have not exceeded their allowed number of free visits before being prompted to choose a subscription plan.

BROWSER ID	USAGE COUNTER
28ec523f092	3
58c9f5702fd	6
c59523926d	10

Table 4.1: User Data Collected in the Database

Now that we have established a solid business plan, we can move forward and delve into the technical details of integrating a payment service into our ChatGPT application. Before we can do that, however, we need to initialize a SQL database.

Initializing a SQL Database

A SQL database is essential to keep track of the number of visits that a user performs on our application, which will in turn enable us to implement a payment mechanism using the Stripe API. By having a database, we can easily store and retrieve data related to our users and their interaction with our application, allowing us to manage the payment process seamlessly.

Now, let's open our Code Bug Fixer application's `app.py` file in PyCharm and import all the necessary libraries to access Stripe and a SQL database:

app.py

```python
from flask import Flask, request, render_template
import openai
import config
import hashlib
import sqlite3
import stripe
```

We have just added the following libraries to our `app.py` file:

- `hashlib`: Provides interfaces to secure hash algorithms. It is used to generate hash values of data. In our case, we will use `hashlib` to hash user information before storing them in the database for security purposes.
- `sqlite3`: This library provides a lightweight disk-based database that doesn't require a separate server process and allows us to access the database using SQL commands. We will use it to create and manage a database to store user information.
- `stripe`: This is a third-party library that provides a Python client for the Stripe API, which allows us to handle payments in our application. We will use it to process payments made by users through our application.

While the `sqlite3` and `hashlib` are built-in libraries in Python, you will need to install `stripe`. You can simply do that by opening a new PyCharm terminal by going to **View | Tool Windows | Terminal** and typing the following:

```
$ pip install stripe
```

After successfully installing Stripe, you can proceed to configure the Stripe test key. To do so, simply navigate to the Stripe dashboard, and then head over to the **Developers** tab, followed by the **API keys** section. From there, you can click on the option to reveal the test key, which will allow you to copy the test key for use.

To create a new API key entry, make the required modifications to the files listed in your Code Bug Fixer project:

config.py

```
API_KEY = "<YOUR_OPENAI_API_KEY>"
STRIPE_TEST_KEY = "<YOUR_STRIPE_API_TEST_KEY>"
```

app.py

```
openai.api_key = config.API_KEY
stripe.api_key = config.STRIPE_TEST_KEY
```

This code will add your Stripe API test key to the `config.py` file and then retrieve this key in the `app.py` file, allowing your application to communicate with the Stripe APIs using the specified keys securely.

The next step is to add the `initialize_database()` function just under the API keys in `app.py`. This function will create a SQLite database and a table of users with two columns for `fingerprint` and the `usage_counter`, as shown in *Table 4.1*:

```
def initialize_database():
    conn = sqlite3.connect('app.db')
    c = conn.cursor()
    c.execute(
        '''CREATE TABLE IF NOT EXISTS users (fingerprint text primary key, usage_counter int)''')
    conn.commit()
    conn.close()
```

The preceding function establishes a connection to a newly created `SQLite` database named `app.db`, using the `sqlite3` library in Python. Then, it creates a **cursor object** called c, which is used to execute SQL commands and fetch results from the database. The cursor object allows you to perform various operations on the database such as creating tables, inserting data, and updating data.

Then, we use the cursor object to execute a SQL command that creates a table named `users` in the connected SQLite database. This table has two columns, `fingerprint` and `usage_counter`; the `fingerprint` column will hold the user browser ID, and `usage_counter` will hold the number of application usages for a specific user. The `primary key` keyword specifies that the `fingerprint` column is the primary key of the table.

Finally, we can `commit` the changes made to the database by the previous SQL command so that they become permanent, and `close` the database connection, freeing up any resources that were used by the connection.

This is how you can initialize a SQL database for the Code Bug Fixer application. Those are all necessary libraries to create a SQL database and configure the Stripe test key. In the next step, you will discover the process of obtaining the `fingerprint` browser, which will aid you to recognize individual users who utilize your application.

Getting a Browser Fingerprint ID

In order to track and identify unique users of your web application, you need a way to obtain their browser fingerprint. A browser fingerprint is a unique identifier generated by the browser based on various parameters, such as browser type, screen resolution, and installed fonts. In this section, we will explore how to obtain the browser fingerprint ID in Python.

It is considered a good practice to have a dedicated Python function for each individual task in our application, and generating a browser fingerprint is no exception. Therefore, it is appropriate to create a new function called `get_fingerprint()` under the `initialize_database()` function:

```python
def get_fingerprint():
    browser = request.user_agent.browser
    version = request.user_agent.version and float(
        request.user_agent.version.split(".")[0])
    platform = request.user_agent.platform
    string = f"{browser}:{version}:{platform}"
    fingerprint = hashlib.sha256(string.encode("utf-8")).hexdigest()
    print(fingerprint)
    return fingerprint
```

The `get_fingerprint()` function is a Flask view function that is responsible for generating, in most cases, a unique browser fingerprint for each user who interacts with the application. A fingerprint is a hash of a string that uniquely identifies a user based on their browser type, version, and platform.

> **Important Note**
> The browser fingerprint is not 100% guaranteed to be unique for every user, but browser fingerprinting can often generate a relatively unique identifier that distinguishes one user from another. Identifiers such as an IP address or device-specific identifiers such as MAC addresses are more suitable for real-world applications.

First, the function gets the `user_agent` object from the request object using `request.user_agent`. This object contains information about the user's browser, platform, and version.

Next, the function constructs a string from the browser, version, and platform information by concatenating them together, separated by colons (:). This string is used as the input to the `hashlib.sha256()` function, which generates a hash of the input string using the **SHA-256** algorithm. The resulting hash is a 64-character hexadecimal string that represents the unique browser fingerprint. We also add a `print()` statement so that we can verify the fingerprint in our PyCharm logs.

The function returns the generated fingerprint string. We will later store the fingerprint in the SQLite database, along with the usage counter for each user, so that the application can keep track of how many times a user has accessed the application. This information is used to determine whether the user needs to pay to continue using the application.

Now, it is time to cover the final part of our user tracking mechanism by getting the number of app utilizations per user in the next section.

Tracking Application Users

In this section, we will delve into the usage counter functionality of the application's backend. Specifically, we will examine the `get_usage_counter()` and `update_usage_counter()` functions, which are responsible for retrieving and updating the usage counter associated with a user's browser fingerprint ID. These functions play a crucial role in determining when a user has exceeded their usage limit and should be prompted to make a payment to continue using the application.

The `get_usage_counter()` function is responsible for retrieving the usage counter for a particular browser fingerprint from the SQLite database. The counter keeps track of how many times a user with that fingerprint has submitted a code error:

```
def get_usage_counter(fingerprint):
    conn = sqlite3.connect('app.db')
    c = conn.cursor()
    result = c.execute('SELECT usage_counter FROM users WHERE
                       fingerprint=?', [fingerprint]).fetchone()
    conn.close()
    if result is None:
        conn = sqlite3.connect('app.db')
        c = conn.cursor()
        c.execute('INSERT INTO users (fingerprint, usage_counter)
                  VALUES ' '(?, 0)', [fingerprint])
        conn.commit()
        conn.close()
        return 0
    else:
        return result[0]
```

The function takes `fingerprint` as an argument because it is used to retrieve the usage counter for the given browser fingerprint. The fingerprint serves as the unique identifier for each user of the application, and the function looks up the usage counter associated with that fingerprint in the database. It creates a connection to the **SQLite** database named `app.db` and then creates a cursor object that can execute `SQLite` commands on the database.

Then, the `c.execute()` command creates a new database table called `users` with two columns named `fingerprint` and `usage_counter`. It only creates the table if it doesn't already exist.

The `result` executes a SQL query to fetch the value of the `usage_counter` column for the given `fingerprint` from the `users` table. It does so by using parameterized queries and the `fetchone()` method. If no record is found for the given fingerprint, the result will be set to `None` for new users.

Once the connection with the database is closed, the function checks whether the result of the previous database query is `None` or not. If it is `None`, it means there is no record for the provided `fingerprint` in the `users` table. In this case, the function does the following:

1. Connects to the database.
2. Creates a cursor object.
3. Inserts a new record for `fingerprint` with a `usage_counter` value of 0.
4. Commits the changes to the database.
5. Closes the connection.
6. Returns 0.

If the result is not `None`, it means that there is already a record for the provided `fingerprint` in the `users` table. In this case, the function returns the value of the `usage_counter` column of the record. In essence, this function aims to either return the value of 0 for new users or the count of usages for those already in the database.

The `update_usage_counter()` function, on the other side, is responsible for updating the usage counter in the database for a given browser fingerprint. The function takes two arguments – the browser fingerprint and the updated usage counter value:

```
def update_usage_counter(fingerprint, usage_counter):
    conn = sqlite3.connect('app.db')
    c = conn.cursor()
    c.execute('UPDATE users SET usage_counter=? WHERE fingerprint=?',
              [usage_counter, fingerprint])
    conn.commit()
    conn.close()
```

Once connected to the database and an edition cursor has been created, the function is responsible for updating the usage counter after every use of our Code Bug Fixer app. It uses the `execute` method of the cursor object to execute a SQL statement that updates the `usage_counter` field for the user with the provided `fingerprint`.

The SQL statement uses `placeholders` ? to indicate where the values of `usage_counter` and `fingerprint` should be inserted. The values to be inserted are passed as a list in the second argument of `execute()` in the order they appear in the SQL statement. The `WHERE` clause ensures that the update is only applied to the row matching the specified `fingerprint`.

To sum up, the `get_usage_counter()` function retrieves the usage counter for a user's browser fingerprint ID from the SQLite database, while the `update_usage_counter()` function updates the usage counter value in the database for a given fingerprint after every use of the Code Bug Fixer app. These functions are crucial to determine when a user has exceeded their usage limit and should be prompted to make a payment to continue using the application. We can now implement all the functions we have created so far into our Code Bug Fixer application `index()` page.

Implementing the Usage Counters

In this section, we will integrate all the functions that we created earlier into the `index()` page of our Code Bug Fixer application. By doing so, we will be able to keep track of the number of times a user has submitted a code error and whether they have reached the limit of three submissions, thus requiring them to pay to continue. Additionally, we will be able to associate each submission with a unique browser fingerprint to prevent users from submitting multiple errors using different aliases:

```
@app.route("/", methods=["GET", "POST"])
def index():
    initialize_database()
    fingerprint = get_fingerprint()
    usage_counter = get_usage_counter(fingerprint)
```

The preceding code snippet performs three essential tasks. Firstly, it initializes the database, then it retrieves the user's browser fingerprint, and fetches their current usage counter from the database. The database table for users will be created if it does not already exist. The fingerprint variable uniquely identifies the user and allows us to track their usage counter.

After our initialization is completed, we need to set a rule that will pass the control to the payment page if the usage counter is higher than a specific number:

```
if request.method == "POST":
    if usage_counter > 3:
        return render_template("payment.html")
```

After that, we check whether the HTTP request method is POST, which indicates that the user has submitted a form on the website. In our case, this means that the user has submitted code for fixing in the Code Bug Fixer. Then, our app will check whether the user's usage counter is greater than 3. If it is, it means the user has exceeded their limit of free usage and should be directed to the payment page. The function returns a rendered template of the payment.html page. We also add a print() statement so that we can verify the counter increment in our PyCharm logs.

After the usage counter is initialized and we have a mechanism to check whether it is greater than the allowed number of usages, the last step is to make sure that the usage counter increments every time the user utilizes the Code Bug Fixer:

```
fixed_code_prompt = (f"Fix this code: \n\n{code}\n\nError:\n\n{error}."
    f" \n Respond only with the fixed code."
)
fixed_code_completions = openai.Completion.create(
    engine=model_engine,
    prompt=fixed_code_prompt,
    max_tokens=1024,
    n=1,
    stop=None,
    temperature=0.9,
)
fixed_code = fixed_code_completions.choices[0].text
usage_counter += 1
print(usage_counter)
update_usage_counter(fingerprint, usage_counter)
```

You can add those increments after the second ChatGPT API completion code, as shown previously. We will first increment the usage_counter variable by one, which means that the user has used the service one more time. After that, we will update the usage_counter value in the database for the user, identified by their browser fingerprint. This ensures that the usage counter is persistent across user sessions and reflects the total number of times the user has used the service. We also add a print() statement so that we can verify the counter increment in our PyCharm logs.

You can now run the Code Bug Fixer application to verify that your usage tracking method works successfully. Once the Code Bug Fixer is up and running, you can place a sample buggy code and an error into the relevant fields, and then click the **Code Fix** button. Perform that operation twice so that your usage counter can increment twice. Once you get the response for ChatGPT API and the **Fixed Code** and **Explanation** fields in your Code Bug Fixer are populated, you can go back to the PyCharm **Run** window and verify that your fingerprint and usage counter are displayed (see *Figure 4.3*).

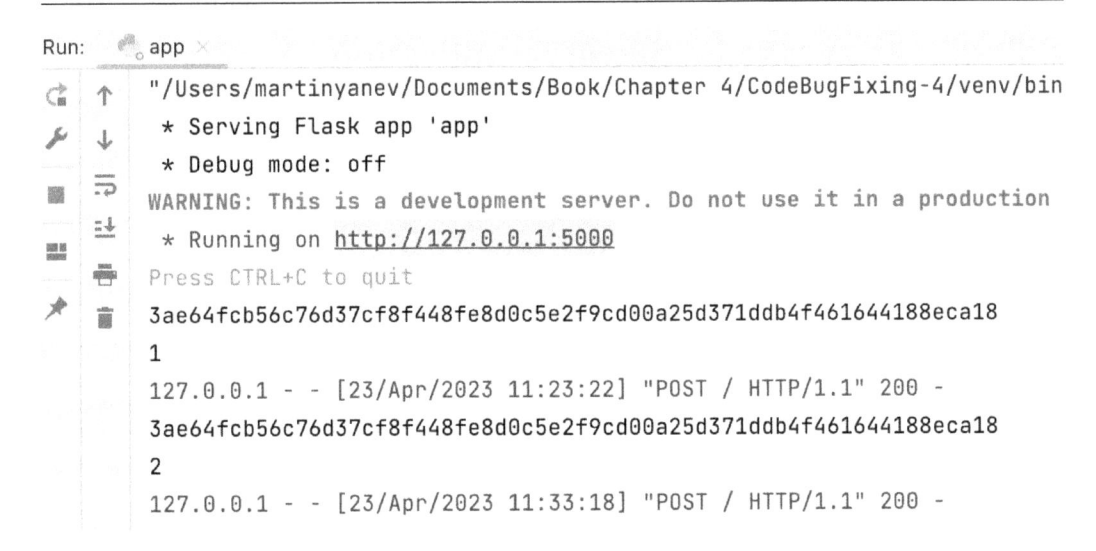

```
Run:        app
     ↑     "/Users/martinyanev/Documents/Book/Chapter 4/CodeBugFixing-4/venv/bin
     ↓     * Serving Flask app 'app'
           * Debug mode: off
           WARNING: This is a development server. Do not use it in a production
           * Running on http://127.0.0.1:5000
           Press CTRL+C to quit
           3ae64fcb56c76d37cf8f448fe8d0c5e2f9cd00a25d371ddb4f461644188eca18
           1
           127.0.0.1 - - [23/Apr/2023 11:23:22] "POST / HTTP/1.1" 200 -
           3ae64fcb56c76d37cf8f448fe8d0c5e2f9cd00a25d371ddb4f461644188eca18
           2
           127.0.0.1 - - [23/Apr/2023 11:33:18] "POST / HTTP/1.1" 200 -
```

Figure 4.3: The Browser Fingerprint and Usage Counter Logging

3ae64fc… is your specific browser fingerprint, while the number represents the number of times you currently used the application. Since you performed two requests to the ChatGPT API, the counter incremented twice.

To confirm the creation of a new database, you can check for a file named app.db in your project directory. This file is where all user data will be stored and will persist even if you shut down and restart the application.

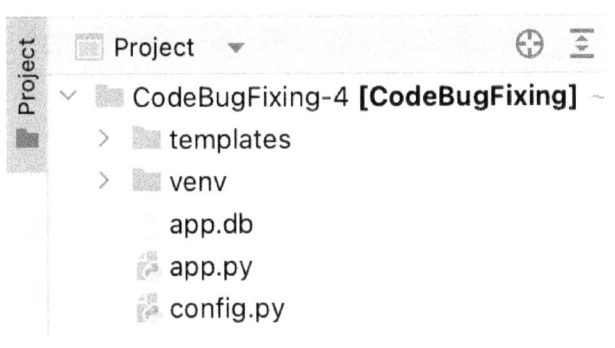

```
Project
  CodeBugFixing-4 [CodeBugFixing]
    > templates
    > venv
      app.db
      app.py
      config.py
```

Figure 4.4: The Database Display

This was the final step to add the main backend functionality to our Code Bug Fixer application. In the next section, you will learn how to build the /charge page, where users will be redirected when their free trial ends.

Adding Payments to a ChatGPT Application

In this section, I will guide you through the process of creating the payment page and functions in the Code Bug Fixer. We will create a payments page connected with Stripe to offer users three different subscription plans:

- **Monthly plan**: Users will be billed $5 every month
- **Quarterly plan**: Users will be billed $12 every quarter
- **Annual plan**: Users will be billed $50 every year

We will also create a confirmation page that will confirm the plan that a user has purchased by using a simple statement such as *"You have successfully paid $12 for the quarterly plan for unlimited access to the Code Bug Fixer."*

Next, you will learn how to create the `payment.html` file.

Building the Payments Page

Here, we will create a complete HTML document that includes a form to collect payment information from users. We will use the **Bulma CSS** framework to style the page and include **jQuery** and the Stripe API to handle the payment processing.

The page will be divided into three columns, each displaying a different payment plan option. Each option includes a card with a title, subtitle, and description of the plan. The payment form is located in the footer of each card, and it includes hidden input fields for the plan type and payment amount. The Stripe API is used to generate a payment button that collects payment information and initiates payment processing (see *Figure 4.5*).

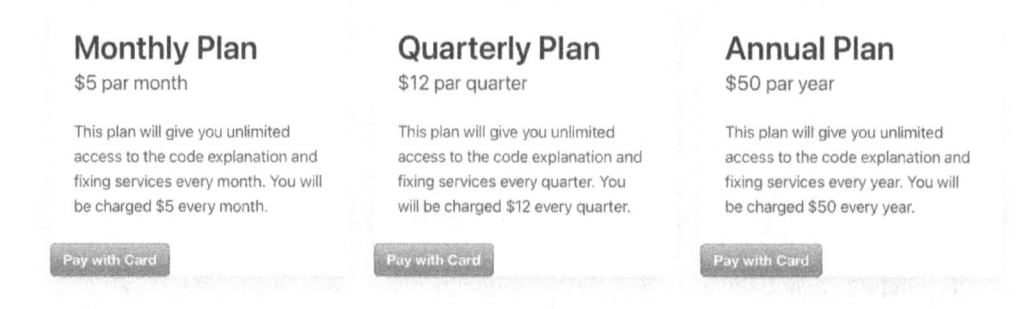

Figure 4.5: The Payment Page

To generate the **Payments** page, create two new files inside the `templates` folder. Those two files will be named `payments.html` and `charge.html`. Once you do that, the Code Bug Fixer project structure will be as follows:

```
CodeBugFixer/
├── templates/
│   ├── charge.html
│   ├── index.html
│   └── payment.html
├── venv/
├── app.db
├── app.py
└── config.py
```

We will start by building the head of our `payments.html` page:

```
<!DOCTYPE html>
<html lang="en">
<head>
    <meta charset="UTF-8">
    <meta name="viewport" content="width=device-width,
        initial-scale=1.0">
    <link rel="stylesheet" href="https://cdn.jsdelivr.net/npm/
        bulma@0.9.0/css/bulma.min.css">
    <script src="https://ajax.googleapis.com/ajax/libs/
        jquery/3.5.1/jquery.min.js"></script>
    <script src="https://js.stripe.com/v3/"></script>
    <title>Payment</title>
</head>
</html>
```

The head contains metadata and external resources that are necessary for a document to be displayed correctly. The character set specifies the character encoding used in the document, which is `UTF-8` in this case, and the viewport meta tag ensures that the document is displayed correctly on different devices with varying screen sizes.

The `link` tag is used to import external frameworks. We will use the Bulma CSS framework, which provides a set of pre-designed CSS styles to build responsive web pages quickly and easily.

Then, we will import the jQuery library, which is a popular JavaScript library that simplifies the process of manipulating HTML documents and handling events. The second import is the Stripe API library, which provides functionality to process online payments.

Now, under `</head>`, we can move to build the main body of the HTML file, which is enclosed within the `<body>` tags:

```
<body>
    <section class="section">
        <div class="container">
            <h1 class="title">Payment Options</h1>
            <div class="columns">
          </div>
        </div>
    </section>
</body>
```

We will use the `<section>` element, indicating that it is a separate section of the page that can be styled independently of other elements. There is a `<div>` element with a class of `columns`. This element is used to create a grid system to lay out content in columns. This is a common approach to creating responsive layouts, where the number of columns may vary depending on the screen size or device being used. The columns in this case will contain the different payment plan options that the user can select from, each with its own set of features and pricing.

Now, inside the `columns` `<div>` element, we can create three columns that represent the three payment plans mentioned earlier:

You can find the complete `payments.html` file here: `https://github.com/PacktPublishing/Building-AI-Applications-with-ChatGPT-APIs/blob/main/Chapter04%20CodeBugFixer/templates/payment.html`:

```
<div class="column">
    <div class="card">
        <div class="card-content">
            <p class="title">Monthly Plan</p>
            <p class="subtitle">$5 par month</p>
            <p>This plan will give you unlimited access
                to the code explanation and fixing services every
                month.
                You will be charged $5 every month.</p>
        </div>
        <footer class="card_footer">
            <form action="/charge" method="post">
                <input type="hidden" name="plan" value="monthly">
                <input type="hidden" name="amount" value="500">
                <script
                    src="https://checkout.stripe.com/checkout.js"
                    class="stripe-button"
                    data-key="<YOUR_PUBLIC_KEY>"
```

```html
                    data-amount="500"
                    data-name="Monthly Plan"
                    data-description="$5 per month"
                    data-image="https://stripe.com/img/
                        documentation/checkout/marketplace.png"
                    data-locale="auto"
                    data-zip-code="false">
                </script>
            </form>
        </footer>
    </div>
</div>
<div class="column">
    <div class="card">
        <div class="card-content">
            <p class="title">Quarterly Plan</p>
            <p class="subtitle">$12 par quarter</p>
            <p>This plan will give you unlimited access
                to the code explanation and fixing services every
                quarter.
                You will be charged $12 every quarter.</p>
        </div>
        <footer class="card_footer">
            <form action="/charge" method="post">
                <input type="hidden" name="plan" value="quarterly">
                <input type="hidden" name="amount" value="1200">
                <script
                    src="https://checkout.stripe.com/checkout.js"
                    class="stripe-button"
                    data-key="<YOUR_PUBLIC_KEY>"
                    data-amount="1200"
                    data-name="Quarterly Plan"
                    data-description="$12 per month"
                    data-image="https://stripe.com/img/documentation/
                        checkout/marketplace.png"
                    data-locale="auto"
                    data-zip-code="false">
                </script>
            </form>
        </footer>
    </div>
</div>
<div class="column">
    <div class="card">
```

```html
                    <div class="card-content">
                        <p class="title">Annual Plan</p>
                        <p class="subtitle">$50 par year</p>
                        <p>This plan will give you unlimited access
                            to the code explanation and fixing services every
                            year.
                            You will be charged $50 every year.</p>
                    </div>
                    <footer class="card_footer">
                        <form action="/charge" method="post">
                            <input type="hidden" name="plan" value="yearly">
                            <input type="hidden" name="amount" value="5000">
                            <script
                                src="https://checkout.stripe.com/checkout.js"
                                class="stripe-button"
                                data-key="<YOUR_PUBLIC_KEY>"
                                data-amount="5000"
                                data-name="Yearly Plan"
                                data-description="$50 per month"
                                data-image="https://stripe.com/img/documentation/
                                    checkout/marketplace.png"
                                data-locale="auto"
                                data-zip-code="false">
                            </script>
                        </form>
                    </footer>
                </div>
            </div>
```

> **Important Note**
> Ensure that you replace the "`<YOUR_PUBLIC_KEY>`" tag with the public key obtained from your Stripe account.

The first `<div>` element with a `column` class is responsible for creating a card-like element that presents information about the monthly plan offered to the user. The card contains information about the name of the plan, the subscription fee, and what the user can expect from this plan.

The `<div>` element with a `card` class is used to create the card that presents information about the monthly subscription plan. Inside the card, the card content is defined with the `card-content` class. The card content consists of three paragraphs, the first containing the title of the plan, `Monthly Plan`, the second containing the subscription fee `$5 per month`, and the third providing a description of the plan, which highlights the benefits of subscribing to the plan.

Inside the footer, a `form` element is defined, which is used to submit the subscription request to the server. The form's action attribute is set to `/charge`, which indicates that the subscription request will be sent to the `/charge` route on the server. We will build the `/charge` page backend function later. This function will ensure that a confirmation is shown to the users, once a payment plan has been purchased.

The form contains two hidden input fields used to send the plan's name and value. In this case, the plan's name is set to `monthly`, while the amount attribute has a value set to `500`, which represents the subscription amount in cents. This information will be used to render the confirmation page.

Finally, a script tag is included inside the form element, which loads a Stripe checkout script. This script is responsible for creating a **secure payment form** that allows the user to enter their payment details and complete the subscription process. The script is configured with various attributes, including the Stripe API key, the subscription amount, the plan name and description, and an image to be displayed on the payment form. The script also sets the `data-locale` attribute to `auto`, which ensures that the payment form's language will be automatically set based on the user's location. The `data-zip-code` attribute is set to `false`, which means that the payment form will not require the user to enter their zip code.

As you can see in the code snippet, the columns for the quarterly and yearly plans are built in the same way as the monthly plan. The only differences are the values for the plan's name, subtitle, and cost, as well as the values for the hidden input fields for the plan and the amount to be charged.

You can verify that your `payment.html` page works properly by displaying it in any browser. This can be easily done with PyCharm. You can hover over the HTML file and choose your favorite browser from the preview options located in the top-right corner of the **Edit** window (see *Figure 4.6*). You should then see a payment page, similar to the one displayed in *Figure 4.5*.

Figure 4.6: Displaying an HTML file in the Browser Using PyCharm

This is how you can build a payments page that includes a form to collect payment information from users. We styled the payments page using the Bulma CSS framework, and the payment processing is handled using jQuery and the Stripe API. The page is divided into three columns, each displaying a different payment plan option, and the payment form is in the footer of each card. The Stripe API is used to generate a payment button that collects payment information and initiates payment processing.

In the next section, you will learn how to create a charge function in your application that handles user payments, using the Stripe API, and returns a payment confirmation page.

Confirming User Payments

In the previous section, you learned that when a user chooses to buy a payment plan to access your application, we will promptly trigger the /charge page and furnish it with the name of the selected plan, as well as the corresponding payment amount in cents.

We can build the charge() function in our app.py file under the index() function. This function is part of the Code Bug Fixer web application and handles the charge process when a user selects a pricing plan and submits their payment information. The function is triggered when the user clicks the **Pay with Card** button in the pricing plan section of payment.html:

```python
@app.route("/charge", methods=["POST"])
def charge():
    amount = int(request.form["amount"])
    plan = str(request.form["plan"])

    customer = stripe.Customer.create(
        email=request.form["stripeEmail"],
        source=request.form["stripeToken"]
    )

    charge = stripe.PaymentIntent.create(
        customer=customer.id,
        amount=amount,
        currency="usd",
        description="App Charge"
    )

    return render_template("charge.html", amount=amount, plan=plan)
```

You can find the complete app.py file here: https://github.com/PacktPublishing/Building-AI-Applications-with-ChatGPT-APIs/blob/main/Chapter04%20CodeBugFixer/app.py.

The `@app.route("/charge", methods=["POST"])` decorator creates a route to handle a POST request sent to the /charge endpoint. This means that when the form in the HTML template is submitted, it will send a POST request to this endpoint.

Both the `amount` and `plan` variables are assigned values that were previously sent by the user via a payment form, and they are used later in the function to create a new customer and charge the customer the appropriate amount based on the selected plan.

Then, we can create a new Stripe customer object using the Stripe API. The `stripe.Customer.create()` method takes two arguments – the email address of the customer and the payment source. In this case, the email address is obtained from the `stripeEmail` parameter in the POST request sent by the Stripe checkout form, and the payment source is obtained from the `stripeToken` parameter.

The `stripeToken` parameter is a unique identifier for the payment information provided by the user in the checkout form, such as credit card details or a payment app. Stripe uses this token to securely charge the user's payment method for the specified amount. By passing the `stripeToken` parameter to the source argument of `stripe.Customer.create()`, the payment information is associated with the newly created customer object in Stripe.

We can then use the Stripe API to create a charge object that is associated with the customer who provided their payment information. The `stripe.PaymentIntent.create()` method creates a new charge object in the Stripe API with the following arguments:

- `customer`: This is the ID of the Stripe customer object associated with the payment. The `customer.id` attribute is used to retrieve the ID of the customer object created in the previous step.
- `amount`: This is the amount of the charge in cents. The amount variable is set to the value passed in the POST request from the form.
- `currency`: This is the currency of the charge. In this case, it is set to USD.
- `description`: This is a brief description of the charge. In this case, it is set to **App Charge**.

After creating the charge, the function uses Flask's `render_template()` function to render the `charge.html` template and pass in the amount and plan variables. The `charge.html` template will be used to display a message to the user, indicating that their payment was successful.

Our final task when building the application is to create the `charge.html` file. This file will be used to display a confirmation message to the user after a successful charge has been made. The `render_template` function used in the charge function of the `app.py` file specifies that the `charge.html` file will be used to render the message.

You can now open the `charge.html` file that we created in the `templates` folder and add the following code:

```html
<!DOCTYPE html>
<html lang="en">
<head>
    <meta charset="UTF-8">
    <title>Payment Confirmation</title>
</head>
<body>
<h1>Payment Confirmation</h1>
<p>You have successfully paid ${{ amount / 100 }} for the {{ plan }} plan for unlimited access to the Code Bug Fixer</p>
</body>
</html>
```

In this simple HTML page, the `<body>` section contains a heading that says `Payment Confirmation`. The paragraph below the heading uses curly braces to display the amount and plan variables passed from the `charge()` function. Specifically, it displays the amount variable divided by `100` (because the amount variable is in cents) and the `plan` variable for the user to confirm the payment they have made.

When the `charge()` function is called and executed, it returns the `charge.html` file as a response, with the amount and plan variables passed as arguments to be rendered in the appropriate places in the HTML code.

Now that the payments infrastructure has been added to your app, you can test it by navigating to the relevant pages and clicking on the payment buttons. You can follow the following steps:

1. Run the `app.py` file to start up your Code Bug Fixer.
2. Create more than three bug-fixing requests to the ChatGPT API to be prompted to the `Payments` page (see *Figure 4.5*).
3. Click on the **Pay with Card** button on one of the payment plans.
4. Enter the following sample credit card details in the pop-up window (see *Figure 4.7*):

    - **Email**: `mrsmith@gmail.com`
    - **Card number**: `4242 4242 4242 4242`
    - **Expiry date**: `09 / 30`
    - **Security code**: `424`

5. Click the **Pay** button:

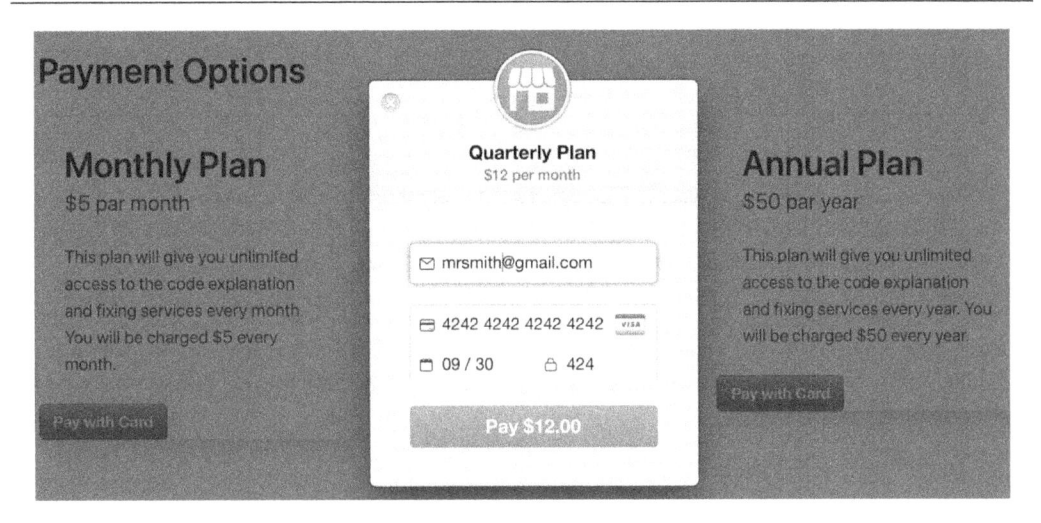

Figure 4.7: Stripe Payment Information

Once you have submitted your payment, you should be redirected to a payment confirmation page that displays a message indicating that your payment has been successfully processed, as shown in *Figure 4.8*:

Payment Confirmation

You have successfully paid $12.0 for the quarterly plan for unlimited access to the Code Bug Fixer

Figure 4.8: The Confirmation Page

In this section, you saw how to confirm user payments using the Stripe API in a Code Bug Fixer web application. We built `charge()` to handle the charge process when a user selects a pricing plan and submits their payment information. We also tested the payment infrastructure of the app using sample credit card details.

Summary

This chapter focused on the implementation of a payment infrastructure into a web application using the Stripe API. It provided instructions on how to set up a Stripe account, create API keys, and configure the payment settings. You saw the importance of selecting the appropriate business strategy, such as subscription or one-time payment, before implementing payment options. You also saw how to track user visits and usage using a SQL database and how to create payment plans on a payment page. Additionally, the chapter outlined the functions required to retrieve and update the usage counter and described how to implement them to track a user's payment status.

You learned how to build the `charge()` function, which handles the payment process when a user selects a pricing plan and submits their payment information. We covered the use of the Stripe API to create a new customer and charge object and render the `charge.html` template to display a confirmation message to the user. This section also provided instructions on how to test the payment feature using sample credit card details. The chapter provided a comprehensive guide on implementing a payment infrastructure in a web application, integrating the Stripe API and the ChatGPT API, from creating a Stripe account to handling payments and confirming user payments.

In *Chapter 5, Quiz Generation App the ChatGPT and Django*, you will learn how to integrate Cthe hatGPT API with **Django**, a full stack web framework that comes with many built-in features and is designed to handle larger and more complex web applications than Flask. Django includes everything from URL routing, database ORM, admin interface, to authentication and security features, providing a more comprehensive framework for web development. We will integrate Djnago with the powerful OpenAI GPT-3.5 turbo model for chat completions and explore how to keep track on the chat context.

5
Quiz Generation App with ChatGPT and Django

In this chapter, we will delve into the exciting world of combining the power of **ChatGPT**, a cutting-edge language model, with **Django**, the widely acclaimed Python framework for app development. Together, we will explore how to build a dynamic and interactive exam generation application that leverages artificial intelligence.

In the previous chapters, we primarily focused on Flask, a lightweight and basic web framework. However, in this chapter, we will focus on Django, a robust and advanced framework that has been instrumental in constructing some of the most renowned and widely used applications, including Instagram, Dropbox, and Pinterest. You will have the opportunity to explore the capabilities of Django, which include features such as database management, authentication system, admin interface, and form handling.

You will learn how to build a Django project from scratch, including setting up the environment and creating the foundational components for your application. We will focus on creating the framework and views for a quiz generation app. You will explore the integration of ChatGPT and Django, enabling you to use AI for quiz generation. To ensure a comprehensive learning experience, we will cover two essential views within the application. One view will allow users to generate quizzes by inputting study material and executing the ChatGPT API, resulting in the generation of relevant questions that will be stored in a database. The other view will enable users to conveniently download any previously generated tests.

In this chapter, you will explore the following:

- Installing Django and creating your first running project
- Building Django views for an exam generation application
- Integrating the ChatGPT API with Django and intercepting ChatGPT responses in the Django backend
- Utilizing Bootstrap templates to create a visually appealing interface

- Storing and fetching ChatGPT responses in a secure database
- Adding file download functionality to your application

By the end of this chapter, you will have the knowledge and skills to employ the ChatGPT API to generate examination questions derived from any provided study material.

Technical Requirements

You will need to cover some basic software installations before continuing with this chapter. In addition, the installation of the Django web framework will be demonstrated in the next section.

The project entails the following technical prerequisites:

- Python version 3.7 or higher installed on your local machine
- A code editor, with PyCharm recommended for an optimal experience
- An OpenAI API key to access the necessary API functionalities

You can access the code examples used in this chapter on GitHub at the provided repository: `https://github.com/PacktPublishing/Building-AI-Applications-with-ChatGPT-APIs/tree/main/Chapter05%20QuizApp/quiz_project`

Building a Django Project

In this section, we will embark on the exciting journey of building a Django project that forms the foundation of our quiz generation application. We will guide you through the step-by-step process of setting up and structuring your Django project, ensuring that you have solid groundwork to build upon. By the end of this section, you will have a fully functional Django project that can facilitate the automated generation of quizzes based on study materials.

Our adventure begins with the installation of Django and the creation of a new Django project. We will walk you through the process of setting up your development environment, including the installation of Python and the Django framework. With Django in place, we will use the command-line interface to generate a new Django project, providing you with the necessary directory structure and initial configuration files.

We can start by launching PyCharm and clicking on **New Project** or going to **File | New Project** to create a new project. You will be prompted to the **New Project** window, in which you name your project `QuizApp` and click **Create**.

To create your PyCharm project, you can follow these steps (see *Figure 5.1*):

1. Launch PyCharm.
2. Click on **New Project** or navigate to **File | New Project** to create a new project.

3. The **New Project** window will appear.
4. Provide a name for your project, such as QuizApp.
5. Click on **Create** to proceed.

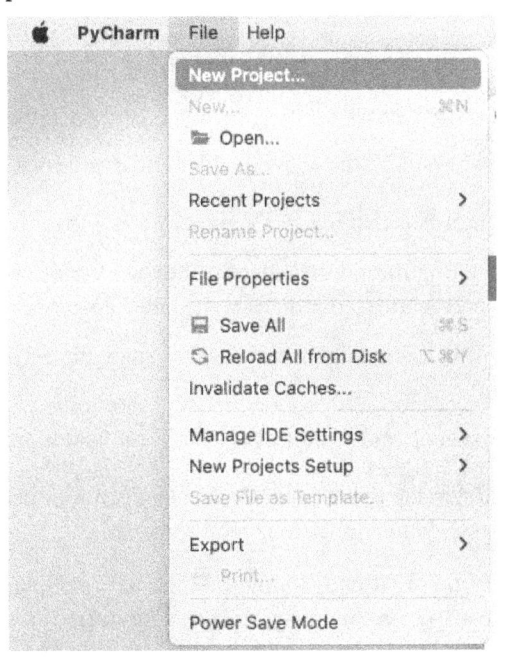

Figure 5.1: The PyCharm File Menu

You can now install Django in your local Python environment. To do so, look for the **Terminal** tab located at the bottom of the PyCharm window. If you don't see it, go to the menu bar and click on **View | Tool Windows | Terminal** to enable it. From the terminal, run the following command to install Django using pip:

```
$pip install Django
```

Next, you run the following command to create a new Django project in the terminal:

```
$django-admin startproject quiz_project
```

When you run this command, Django's command-line utility, called django-admin, creates a new project directory with the specified name quiz_project. This directory will contain the necessary files and folders to start a Django project.

The `startproject` command initializes the project structure by generating the following files:

- `manage.py`: A command-line utility that allows you to interact with various Django commands and manage your project.
- `quiz_project`: The project directory, which will have the same name as the one specified in the command. This directory serves as the root of your Django project and contains configuration files and other project-specific components.

Inside the project directory, you will find the following files and directories:

- `__init__.py`: An empty file that marks the directory as a Python package
- `settings.py`: The configuration file where you define various settings for your Django project, including database settings, middleware, installed apps, and more
- `urls.py`: The URL configuration file that defines the mapping between URLs and views for your project
- `wsgi.py`: The **Web Server Gateway Interface (WSIG)** configuration file used for deployment

You can further customize and develop your Django project by defining models, views, and templates and configuring settings based on your application's requirements.

In Django, a project is a collection of settings, configurations, and multiple apps that work together to create a web application. An app, on the other hand, is a modular component within a Django project that serves a specific purpose or functionality. For this reason, in our `quiz_project` we can create a new application as follows.

```
$cd quiz_project
$python manage.py startapp quiz_app
```

The purpose of our newly created application will be to generate AI questions and enable users to download them. A new directory is generated with the specified app name `quiz_app`. This directory contains the necessary files and folders to develop your Django app. Let's explore the typical project structure and files within the app directory:

- `admin.py`: This file is used to register your app's models with the Django admin interface. You can customize how your models are displayed and interacted with on the admin site.
- `apps.py`: This file defines the app configuration, including the name of the app, and uses initialization functions when the application is started.
- `models.py`: Here, you define your app's data models using Django's **object-relational mapping (ORM)**. Models represent the structure of your data and define the tables in your database.
- `tests.py`: This file is used to write tests for your app. You can create test cases and run them to ensure the functionality of your app.

- `views.py`: This file contains the views for your app, which define the logic to process user requests and return responses. Its views handle user interactions and provide the necessary data to render templates.
- `migrations/`: The folder is used to store database migration files. Migrations are a way to manage changes to your database schema over time. They allow you to track and apply incremental changes to your database structure, such as creating new tables, modifying existing tables, and adding or removing columns.

The complete high-level project structure of the Quiz Generation app is as follows:

```
quiz_project/
├── quiz_app
│   ├── migrations/
│   ├── __init__.py
│   ├── admin.py
│   ├── apps.py
│   ├── models.py
│   ├── tests.py
│   └── views.py
├── quiz_project/
│   ├── settings.py
│   ├── urls.py
│   ├── wsgi.py
│   └── __init__.py
└── manage.py
```

By default, Django includes several built-in apps such as `auth`, `admin`, `contenttypes`, and `sessions`. These apps have their own migrations that need to be applied to create the required tables holding the default user data in the database.

Django utilizes a default SQLite database to store data. We can run the following command to initialize the database with all existing models:

```
$python manage.py migrate
```

When you run the command, Django will check for any pending migrations in these default apps and apply them if necessary. This ensures that the database schema is properly set up to support Django's built-in functionality, verified by the command output:

```
Operations to perform:
  Apply all migrations: admin, auth, contenttypes, sessions
Running migrations:
  Applying contenttypes.0001_initial... OK
  Applying auth.0001_initial... OK
```

```
Applying admin.0001_initial... OK
Applying admin.0002_logentry_remove_auto_add... OK
Applying admin.0003_logentry_add_action_flag_choices... OK
Applying contenttypes.0002_remove_content_type_name... OK
Applying auth.0002_alter_permission_name_max_length... OK
Applying auth.0003_alter_user_email_max_length... OK
Applying auth.0004_alter_user_username_opts... OK
Applying auth.0005_alter_user_last_login_null... OK
Applying auth.0006_require_contenttypes_0002... OK
Applying auth.0007_alter_validators_add_error_messages... OK
Applying auth.0008_alter_user_username_max_length... OK
Applying auth.0009_alter_user_last_name_max_length... OK
Applying auth.0010_alter_group_name_max_length... OK
Applying auth.0011_update_proxy_permissions... OK
Applying auth.0012_alter_user_first_name_max_length... OK
Applying sessions.0001_initial... OK
```

Once the migrations are all set, you can start the development server to run your Django project locally:

```
$python manage.py runserver

Watching for file changes with StatReloader
Performing system checks...

System check identified no issues (0 silenced).
May 26, 2023 - 18:59:08
Django version 4.2.1, using settings quiz_project.settings'
Starting development server at http://127.0.0.1:8000/
Quit the server with CONTROL-C.
```

When you run this command in the terminal, Django's `manage.py` script launches a lightweight web server, allowing you to run and test your Django application locally. To access your app, you can click on the link provided in the terminal output (http://127.0.0.1:8000/) or type it in your browser. This link includes a local IP address and a port on which you can access your new app (see *Figure 5.2*).

The install worked successfully! Congratulations!

You are seeing this page because DEBUG=True is in your settings file and you have not configured any URLs.

Figure 5.2: The Django Welcome Screen

Seeing the Django welcome page in our browser means that we successfully created our Django project and application. In the next section, we will begin building our application by defining models, views, and templates and configuring the URL routing, according to your project requirements.

Creating the Exam App Frame and Views

In this section, we will focus on building the fundamental structure of your Django application. We will begin by exploring the Django settings, where you will learn how to configure important aspects such as database connections and middleware components. Understanding and properly setting these configurations is essential for the smooth operation of your application.

We will also learn URL handling in Django. You will discover how to define URL patterns using the `urls.py` file, enabling seamless navigation within your application. We will also cover dynamic URLs using regular expressions, allowing flexible and dynamic routing. Additionally, we will guide you through the process of incorporating a base template, which will provide consistent menus, sidebars, and views throughout your application.

Connecting Django Views and URLs

In Django, the relations between views, app URLs, and project URLs form a crucial structure to handle and route web requests. The flow begins with views, which are Python functions or classes responsible for processing specific HTTP requests and returning appropriate responses. Each view corresponds to a particular functionality or page within your application. Those views can be shown to users by being assigned a unique URL. Since, in Django, a project can have more than one application, those URLs are first defined on an app level in `quiz_app/urls.py`. Those URLs are then passed to the project-level `urls.py` file located in the `quiz_project` directory for our project (see *Figure 5.3*).

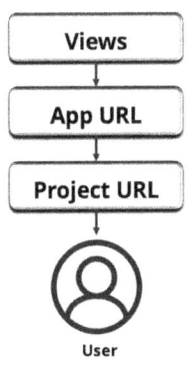

Figure 5.3: Django Views/URLs Architecture

By default, Django automatically generates the `quiz_project/urls.py` file when you initialize your project. However, it is important to note that we will need to manually create a new `urls.py` file inside the `quiz_app` folder. Unlike the project-level `urls.py` file, the `urls.py` file at the app level is not generated automatically, and it is essential to organize and define the URL patterns specific to the functionalities within `quiz_app`.

Now, you can open `quiz_app/views.py` and write the following Python code:

```python
from django.shortcuts import render

def home(request):
    return render(request, 'base.html')
```

This code demonstrates a simple Django view function named home. This view function is responsible for handling a specific type of request, typically an HTTP GET request, and generating an appropriate response.

Within the function, the Django shortcut `render` function is used to render an HTML template. The first parameter, `request`, represents the incoming HTTP request object. This object contains information about the request, such as headers, data, and user session details. The second parameter, `base.html`, specifies the template to be rendered.

Before building the `base.html` file, we need to ensure that the home view can be accessed by the user. To achieve that, we need to specify a unique URL in our `quiz_app/urls.py` file:

```python
from django.urls import path
from . import views

urlpatterns = [
    path('', views.home, name='home'),
]
```

Here, the `urlpatterns` variable is a list that holds the defined URL patterns for the application. In this case, there is a single URL pattern specified for now. The `path` function is used to define a URL pattern. It takes three arguments – the first argument is the URL pattern itself, which is represented by an empty string, `''`, in this case. This empty string signifies the root URL or the base URL of the application.

The second argument, `views.home`, refers to the view function that will handle the request for this URL pattern. The third argument, `name='home'`, provides a unique name for this URL pattern. This name can be used to reference the URL pattern from other parts of the application, such as templates or other URL configurations.

Finally, we can import this application-level URL into the project level by modifying `quiz_project/urls.py`:

```python
from django.contrib import admin
```

```
from django.urls import include, path

urlpatterns = [
    path('admin/', admin.site.urls),
    path('', include('quiz_app.urls')),
]
```

The provided code showcases the configuration of URL patterns in our Django project. Just like in the application-level URL file, here the `urlpatterns` variable holds a list of URL names for the project. In this case, there are two URL patterns specified.

The first URL pattern is defined using the `path` function with the `admin/` argument. This associates the `admin/` URL pattern with the Django admin interface, enabling access to the admin dashboard and related functionalities. The Django admin page is usually set by default and is not related to the functionality of our quiz application.

The path function `path('', include('quiz_app.urls'))` takes the app-level URLs from `quiz_app/urls.py`. The first argument, an empty string, `''`, signifies the root URL or base URL of the application. This means that when a user accesses the root URL of the project, this URL pattern will be matched.

The second argument, `include('quiz_app.urls')`, instructs Django to include the URL patterns defined in the `quiz_app.urls` module. This means that any URLs specified within the `quiz_app` application will be matched and handled accordingly.

This is what the hierarchical structure of URL handling looks like. We started from views that process requests to app-level URLs that define specific URL patterns, and finally, to project-level URLs that route requests to the appropriate app-level URLs. The process was illustrated with code examples, highlighting the significance of correctly configuring URLs at both the app and project levels for smooth navigation and functionality within a Django application.

In the upcoming section, we will delve into building HTML templates, including the essential `base.html` file. Templates play a crucial role in defining the visual structure and layout of web pages in a Django application. By constructing and customizing HTML templates, we can create a consistent and visually appealing user interface for our quiz application.

Developing Django Templates

In this section, we will focus on building the `base.html` template and incorporating CSS into our Django application. The `base.html` template serves as the foundation for the visual structure and layout of our web pages. To enhance the design and styling of our application, we will utilize external CSS resources. One valuable resource is the Bootstrap framework, which offers a wide range of pre-designed templates and components. We will go through the process of finding suitable templates from the official Bootstrap website (https://getbootstrap.com/docs/5.3/examples/), where you can explore various examples and choose the ones that align with your desired aesthetics and functionality.

You can easily access the code behind any of the Bootstrap templates if you use **Google Chrome**. For instance, for this project, we can use the **Dashboard template** that you can access here: `https://getbootstrap.com/docs/5.3/examples/dashboard/`. As you can see in *Figure 5.4*, the HTML code can be accessed by right-clicking on the **Dashboard** template and choosing the **View Page Source** option.

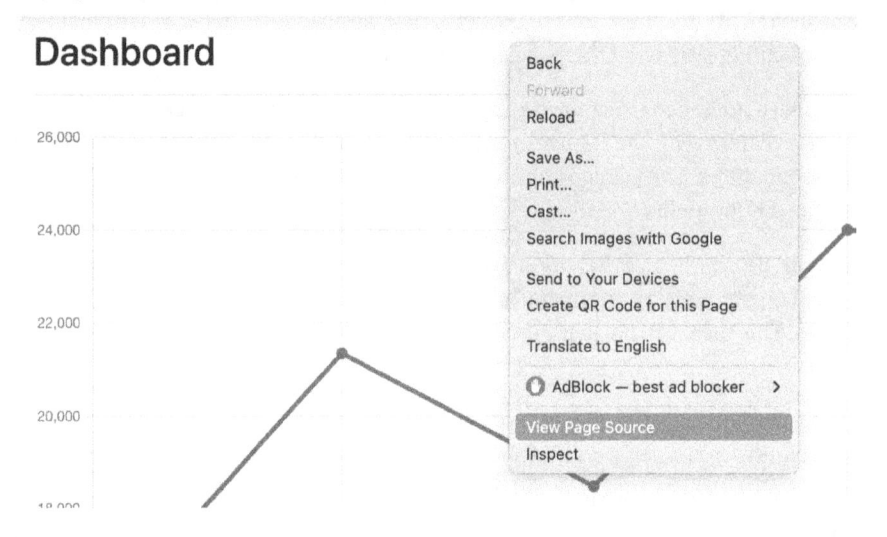

Figure 5.4: Viewing the Page Source in Chrome

By following this approach, you can extract specific sections from this template and incorporate them into your own application, allowing for easy customization and extension. This process establishes a solid foundation for your Django app.

To begin, you can create a `templates` folder in a separate location outside of both your application and project folders, adhering to the recommended structure outlined as follows. This organized setup ensures efficient management of your template files:

```
quiz_project/
├── quiz_app
├── quiz_project/
└──   templates
```

Within the `templates` directory, you will create a new HTML file named `base.html`, serving as the foundation for your application's structure. In this file, you can begin by including relevant links and defining the header section that sets the overall context for your application:

```
{% load static %}
```

```html
<html lang="en" data-bs-theme="auto">
<head>
  <script src="/docs/5.3/assets/js/color-modes.js"></script>
  <meta charset="utf-8">
  <meta name="viewport" content="width=device-width, initial-scale=1">
  <title>Quiz App</title>

  <!-- Bootstrap CSS -->
  <link href="{% static 'css/bootstrap.min.css' %}" rel="stylesheet" />

<!--  ; Custom styles for this template &ndash;&gt;-->
  <link href="{% static 'css/dashboard.css' %}" rel="stylesheet" />
</head>
```

The first line, `{% load static %}`, is a Django template tag that allows us to load static files, such as CSS style sheets and JavaScript scripts, into our HTML template. It enables us to access and utilize these files within our Django project. Later in this section, we will create the .css files, and they will be automatically passed to the HTML.

Then, the data-bs-theme attribute is used for automatic theme handling. This attribute is often used with Bootstrap, a popular CSS framework, to automatically switch between light and dark themes based on the user's device settings.

The head section contains various meta tags and external script and style sheet references. These meta tags provide information about the character encoding and viewport settings for the web page. They ensure that the web page is rendered properly and adjusts its layout to fit different screen sizes.

Next, we include external CSS style sheets. The `{% static 'css/bootstrap.min.css' %}` and `{% static 'css/dashboard.css' %}` tags refer to the static CSS files that we will create in our Django project. These CSS files provide styling rules and formatting instructions that define the visual appearance of elements on the web page.

Once the header is completed, we can now enter the following code snippet to build the body of our page:

```html
<body>
  <header class="navbar navbar-dark sticky-top bg-dark flex-md-nowrap
      p-0 shadow">
    <a class="navbar-brand col-md-3 col-lg-2 me-0 px-3 fs-6" href="#">
        Quiz App</a>
    <div class="navbar-nav">
    </div>
  </header>

  <div class="container-fluid">
    <div class="row">
```

```html
          <nav id="sidebarMenu" class="col-md-3 col-lg-2 d-md-block
            bg-body-tertiary sidebar collapse">
          <div class="position-sticky pt-3 sidebar-sticky">
            <ul class="nav flex-column">
              <li class="nav-item">
                <a class="nav-link active" aria-current="page" href="">
                  <span data-feather="home" class="align-text-bottom">
                    </span>
                  Questions Generator
                </a>
              </li>
              <li class="nav-item">
                <a class="nav-link active" aria-current="page"
                    href="/history">
                  <span data-feather="file" class="align-text-bottom">
                    </span>
                  My Quiz
                </a>
              </li>
            </ul>
          </div>
        </nav>
      </div>
    </div>
  </body>
</html>
```

Here, the body consists of a `<header>` section that contains a navigation bar. The navigation bar includes a brand name for the quiz app. The `<div class="navbar-nav">` element can be used to add additional navigation items if needed.

Inside this navigation, there is a `<nav id="sidebarMenu">` element that serves as a sidebar menu. It contains a list of navigation items that can be customized as needed. Each navigation item is represented by `<li class="nav-item">` with an associated link. We will have two main links inside the sidebar:

- The **Questions Generator** tab: This shows the ChatGPT quiz generation tool
- The **My Quiz** tab: This shows all the quizzes that the user created so far, ready to be downloaded

Now that your `base.html` has been completed, we can add the style files. To do that, create two new directories called `static` and `css` inside your `quiz_project`, as shown here:

```
quiz_project/
├── quiz_app
├── quiz_project/
```

```
|   ├── static/
|   └── css/
|       ├── dashboard.css
|       └── bootstrap.min.css
└── templates
```

Instead of writing the style files on our own, we can simply download the CSS files from the **Dashboard** template source code discussed earlier. Once downloaded, you can paste them into your `css` folder. You can find the links to each of the CSS files required for our project here:

- `dashboard.css`: https://getbootstrap.com/docs/5.3/examples/dashboard/dashboard.css
- `bootstrap.min.css`: https://getbootstrap.com/docs/5.3/dist/css/bootstrap.min.css

Alternatively, you can access all project files at our GitHub repository: https://github.com/PacktPublishing/Building-AI-Applications-with-ChatGPT-APIs.

Now, let's see how to integrate these HTML and CSS files into our Django project. By modifying the `settings.py` file, we can specify the directories where Django should look for static files, including HTML templates and CSS files. This configuration will ensure that our Django application can access and utilize the desired templates and CSS styles, providing a visually appealing and cohesive user experience throughout the entire application.

Firstly, to add the HTML files to your project, you can simply reference the `templates` directory inside the `settings.py` file. To do that, find the `TEMPLATES` dictionary and edit the `DIRS` key, as follows:

```
TEMPLATES = [
    {
        'BACKEND': 'django.template.backends.django.DjangoTemplates',
        'DIRS': [os.path.join(BASE_DIR, 'templates')],
        'APP_DIRS': True,
        'OPTIONS': {
            'context_processors': [
                'django.template.context_processors.debug',
                'django.template.context_processors.request',
                'django.contrib.auth.context_processors.auth',
                'django.contrib.messages.context_processors.messages',
            ],
        },
    },
]
```

This is used to construct the absolute path to the `templates` directory within your Django project. `BASE_DIR` refers to the base directory of your Django project, and `templates` is the name of the directory where your template files are stored.

By setting the `DIRS` key, you tell Django to include the `templates` directory as one of the locations to search for template files. This allows you to organize your template files separately from your application directories and provides a central location to store your HTML templates.

We will also need to import the `os` library at the beginning of the `setting.py` file:

```
import os
from pathlib import Path
```

Secondly, to pass all CSS files to your Django project, you can scroll to the bottom of `settings.py` and add the following:

```
# Static files (CSS, JavaScript, Images)
# https://docs.djangoproject.com/en/4.2/howto/static-files/

STATIC_URL = 'static/'
STATICFILES_DIRS = [os.path.join(BASE_DIR, 'quiz_project /static')]
STATIC_ROOT = os.path.join(BASE_DIR, 'static')

# Default primary key field type
# https://docs.djangoproject.com/en/4.2/ref/settings/#default-auto-field

DEFAULT_AUTO_FIELD = 'django.db.models.BigAutoField'
```

Here, `STATICFILES_DIRS` tells Django where to find static files during development, while `STATIC_ROOT` specifies the directory where static files will be collected for deployment. These settings ensure that your static files are organized and accessible, both during development and in a production environment. This will allow us to pick those CSS files for our project.

This section explained the process of developing Django templates by building a `base.html` template, incorporating CSS resources such as Bootstrap, and configuring the `settings.py` file to manage static files and templates in a Django project. After completing the steps outlined, you are now ready to run your Django application in the next section.

Running Your Django Application

Once you have completed the steps covered in the previous section, you can now run your Django project. To run a Django application, you will need to access again your PyCharm terminal or navigate to the root directory, `quiz_project`, of your Django project. This is the directory that contains the `manage.py` file. Once you're in the correct directory, execute the following command:

```
$python manage.py runserver
```

This command starts the development server, which allows you to run your Django application locally for testing and development purposes.

> **Important Note**
>
> An important note to keep in mind is that Django's development server has a useful feature called **auto-reloading**. This means that you can leave the server running while you make changes to your code, and the server will automatically detect these changes and apply them without requiring a manual restart.

Once the Django development server is running, you can access your application by opening a web browser and entering the following URL: `http://127.0.0.1:8000/` (see *Figure 5.5*). By default, Django runs the server on localhost `127.0.0.1` and uses port `8000`. The preceding URL will point your browser to the home page of your Django application.

Figure 5.5: The Quiz App Initial Page View

In our Django application, we can observe three distinct sections. Firstly, at the top, we have the header area displaying the name **Quiz App** against a dark background. On the left-hand side, we find a navigation bar with two tabs that we incorporated into the `base.html` file – **Questions Generator** and **My Quiz**. These tabs facilitate easy navigation between different features of our application. The **Questions Generator** tab directs users to a section where they can construct quizzes, while the **My Quiz** tab presents a view to download quizzes. Finally, on the right-hand side of the navigation bar, we have the working area, where users can interact with and explore the contents of the **My Quiz** and **Questions Generator** functionalities.

This is what the initial view of your application looks like, with a sleek and modern interface showcasing a user-friendly design. In the next section, our attention can now be directed toward developing the fundamental aspect of the app, which involves creating the core ChatGPT quiz generation component.

Integrating ChatGPT and Django for Quiz Generation

In this section, we will explore the exciting task of generating questions using the ChatGPT API within your Django application. This powerful functionality will allow you to create interactive quizzes based on user-provided text input. By handling POST requests from the user and leveraging the capabilities of the ChatGPT API, you will be able to dynamically generate insightful questions that enhance user engagement and knowledge acquisition.

The process begins by incorporating a field in your Django application where users can input text. Once the user submits the text by clicking the submit button, the magic unfolds as your application utilizes the ChatGPT API to generate relevant and contextually accurate questions based on the provided text. These questions are seamlessly displayed to the user, enabling an interactive and educational experience. By automating the question generation process, you can save time and effort while providing valuable content to your users. So, let's dive in and explore the steps involved in handling POST requests, building the ChatGPT API function for question creation, and ultimately, displaying the generated questions to your users in a user-friendly and intuitive manner.

Building the Quiz Generation Text Area and Submit Button

In a slight departure from the chronological order, we will begin by making modifications to the base.html file to incorporate the necessary components for our question generation feature. Specifically, we will add a text area where users can input their desired text, and a submit button that triggers the question generation process. You can add those fields under the navigation bar menu code (under the `</nav>` tag), as shown in the following code:

---

base.html

```
    </nav>
      <main class="col-md-9 ms-sm-auto col-lg-10 px-md-4">
        {% block content %}
        <h1>Create a Quiz</h1>
        <form method="post" action="">
          {% csrf_token %}
          <textarea name="text" rows="5" cols="50"
            placeholder="Enter some text..."></textarea>
          <br>
          <input type="submit" value="Generate Questions">
        </form>
            {% if questions %}
                <h2>Generated Questions:</h2>
                    {{ questions|linebreaks }}
            {% endif %}
       {% endblock %}
```

```
            </main>
        </div>
    </div>
  </body>
</html>
```

This represents the section of the `base.html` file that is responsible for displaying the user interface elements related to the question generation feature in our Quiz Generation application.

In the code, we can observe the usage of HTML tags and Django template syntax. The `<main>` tag defines the main content area. Inside the `<main>` tag, we have a Django template block defined by `{% block content %}` and `{% endblock %}`, which allows dynamic content insertion. This will ensure that we can connect this block with our Django views later.

In this block, we begin by displaying a heading, **Create a Quiz**, to provide a clear title for the question generation section. Next, we encounter a form that is responsible for handling the user's input and submitting it for question generation. The `{% csrf_token %}` template tag ensures the security of the form submission.

Inside the form, we find `textarea`, which serves as the input field where users can enter the text from which they want questions to be generated. It has specified rows and columns attributes to define the size of the text input area. Additionally, there is placeholder text, `Enter some text...`, to provide instructions to the user.

Following `textarea`, we have a submit button with the title `Generate Questions`, which users can click to initiate the question generation process. When the form is submitted, the user's input will be sent to the appropriate view for further processing.

After the form, there is a `{% if questions %}` statement, which checks whether there are generated questions available. If there are, a heading, **Generated Questions**, is displayed, followed by the generated questions themselves, which are rendered using `{{ questions|linebreaks }}`. This syntax ensures that line breaks within the generated questions are properly displayed under the text field.

Finally, we can add a new style sheet, which we will build later, to the `base.html` file inside its `head`:

```
<!--   &lt;!&ndash; Custom styles for this template &ndash;&gt;-->
  <link href="{% static 'css/dashboard.css' %}" rel="stylesheet" />
  <link rel="stylesheet" type="text/css" href="{% static 'css/quiz_
    style.css' %}">
</head>
```

When you launch your Quiz Generator at this point, you will see that while all the fields are visible, their visual presentation may not be aesthetically pleasing. This is because we have only incorporated HTML elements thus far. To enhance their appearance, we need to introduce some CSS styling. To do that, you can create a new CSS file called `quiz_style.css` inside the `quiz_project/static/css` directory. You can find the CSS file content here: `https://github.com/PacktPublishing/Building-AI-Applications-with-ChatGPT-APIs/blob/main/Chapter05%20QuizApp/quiz_project/quiz_project/static/css/quiz_style.css`

Here, we define the styles for the `body`, `container`, and `main` elements. The body element is set to use the Arial font family and has a white background. The container class specifies a maximum width of `960px`, while the main element that holds our application also has a box shadow effect and a border radius of `5px`.

Then, we can define the styles for the `textarea` and `submit` button elements. The `textarea` element is set to have a width of `70%` of its parent container with a light gray color. The `input[type="submit"]` element, which represents a submit button, has a blue background color, and the cursor changes to a pointer when hovering over it.

The `Responsive styles` section uses media queries to apply specific styles when the maximum width of the viewport is `767px` or less. In this case, it reduces the padding of the `.container` and `main` elements, decreases the font size of headings to `20px`, and adjusts the padding of the `textarea` and `input[type="submit"]` elements. These styles ensure that the Quiz Generator application is visually appealing and adapts well to different screen sizes, providing a better user experience.

So far, we have successfully constructed the entire user interface for the Quiz Generation feature of our application. Our next step is to integrate the ChatGPT API service and implement the necessary views.

Creating ChatGPT API Views with Django

Now that we have completed the frontend, we will explore how to incorporate this powerful ChatGPT API into our Django views, enabling us to harness the capabilities of ChatGPT to generate quiz questions.

Asking ChatGPT to generate a response in a specific structure can be a challenging task, as we need to define very specific instructions about how the questions in our quiz should be generated. Having that in mind, our ChatGPT prompt should meet the following requirements:

- A variable holding the text that we want to create questions for should be passed as a separate variable. That will enable our app to work with different types of text.
- The prompt should consist of instructions that specify the following:
  - The number of questions
  - Where and how the correct answer should be displayed
  - What type of question ChatGPT should generate (multiple-choice, open-answer, etc)

It is a good practice to create such requirements every time you want to design a ChatGPT prompt and test whether the API response meets the expected response, based on your prompt definition.

Inside the quiz_app folder of your Django project, you will need to create two essential files – config.py and services.py. The config.py file serves as a container for your ChatGPT API key, allowing you to securely store and access it within your application. This key is crucial to establish a connection with the ChatGPT API service. The services.py file, on the other hand, plays a pivotal role in housing the necessary functions that will enable you to interact with the ChatGPT API within your Django views. These functions will facilitate communication with the API, allowing you to generate quiz questions dynamically based on user input:

services.py

```
import openai
from . import config

# API Token
openai.api_key = config.API_KEY
def generate_questions(text):

    # Define your prompt for generating questions
    prompt = f"Create a practice test with multiple choice questions
            on the following text:\n{text}\n\n" \
            f"Each question should be on a different line. Each
                question should have 4 possible answers. " \
            f"Under the possible answers we should have the correct
                answer."

    # Generate questions using the ChatGPT API
    response = openai.Completion.create(
        engine='text-davinci-003',
        prompt=prompt,
        max_tokens=3500,
        stop=None,
        temperature=0.7
    )

    # Extract the generated questions from the API response
    questions = response.choices[0].text
    return questions
```

config.py

```
API_KEY = "YOUR_API_KEY"
```

Here, we have a Python function that utilizes the OpenAI library to interact with the ChatGPT API to generate quiz questions. First, the necessary dependencies are imported, including the OpenAI library and the local `config` module, which holds the API key. The API key is set using the imported `config.API_KEY` value to establish a connection with the ChatGPT API.

The `generate_questions` function takes a text input as a parameter, which represents the content or context from which questions will be generated. The function prepares a prompt by incorporating the provided text into a specific format that instructs the AI model to create multiple-choice questions, based on the given content.

As you can see, the design of the given ChatGPT prompt focuses on providing clear instructions to generate a practice test with multiple-choice questions, based on a given text. Here's the reasoning behind the design:

- **Clear instructions**: The prompt begins by clearly stating the purpose of the task – to create a practice test with multiple-choice questions. This helps set the context and expectations for the generated content.
- **Introduction to the text**: The prompt includes the placeholder {text} to indicate that the given text should be inserted at that point. This allows the user to provide the specific text on which the questions will be based.
- **Structured format**: The prompt specifies that each question should be on a separate line. This helps create a structured layout for the practice test, making it easier to read and be understood by humans and other Python scripts.
- **Multiple-choice format**: The prompt states that each question should have four possible answers. This indicates that the generated questions should follow the multiple-choice question format commonly used in tests and quizzes.
- **Indicating the correct answer**: The prompt mentions that under the possible answers, the correct answer should be provided. This ensures that the generated questions include the correct answer along with the options, allowing learners to easily identify the correct response.

Using the ChatGPT API, the function sends a request to the API with the prepared prompt. The API response contains the generated questions. The function extracts these questions from the API response and returns them as a string variable.

The `questions` variable can be now used inside the `views.py` file to pass the generated questions to be displayed in our `base.html` frontend file:

views.py

```
from django.shortcuts import render

from .services import generate_questions


def home(request):
```

```
    if request.method == 'POST':
        text = request.POST['text']
        questions = generate_questions(text)
        context = {'questions': questions}
        return render(request, 'base.html', context)
    return render(request, 'base.html')
```

Here, we upgrade the home function that handles the rendering of the home page and the generation of quiz questions based on user input. Upon receiving a request, the view function checks the HTTP method of the request. If it is a POST request, indicating that the user has submitted a form, the function proceeds to extract the text input from the request's POST data using the text key. In fact, the submission is initiated by selecting the **Submit** button while the text is inside the text files of our Question Generation app.

The extracted text is then passed as an argument to the generate_questions function, which we previously defined in the services.py file. This function utilizes the ChatGPT API to generate quiz questions based on the provided text. The generated questions are stored in the questions variable.

To display the generated questions on the web page, a dictionary called context is created with the questions key and the corresponding value containing the generated questions. This context dictionary is passed as an argument to the render function, along with the request object and the template file, base.html. The rendered page will have access to the questions variable and can display it appropriately.

By implementing this code in your Django application's views.py file, the home view function will handle the generation of quiz questions, based on user input, and render the home page with the generated questions displayed if a POST request is received.

Before testing your Django application and utilizing the ChatGPT API, you need to ensure that the OpenAI library is installed. The OpenAI library provides the necessary tools and functionalities to interact with the ChatGPT API. To install the library, you can type the following command in the terminal window:

```
pip install openai
```

To test your Quiz Generator application, follow these steps:

1. Ensure that your Django development server is running. If it's not already running, navigate to the root directory of your Django project in the terminal or Command Prompt and execute the following command:

   ```
   $python manage.py runserver.
   ```

2. Open a web browser and enter the URL http://127.0.0.1:8000/. This will direct you to the home page of your Quiz Generator application.

3. On the home page, you will see a text area where you can enter some text. Paste or type the desired text for which you want to generate quiz questions (see *Figure 5.5*).

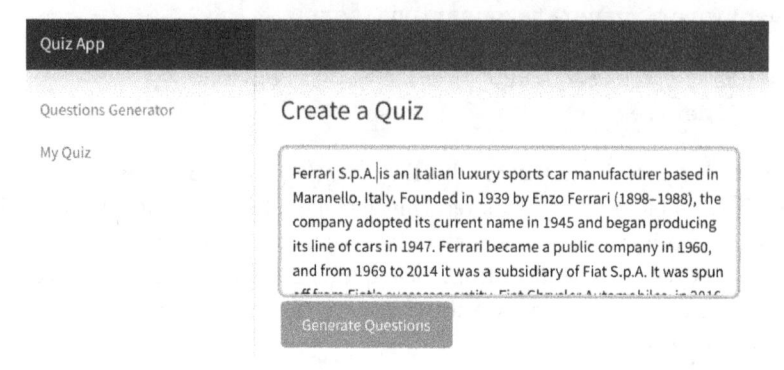

Figure 5.6: Adding Text to the Quiz Generation App

4. Once you have entered the text, click the **Generate Questions** button. This will submit the form and trigger a `POST` request to the server.
5. The server will process the request and generate quiz questions based on the provided text, using the ChatGPT API. The generated questions will be displayed below the text area (see *Figure 5.7*).

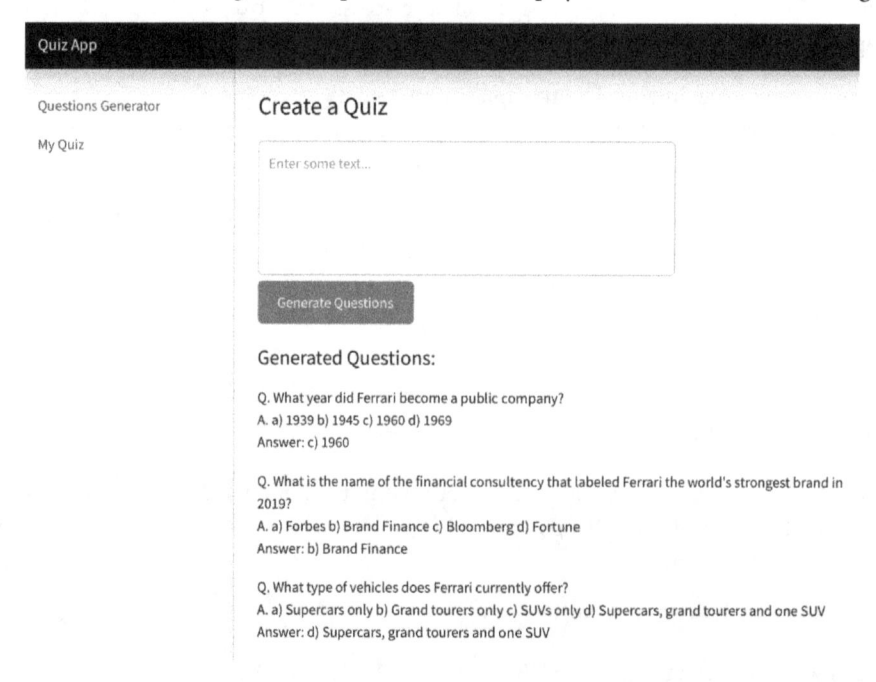

Figure 5.7: Questions Displayed by the Quiz Generation App

By following these steps, you can now test your Quiz Generator application and see how it generates questions based on the text input. Feel free to experiment with different inputs to explore the capabilities of your application.

In this section, we explored the integration of ChatGPT and Django for quiz generation. We covered the creation of a user interface for question generation, incorporating CSS styling for visual appeal, implementing ChatGPT API views using Django, and testing the Quiz Generator application by entering text and generating questions based on it. We can now build a database to store the generated questions and enable users to download them, which we will cover in the next section.

Storing and Downloading Generated Quizzes

In this next section, you will learn how to build the quiz download functionality for your Quiz Generation app. By incorporating a database and creating a dedicated page for downloading quizzes, you will empower your users to access and utilize the quizzes they generate. This feature will enhance the overall user experience by providing a seamless way to save and retrieve quizzes, enabling users to revisit and share their generated content effortlessly.

We will explore the process of saving generated quizzes in a database using Django's models and database management capabilities. By defining the appropriate database structure and implementing the necessary views and templates, you will be able to create a user-friendly page where users can browse and download their generated quizzes. With this functionality in place, your Quiz Generation App will offer a comprehensive solution to generate, store, and access quizzes, further enriching the interactive and educational experience for your users.

Saving the Quizzes in an SQLite Database

One of the key aspects of building the quiz download functionality is the ability to save the generated quizzes in a database. SQLite provides a simple and efficient solution for this purpose. SQLite is a lightweight, serverless, and self-contained database engine that requires minimal setup and configuration. It is ideal for smaller-scale applications and offers seamless integration with Python.

To begin, you will need to modify the `generate_questions()` function to incorporate database functionality. Within this function, you can include code to save the generated quiz questions and options into the SQLite database. By defining appropriate table structures using Django's models, you can easily map the quiz data to the corresponding fields in the database.

In addition to modifying the `generate_questions()` function, you will also need to create a separate function to initialize the database. This function will handle tasks such as creating the necessary tables and establishing a database connection. To create it, open your `services.py` file, where you can write the initialization function under your `API_KEY` definition:

```
import sqlite3
import openai
```

```python
from . import config
# API Token
openai.api_key = config.API_KEY

def initialize_database():
    # Connect to the SQLite database
    conn = sqlite3.connect('questions.db')
    cursor = conn.cursor()

    # Create the table if it doesn't exist
    cursor.execute('''CREATE TABLE IF NOT EXISTS questions
                    (id INTEGER PRIMARY KEY, key TEXT UNIQUE, value
                    TEXT)''')
    conn.commit()
    conn.close()
```

The `initialize_database()` function is responsible for setting up the SQLite database to store the generated quizzes. It begins by establishing a connection to the SQLite database named `questions.db`. Then, the cursor serves as a handle for executing SQL statements and fetching results from the database. It allows us to execute SQL commands and retrieve data from the database.

The function then checks whether a table named `questions` exists in the database. This statement creates a table with three columns – `id`, `key`, and `value`. The `key` column will later take the first two words from the text you pass to ChatGPT and use them as a quiz name, while the `value` column will hold the complete quiz.

After executing the table creation statement, the changes are committed to the database using `conn.commit()`. This ensures that the table creation is finalized and persisted in the database before the connection to the database is closed, using `conn.close()` to free up system resources and maintain good coding practices.

Additionally, make sure to import the SQLite package to enable the utilization of the database functionalities.

Now, we can modify our `generate_questions()` function to incorporate the database:

```python
def generate_questions(text):
    initialize_database()
    # Connect to the SQLite database
    conn = sqlite3.connect('questions.db')
    cursor = conn.cursor()

    # Define your prompt for generating questions
    prompt = f"Create a practice test with multiple choice questions
            on the following text:\n{text}\n\n" \
            f"Each question should be on a different line. Each
            question should have 4 possible answers. " \
```

```python
            f"Under the possible answers we should have the correct
                answer."

    # Generate questions using the ChatGPT API
    response = openai.Completion.create(
        engine='text-davinci-003',
        prompt=prompt,
        max_tokens=3500,
        stop=None,
        temperature=0.7
    )

    # Extract the generated questions from the API response
    questions = response.choices[0].text

    # Generate a unique key for the question
    base_key = ' '.join(text.split()[:2])
    key = base_key
    index = 1
    while key_exists(cursor, key):
        key = f"{base_key} {index}"
        index += 1

    # Insert the questions into the database
    value = questions
    cursor.execute("INSERT INTO questions (key, value) VALUES (?, ?)",
                   (key, value))
    conn.commit()

    return questions

def key_exists(cursor, key):
    cursor.execute("SELECT COUNT(*) FROM questions WHERE key = ?",
                   (key,))
    count = cursor.fetchone()[0]
    return count > 0
```

Firstly, the function establishes a connection to the SQLite database named `questions.db` using the `sqlite3.connect()` method, similar to the previous function.

To ensure the uniqueness of each question, the function generates a unique key by combining the first two words of the input text. If a question with the same key already exists in the database, it appends a numerical index to the key until a unique key is obtained. We verify the key by using the `key_exists()` method.

The function then inserts the generated questions into the SQLite database using the `cursor.execute()` method. The key and value (`questions`) are passed as parameters to the SQL query. Once the insertion is complete, the function calls `conn.commit()` to save the changes made to the database.

The `key_exists()` function takes a cursor object and a key as parameters, executes an SQL query to count the number of rows with the given key in the `questions` table, and returns `True` if a key exists in the table, or `False` otherwise. This function provides a convenient way to check for the existence of a key in the database before inserting new data or performing other operations.

To fetch the database, we can create the `print_all_questions()` function. It retrieves all the rows from the `questions` table in the SQLite database and returns them as a result:

```
def print_all_questions():
    initialize_database()
    conn = sqlite3.connect('questions.db')
    cursor = conn.cursor()
    # Retrieve all rows from the database
    cursor.execute("SELECT * FROM questions")
    rows = cursor.fetchall()
    return rows
```

First, the function executes an `SQL SELECT` statement using the the `SELECT * FROM questions` query. This query selects all the columns from the `questions` table.

After executing the `SELECT` statement, the function retrieves all the rows returned by the query. The `fetchall()` method returns the result as a list of tuples, where each tuple represents a row from the table. Later, we will use this function as a part of the download functionality to download our quizzes from the database.

Building the Download Quiz View

Now, it's time to explore the process of integrating download quiz views into your Django application. The download quiz views are essential to enable users to access and obtain the quizzes generated by the Quiz Generation app. First, navigate to the `views.py` file and add the following code under the `home` function:

```
def history(request):
    return render(request, 'download.html')

data = print_all_questions()

class TestListView(TemplateView):
    template_name = 'download.html'
```

```python
    def get_context_data(self, **kwargs):
        context = super().get_context_data(**kwargs)
        context['data'] = data
        return context

def download(request, test_id):
    test = next((t for t in data if t[0] == test_id), None)
    if test:
        header = test[1]
        questions = test[2]
        filename = f'test_{test_id}.txt'
        with open(filename, 'w') as f:
            f.write(questions)
        file_path = os.path.join(os.getcwd(), filename)
        response = HttpResponse(open(file_path, 'rb'),
            content_type='text/plain')
        response['Content-Disposition'] = f'attachment;
            filename="{header}.txt"'
        return response
    else:
        return HttpResponse("Test not found.")
```

The provided code demonstrates the additional functions included in the `views.py` file of our Django Quiz Generator. Let's go through each function and its purpose:

1. The `history` function is a view function that renders the `download.html` template, which we will build in the next section. When a user visits the specified URL associated with this function, the template will be displayed, allowing them to view the history of quizzes available to download.

2. The `data` variable is assigned the value returned by the `print_all_questions()` function. This function retrieves all the rows from the database containing the generated quizzes. By storing the data in the data variable, it can be used later to populate the context for the `TestListView` view.

3. The `TestListView` class is a subclass of `TemplateView`, which provides a generic class-based view. It defines the template that will be used to display the downloaded quizzes – in this case, the `download.html` template. The `get_context_data()` method is overridden to add the `data` variable to the context, making it available in the template for rendering.

4. The `download()` function handles the download functionality for a specific quiz, identified by its `test_id`. It first searches for the quiz in the `data` variable using the `test_id`. If the quiz is found, the header, questions, and filename are extracted. The questions are then written to a text file with the appropriate filename. The file path is determined, and an `HttpResponse` object is created with the file content and content type. The Content Disposition header is set

to specify the filename for the downloaded file. Finally, the response is returned to initiate the file download. If the quiz is not found, an `HttpResponse` object is returned, with a message indicating that the test was not found.

Finally, at the beginning of the `views.py` file, you can add all the necessary imports for those functions to operate properly:

```
import os

from django.http import HttpResponse
from django.shortcuts import render
from django.views.generic import TemplateView

from .services import generate_questions, print_all_questions
```

As you can see, the `HttpResponse` and `render` functions are imported from the Django framework. These functions are essential to generate and return HTTP responses. The `HttpResponse` class allows you to create custom HTTP responses, while the `render` function is used to render HTML templates and return the result as an `HttpResponse` object. The `TemplateView` class will be used later as a class-based view that will render the templates for the download view.

By adding these functions to your `views.py` file, you enable the rendering of the download history page and the listing of quizzes in the `download.html` template. In the next section, we will create the download template and add all necessary URLs to make the **My Quiz** download page accessible to the users.

Designing the Download Template

If you have a close look at your `base.html` file, you will see that there are two buttons displayed inside the navigation bar – **Questions Generator** and **My Quiz**. We already ensured that once the user clicks on **Questions Generator**, they can see the `home` view, allowing them to generate quizzes using the ChatGPT API. In this section, we will focus on the **My Quiz** page. We will ensure that once the user clicks the **My Quiz** button, they are sent to the `127.0.0.1/history` page. This page will show all views related to our download functionality, which we built in the previous section.

To do that, we need to create a new HTML file that will be rendered once the user clicks on the **MyQuiz** button. This HTML will be almost an exact copy of the `base.html`, with the only difference being that it will run a different set of functions (the download functions) in its `main` area. You can create your `downloads.html` file inside the `templates/` directory:

```
{% load static %}
<html lang="en" data-bs-theme="auto">
<head>
    <script src="/docs/5.3/assets/js/color-modes.js"></script>
```

```html
      <meta charset="utf-8">
      <meta name="viewport" content="width=device-width, initial-scale=1">
      <title>Quiz App</title>

      <!-- Bootstrap CSS -->
      <link href="{% static 'css/bootstrap.min.css' %}" rel="stylesheet" />

      <!-- Custom styles for this template -->
      <link href="{% static 'css/dashboard.css' %}" rel="stylesheet" />

</head>

<body>
   <header class="navbar navbar-dark sticky-top bg-dark flex-md-nowrap
     p-0 shadow">
     <a class="navbar-brand col-md-3 col-lg-2 me-0 px-3 fs-6"
       href="#">Quiz App</a>
     <div class="navbar-nav">
     </div>
   </header>

   <div class="container-fluid">
     <div class="row">
       <nav id="sidebarMenu" class="col-md-3 col-lg-2 d-md-block
         bg-body-tertiary sidebar collapse">
       <div class="position-sticky pt-3 sidebar-sticky">
         <ul class="nav flex-column">
           <li class="nav-item">
             <a class="nav-link active" aria-current="page" href="/">
               <span data-feather="home" class="align-text-bottom">
                 </span>
               Questions Generator
             </a>
           </li>
           <li class="nav-item">
             <a class="nav-link active" aria-current="page"
               href="/history">
               <span data-feather="file" class="align-text-bottom">
                 </span>
               My Quiz
             </a>
           </li>
         </ul>
       </div>
     </nav>
```

```html
        <main class="col-md-9 ms-sm-auto col-lg-10 px-md-4">
          <h1>Download Quiz</h1>
          <ul>
          {% for test in data %}
            <li><a href="/download/{{ test.0 }}" class="test-header">
              {{ test.1 }}</a></li>
          {% endfor %}
          </ul>
        </main>
      </div>
    </div>
   </body>
</html>
```

After the navigation bar, where our working area is located, we can create a section where users can download quizzes. We can generate a list of quiz download links based on the data provided, displaying the quiz headers as clickable links for users to access and download the quizzes.

Inside the `<main>` element, there is an `<h1>` heading tag that displays the text `Download Quiz`. This heading provides a clear title for the section, indicating its purpose to the users.

Below the heading, there is a `<ul>` element that represents an unordered list. Within this list, there is a loop construct using Django's template syntax, denoted by `{% for test in data %}` and `{% endfor %}`. This loop iterates over the `data` variable, which contains a list of quizzes or test data.

For each iteration of the loop, a new list item, `<li>`, is generated. Inside the list item, there is an anchor (`<a>`) tag that serves as a hyperlink. The `href` attribute of the anchor tag is dynamically generated using Django's template syntax and the `test` variable. This link points to the `/download/` URL, followed by the test.

This section of `download.html` generates a main content area with a heading and a list of quiz download links. The loop ensures that each quiz in the `data` variable is represented as a separate list item with an appropriate hyperlink and display text.

As a final step to set up the `My Quiz` page in your Django project, we need to modify the `urls.py` files. Those files are responsible for routing requests to the appropriate views. You need to define a URL pattern that maps to the history view, which will display the **My Quiz** page. By updating the `urls.py` files, users will be able to access the **My Quiz** page and view their downloaded quizzes:

quiz_project/urls.py

```python
from django.contrib import admin
from django.urls import include, path

urlpatterns = [
```

```
    path('admin/', admin.site.urls),
    path('', include('quiz_app.urls')),
    path('history/', include('quiz_app.urls')),
]
```

quiz_app/urls.py

```
from django.urls import path
from . import views
from .views import TestListView, download

urlpatterns = [
    path('', views.home, name='home'),
    path('history/', TestListView.as_view(), name='test_list'),
    path('download/<int:test_id>', download, name='test_download'),
]
```

In the `quiz_project/urls.py` file, we define the URL patterns for the entire project. The `history/` path is mapped to the `quiz_app.urls` module, which contains the URL patterns specific to the quiz application. This configuration allows users to access the **My Quiz** page.

In the `quiz_app/urls.py` file, we define the URL patterns for the quiz application specifically. We add the `history/` path that is mapped to the `TestListView` view class, which is responsible for displaying the **My Quiz** page. Additionally, the `download/<int:test_id>` path is mapped to the download view function, which handles the downloading of specific quizzes that the user selects.

By configuring the URL patterns in these files, you enable users to navigate to different pages of your Quiz app, such as the **Question Generator** page or the **My Quiz** page, from which the download page can be activated by accessing the corresponding URLs.

Configuring the URL files marks the final stage in the creation of your application. To test the Django quiz app, you can run it from the terminal using the following command:

```
$python manage.py runserver
```

Once the application is up and running, you can access it through your web browser. Start by navigating to the **Question Generator** page, where you can generate a few quizzes by providing the necessary inputs. After generating the quizzes, you can reboot the application by restarting the server.

Next, navigate to the **My Quiz** tab, which should be available in the navigation menu. Clicking on this tab will take you to the page where you will see the names of all the quizzes you previously generated. This list will be populated based on the quizzes stored in the database. It provides a convenient overview of the quizzes you have created (see *Figure 5.8*).

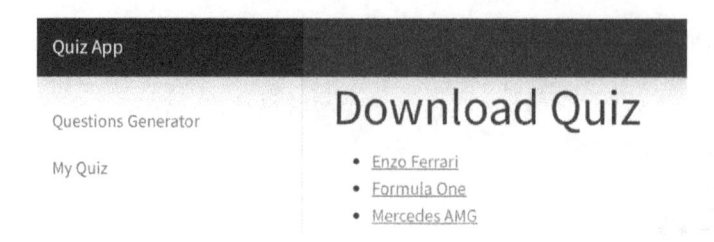

Figure 5.8: Downloading Quizzes from the My Quiz Page

To download a specific quiz as a text file, simply click on the desired quiz from the list. This action will trigger the download functionality implemented in the application. The quiz will be downloaded as a text file, which you can save to your local machine. This allows you to access and review the quiz offline, print it, or share it with others if needed.

This is how we integrated the download quiz views into our Django application. We added functions to the `views.py` file, such as `history` to render the download history page, `TestListView` to display downloaded quizzes, and `download` to handle quiz downloads. These functions enable users to access and obtain quizzes generated by the Quiz Generation app. We also created the `downloads.html` template, modified from `base.html`, to display the download functionality. The `urls.py` files were modified to define URL patterns, allowing access to the **My Quiz** page and quizzes to be downloaded. To test the application, we generated quizzes using the **Question Generator** page, and then we navigated to the **My Quiz** page to view and download our quizzes.

Summary

In this chapter, the focus was on building a Django project for a quiz generation application. We provided a step-by-step guide to set up and structure the project, including the installation of Django and important aspects such as database initialization, running a development server, and understanding the flow of views and URLs in Django. We also explored the concept of templates and demonstrated how to incorporate external CSS resources such as the Bootstrap framework.

We also explained how to integrate ChatGPT and Django for quiz generation. We illustrated the process of adding a text input field and a submit button to the application's interface, enabling users to generate relevant questions using the ChatGPT API. We also discussed how to test the Quiz Generator application and outlined the next steps, which involve building a database to store the generated questions. You learned how to store the generated quizzes in an SQLite database, using Django's models and database management capabilities, and download the stored quizzes.

This project was a comprehensive guide to building a Django-based quiz generation application, integrating ChatGPT for question generation, and implementing the functionality to download generated quizzes. You gained valuable experience to create your own interactive applications with Django.

In the next chapter, called *Language Translation Desktop App with ChatGPT API and Microsoft Word*, you will learn how to create a language translation desktop app using Python and the ChatGPT API. We will explain how to integrate the ChatGPT API with Microsoft Word to translate Word documents into different languages. The chapter will cover the creation of a user interface using the **Tkinter** library, allowing users to choose a target language and view real-time translations. It will also provide information on implementing language selection and file-browsing features, emphasizing the use of the powerful GPT-3.5 turbo language model for accurate translations.

Part 3: The ChatGPT, DALL-E, and Whisper APIs for Desktop Apps Development

In this part, your attention will be directed toward the creation of desktop applications, broadening your expertise across an array of artificial intelligence APIs. You will explore AI art by seamlessly integrating the ChatGPT and DALL-E APIs to infuse your applications with captivating artistic capabilities. Additionally, you will explore the realm of language translation and transcription through the utilization of the Whisper API. Throughout this part, you will be exposed to various desktop application frameworks such as Tkinter, PyQt, and the Microsoft Office APIs, enabling you to craft robust and feature-rich applications.

This part has the following chapters:

- *Chapter 6, Language Translation Desktop App with the ChatGPT API and Microsoft Word*
- *Chapter 7, Building an Outlook Email Reply Generator*
- *Chapter 8, Essay Generation Tool with PyQt and the ChatGPT API*
- *Chapter 9, Integrating ChatGPT and DALL-E API: Build End-to-End PowerPoint Presentation Generator*
- *Chapter 10, Speech Recognition and Text-to-Speech with the Whisper API*

6
Language Translation Desktop App with the ChatGPT API and Microsoft Word

In today's globalized world, language translation has become an essential tool for businesses and individuals to communicate effectively across borders. Fortunately, with the advancement of **natural language processing** (**NLP**) and machine learning technologies, language translation has become more accurate and accessible than ever before. In this chapter, we will explore how to build a language translation desktop app using the OpenAI ChatGPT API and **Microsoft Word**.

In this chapter, you will learn how to create a desktop application that can translate text in real time using the powerful ChatGPT API. We will walk through the process of integrating the API with Microsoft Word, enabling users to upload Word documents and translate them into a variety of languages. We will also cover how to build a simple user interface using the Python **Tkinter** library, allowing users to select their target language and view the translated text. With these skills, you will be able to develop your own language translation apps and enhance your NLP and machine learning abilities.

In this chapter, we will learn how to do the following:

- Build a language translation desktop app using Python and the ChatGPT API
- Use the Microsoft Word library to extract text from Word documents
- Integrate the ChatGPT API for language translation
- Create a user interface for the desktop app using the Tkinter library
- Implement language selection and file-browsing functionalities
- Test the translation flow using sample texts
- Use the GPT-3.5 turbo language model

By the end of the chapter, you will have acquired the essential knowledge to develop a simple yet functional Desktop application by seamlessly integrating the ChatGPT API with Tkinter and Microsoft Word. With these skills, you will be able to utilize AI-powered language translation and seamlessly incorporate this feature into any application of your choice, providing you with a valuable tool to effectively communicate with individuals from diverse linguistic backgrounds.

Technical Requirements

To complete this language translation desktop app project, you will need the following technical requirements:

- Python 3.7 or later installed on your machine
- A code editor, such as PyCharm (recommended)
- A Python virtual environment
- An OpenAI API key
- Microsoft Word available on your device

In the upcoming section, you will discover how to effectively employ the `docx` Python library to access and extract information from Word documents. This will enable you to seamlessly pass the data to the ChatGPT API and leverage its power to perform translations.

You can locate the code snippets demonstrated in this chapter on the GitHub platform through this link: `https://github.com/PacktPublishing/Building-AI-Applications-with-ChatGPT-APIs/tree/main/Chapter06%20WordTranslator`

Integrating ChatGPT API with Microsoft Office

In this section, we will explore how to set up a PyCharm project and install the `docx` Python library to extract text from **Word** documents. The `docx` library is a Python package that allows us to read and write Microsoft Word (`.docx`) files and provides a convenient interface to access information stored in these files.

The first step is to initiate your work by creating a new PyCharm project. This will enable you to have a dedicated area to craft and systematize your translation app code. Although we have previously discussed how to develop a PyCharm project, I will still outline the steps for you here.

1. Open **PyCharm IDE** on your system.
2. Click on **Create New Project** from the welcome screen or go to **File | New Project** if you're already in the IDE.
3. Keep the default settings.
4. Give your project the name `Translation App`.
5. Click on **Create** to create the project.

To run the language translation desktop app, you will need to install the following libraries:

- `openai`: The `openai` library allows you to interact with the OpenAI API and perform various natural language processing tasks
- `docx`: The `docx` library allows you to read and write Microsoft Word `.docx` files using Python
- `tkinter`: The `tkinter` library is a built-in Python library that allows you to create **graphical user interfaces (GUIs)** for your desktop app

As `tkinter` is a built-in library, there is no need for installation, since it already exists within your Python environment. To install the `openai` and `docx` libraries, access the PyCharm terminal by clicking on **View** | **Tool Windows** | **Terminal**, and then execute the following commands:

```
pip install openai
pip install python-docx
```

To access and read the contents of a Word document, you will need to create a sample Word file inside your PyCharm project. Here are the steps to create a new Word file in PyCharm:

1. In the PyCharm project, right-click on the project directory, select **New**, and create a directory called `files`.
2. Right-click on the `files` folder and select **New** | **File**.
3. In the dialog box that appears, enter a filename with the `.docx` extension – for example, `info.docx`.
4. Press the *Enter* key to create the file.
5. Once the file is created, double-click on it to open it.

You can now add some text or content to this file, which we will later access and read using the `docx` library in Python. For this example, we have created an article about New York City. However, you can choose any Word document containing text that you want to analyze:

> *The United States' most populous city, often referred to as New York City or NYC, is New York. In 2020, its population reached 8,804,190 people across 300.46 square miles, making it the most densely populated major city in the country and over two times more populous than the nation's second-largest city, Los Angeles. The city's population also exceeds that of 38 individual U.S. states. Situated at the southern end of New York State, New York City serves as the Northeast megalopolis and New York metropolitan area's geographic and demographic center - the largest metropolitan area in the country by both urban area and population. Over 58 million people also live within 250 miles of the city. A significant influencer on commerce, health care and life sciences, research, technology, education, politics, tourism, dining, art, fashion, and sports, New York City is a global cultural, financial, entertainment, and media hub. It houses the headquarters of the United Nations, making it a significant center for international diplomacy, and is often referred to as the world's capital.*

Now that you have created the Word file inside your PyCharm project, you can move on to the next step, which is to create a new Python file called `app.py` inside the `Translation App` root directory. This file will contain the code to read and manipulate the contents of the Word file using the `docx` library. With the Word file and the Python file in place, you are ready to start writing the code to extract data from the document and use it in your application.

To test whether we can read Word files with the `docx-python` library, we can implement the following code in our `app.py` file:

```
import docx

doc = docx.Document("<full_path_to_docx_file>")
text = ""
for para in doc.paragraphs:
    text += para.text

print(text)
```

Make sure to replace `<full_path_to_docx_file>` with the actual path to your **Word** document file. Obtaining the file path is a simple task, achieved by right-clicking on your `.docx` file in PyCharm and selecting the **Copy Path/Reference…** option from the drop-down menu.

Once you have done that, run the `app.py` file by single-clicking on the **Run** button and verify the output. This code will read the contents of your Word document and print them to the **Run Window** console. If the text extraction works correctly, you should see the text of your document printed in the console (see *Figure 6.1*). The `text` variable now holds the data from `info.docx` as a Python string.

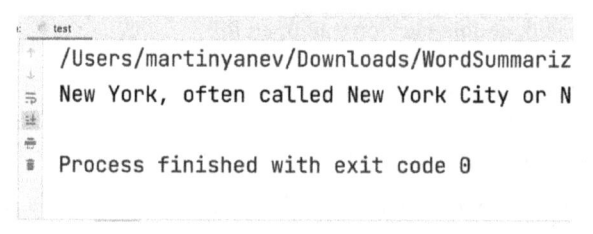

```
/Users/martinyanev/Downloads/WordSummariz
New York, often called New York City or N

Process finished with exit code 0
```

Figure 6.1: Word Text Extraction Console Output

This section provided a step-by-step guide on how to set up a PyCharm project and install the `docx` Python library to extract text from Word documents. The section also included instructions on how to create a new Word file in PyCharm and use the `docx` library to read and manipulate its contents, using Python.

In the upcoming section, we will dive into building the frame of our Tkinter application. You will learn how to create a basic window with widgets and how to use geometry managers to position them on the screen.

Building a User Interface with Tkinter

In this section, we will learn how to use the **Tkinter** library to create a GUI for our text translation application. Tkinter is a standard Python library for creating GUIs, and it provides a simple and efficient way to create windows, buttons, text fields, and other graphical elements.

The **Text Translator** application shown in *Figure 6.2* will be designed to have a simple and user-friendly interface. When you run the application, there will be a button labeled **Browse** and a drop-down menu with a list of languages to translate to.

To translate the text, the user can select the language they want to translate to from the drop-down menu. Once the language is selected, the user can click on the **Browse** button and select the Word file they want to translate. Upon selection, the contents of the file will be translated using the ChatGPT API, and the translated text will be displayed in the large text field in the center of the window. The user can then copy and paste the translated text to use it as needed.

The Text Translator application is designed to be a simple and efficient tool to translate text from one language to another.

> **Important Note**
> We do not need to specify the text from which we want to translate, as the ChatGPT language model is designed to automatically recognize the prompt language.

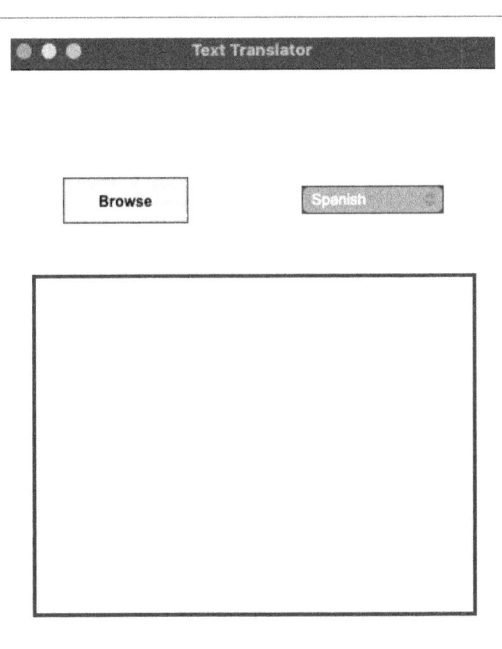

Figure 6.2: The Text Translator Application UI

Now that we are clear about the base design, we can bring it to life with Tkinter. To get started, we'll need to remove the example code that we previously added to our `app.py` file. Simply delete all the lines of code containing the example code so that we can start with a clean slate.

Creating a Tkinter window is the next step in building our text translator application. You can achieve this by writing the following code in `app.py`, which initializes a new instance of the Tk class and sets the application window:

```
import openai
import docx
import tkinter as tk
from tkinter import filedialog
root = tk.Tk()
root.title("Text Translator")
root.configure(bg="white")

header_font = ("Open Sans", 16, "bold")

header = tk.Label(root,
                  text="Text Translator",
                  bg="white",
                  font=header_font,
                  )

header.grid(row=0, column=0, columnspan=2, pady=20)
root.mainloop()
```

To start building the Tkinter app, we first need to import the necessary libraries. We will use the `openai`, `docx`, and `tkinter` libraries for this project. Next, we need to create the main window of our application. We will do this using the `Tk()` method of the `tkinter` library. We will also give our application a title and set its background color to white.

We can also set a header for our application using the `Label()` method of `tkinter`. We can set its text to `Text Translator`, its background color to `white`, and its font to `Open Sans`, with a size of `16` and a `bold` weight. We will then use the `grid()` method to place the header in our application window at a specific position by specifying the `row` and `column` values, spanning two columns and with a small padding.

We will run our application using the `mainloop()` method of `tkinter`. The `mainloop()` method is an infinite loop used to run the application, listen for events such as button clicks or window resizing, and update the display as needed. It continuously listens for events until the user closes the window or exits the application.

After creating the app window, the next step is to add elements to it. One of those elements will be the **Browse** button:

```
browse_button = tk.Button(root, text="Browse",
                          bg="#4267B2", fg="black", relief="flat",
                          borderwidth=0, activebackground="#4267B2",
                          activeforeground="white")

browse_button.config(font=("Arial", 12, "bold"), width=10, height=2)
browse_button.grid(row=1, column=0, padx=20, pady=20)
```

> **Important Note**
> It's important to add all elements before calling the `mainloop()` method, so they are properly included in the application window. `mainloop()` should always be the last line in your `app.py` file.

To create a button widget, you can use the `tk.Button()` method in the `tkinter` library. The button is placed in the root window and has the **Browse** text displayed on it. The bg parameter sets the background color of the button to a dark blue, while `fg` sets the foreground color to `black`. Meanwhile, `relief` is set to `flat` to create a flat appearance, and `borderwidth` is set to 0 to remove the border of the button. We then use the `activebackground` and `activeforeground` parameters to set the colors of the button when it is clicked or hovered over.

Under the **Browse** button, we can create a drop-down menu with a list of languages:

```
languages = ["Bulgarian", "Hindi", "Spanish", "French"]
language_var = tk.StringVar(root)
language_var.set(languages[0])
language_menu = tk.OptionMenu(root, language_var, *languages)
language_menu.config(font=("Arial", 12), width=10)
language_menu.grid(row=1, column=1, padx=20, pady=20)
```

The `languages` list contains a list of languages that the user can select from. You can add any language to that list, and it will be displayed to the users in the drop-down menu.

The `language_var` variable is created as a `StringVar` object and set to the first language in the list. The `set()` method of the `language_var` object is then used to set its initial value to the first element of the `languages` list. This is done so that the default value of the language drop-down menu is the first language in the list, which is `Bulgarian` in this case.

The `OptionMenu` widget is then created with the `language_var` variable and the `*languages` syntax, which unpacks the `languages` list as individual arguments. This sets the available options for the drop-down menu to the languages in the languages list. Then, we configure and position an options menu widget in the second column of the first row of the application window.

The next step is to add the text field to our GUI. To do this, you can add the following code below the **Language** menu in your `app.py` file. This code creates a text field with specific dimensions, colors, and properties, and then places it within the window using grid positioning:

```
text_field = tk.Text(root, height=20, width=50, bg="white", fg="black",
                    relief="flat", borderwidth=0, wrap="word")
text_field.grid(row=2, column=0, columnspan=2, padx=20, pady=20)
text_field.grid_rowconfigure(0, weight=1)
text_field.grid_columnconfigure(0, weight=1)

root.grid_rowconfigure(2, weight=1)
root.grid_columnconfigure(0, weight=1)
root.grid_columnconfigure(1, weight=1)
```

This code will add a text field to the GUI window, which will be used to display the ChatGPT translation of the Word document. Firstly, the `Text` widget object named `text_field` is placed inside the root window. The `Text` widget is used to display and edit text in multiple lines. Then, we use the `grid()` method to position the `Text` widget on the GUI. The `padx` and `pady` parameters add padding around the widget to create some space between it and other widgets in the window.

You can configure `text_field` to to expand the main window horizontally and vertically, using the `grid_rowconfigure()` and `grid_columnconfigure()` methods. This allows the text field to fill up the available space in the window. Then, you can also configure the main window, `root`, to expand it. These settings ensure that the text field remains centered in the window and fills up the available space.

Once your GUI is finalized, you can launch the application, and confirm that your GUI adheres precisely to the style and attributes shown in *Figure 6.2*. By selecting the **Languages** menu with a single click, you can access and choose any language from it.

This is how you can use the Tkinter library to create a GUI for a text translation application. We have created the main window, header, **Browse** button, and drop-down menu with a list of languages.

Despite having completed your GUI, clicking on the **Browse** button with a single click will not trigger any action, as it is not yet connected to any active Python function. We will fix that in the next section, where we will create two core functions that are responsible for opening the Microsoft Word file and performing the translation.

Integrating Microsoft Word Text with the ChatGPT API

In this section, we will provide you with step-by-step instructions on how to create two core functions using Python, which are crucial to building a text translation application. The first function, `translate_text()`, uses **OpenAI's GPT-3.5** language model to translate text from a Microsoft Word file into a target language selected by the user. The second function, `browse_file()`, allows users to browse and select a Word file from their local system and trigger the text translation process. Both functions will be explained in detail with code examples to help you understand and implement them in your own projects.

Translating a Word Text with ChatGPT 3.5 Turbo

In this section, you will learn how to build the `translate_text()` function. This function is responsible for translating the text of a Microsoft Word file into the language chosen by the user through the GUI. We will use the OpenAI API, specifically the GPT 3.5 Turbo model, to translate the text.

Before building the `translate_text()` function, you will need to create a file called `config.py` in your project root directory. This file will contain your OpenAI API token, which is required to use the OpenAI API. The API token should be assigned to a variable called `API_KEY` in the `config.py` file:

config.py

```
API_KEY = "<YOUR_CHATGPT_API_KEY>"
```

app.py

```
import openai
import docx
import tkinter as tk
from tkinter import filedialog
import config

openai.api_key = config.API_KEY
```

This step is necessary to keep the API token secure and prevent it from being accidentally uploaded to a public repository.

With the API key in place, you can now proceed to implement the `translate_text()` function in our `app.py`, as demonstrated in the following code snippet:

```
def translate_text(file_location, target_language):
    doc = docx.Document(file_location)
    text = ""
    for para in doc.paragraphs:
        text += para.text


    model_engine = "gpt-3.5-turbo"

    response = openai.ChatCompletion.create(
```

```
        model=model_engine,
        messages=[
            {"role": "user", "content": "You are a professional
                                         language translator. "
                                        "Below I will ask you to
                                         translate text. "
                                        "I expect from you to give me
                                         the correct translation"
                                        "Can you help me with that?"},
            {"role": "assistant", "content": "Yes I can help you with
                that."},
            {"role": "user", "content": f"Translate the following text
                in {target_language} : {text}"}
        ]
    )

    translated_text = response["choices"][0]["message"]["content"]

    return translated_text
```

The `translate_text()` function takes two parameters – `file_location`, which is the location of the Microsoft Word file to be translated, and `target_language`, which is the language to translate the text into. The first line of the function uses the `docx` module to open the Word document located at `file_location`. The next few lines of code create an empty string text and then loop through each paragraph in the document, concatenating the text from each paragraph to the text string. In other words, we can extract all the text from the Word document and store it in a single string.

Then, the GPT-3.5 API model is used to translate the text. The `model_engine` variable is set to the GPT-3.5 model. A `response` variable is created by calling the `openai.ChatCompletion.create()` method, which sends a prompt message to the API, requesting a response to translate the given text into the specified `target_language`.

The `messages` argument is a list of dictionaries that represent the conversation between the user and the language translator.

The `messages` variable is used to pass a conversation history to the language model for translation. The conversation consists of messages exchanged between a user and an assistant, using the ChatGPT API.

Let's break down the design of the `messages` variable:

- The variable is a list of dictionaries, where each dictionary represents a message with two key-value pairs:

  - `role`: This represents the role of the participant in the conversation. It can be either `user` or `assistant`.

  - `content`: This represents the actual content of the message.

- The conversation follows a pattern, with the first two messages establishing the context and the last message providing the text to be translated:

  - The first message is from the user's role and explains the context of the interaction
  - The second message is from the assistant's role and confirms its ability to help
  - The third message is from the user's role and contains the text to be translated, including the target language

The conversation format is designed to give context to the language model about the task it needs to perform, making it clear that the user wants the assistant to translate the given text into the specified target language.

The `role` key specifies whether the message is from the user or the assistant, and the `content` key contains the actual message text. The final translated text is obtained from the `response` object and returned by the function.

After sending the message with the text to be translated and the target language to the GPT-3.5 API model, the response will be a JSON object containing various information about the response generated by the model. For this model, the actual translation is stored in the `content` field of the first choice in the `choices` list of the response. Therefore, the code extracts the translated text by accessing the `content` field of the first choice and assigns it to the `translated_text` variable, which is then returned by the function.

Once we have processed the translated text into a Python string, we can display it to the user. In addition to that, we need to implement a function to establish the path to our Word file using the **Browse** button. This can be done by building the `browse_file()` function:

```
def browse_file():
    file_location = filedialog.askopenfilename(initialdir="/",
                                                title="Select file",
                                                filetypes=(("Word files", "*.docx"), ("all files", "*.*")))
    if file_location:
        # Get the selected language from the dropdown menu
        target_language = language_var.get()

        translated_text = translate_text(file_location,
            target_language)
        text_field.delete("1.0", tk.END)
        text_field.insert(tk.END, translated_text)
```

The `browse_file()` function creates a file dialog window that allows the user to select a Word file to be translated. If the user selects a file, the function retrieves the selected language from a dropdown menu, and then it calls the `translate_text()` function with the file location and target language as parameters. Once the text has been translated, the function clears the text field and inserts the translated text into it.

The function opens a file dialog window for the user to select a Word file to translate. The `initialdir` parameter sets the initial directory to be displayed when the file dialog opens, and the `title` parameter sets the title of the file dialog window. The `filetypes` parameter specifies the file types that the user can select in the file dialog. In this case, the user can select files with a `.docx` extension. The path of the selected file is stored in the `file_location` variable.

Then, we check whether a file has been selected; if so, then we can retrieve the selected language from a drop-down menu using the `language_var.get()` function. The `translate_text()` function is called, with the selected file location and target language as arguments to translate the text in the file to the target language.

After the text is translated, we can delete any text that may be in the text field and insert the translated text into the text field. The text field is the GUI widget that displays the translated text in our app.

Finally, you can add another parameter to `browse_button`, ensuring that the `browse_file()` function is activated upon a single click of the button:

```
browse_button = tk.Button(root, text="Browse",
                          bg="#4267B2", fg="black", relief="flat",
                          borderwidth=0, activebackground="#4267B2",
                          activeforeground="white",
                          command=browse_file)
```

The `command=browse_file` parameter associates the `browse_file()` function with the `tk.Button` widget. When the button is clicked, the `browse_file()` function will be executed.

To run and test the application in PyCharm, you can simply click on the **Run** button located in the top-right corner of the PyCharm window, or you can use the *Shift + F10* keyboard shortcut. This will start the application and open the GUI window. From there, you can select the target language from the drop-down menu and click on the **Browse** button to select a Word file (see *Figure 6.3*).

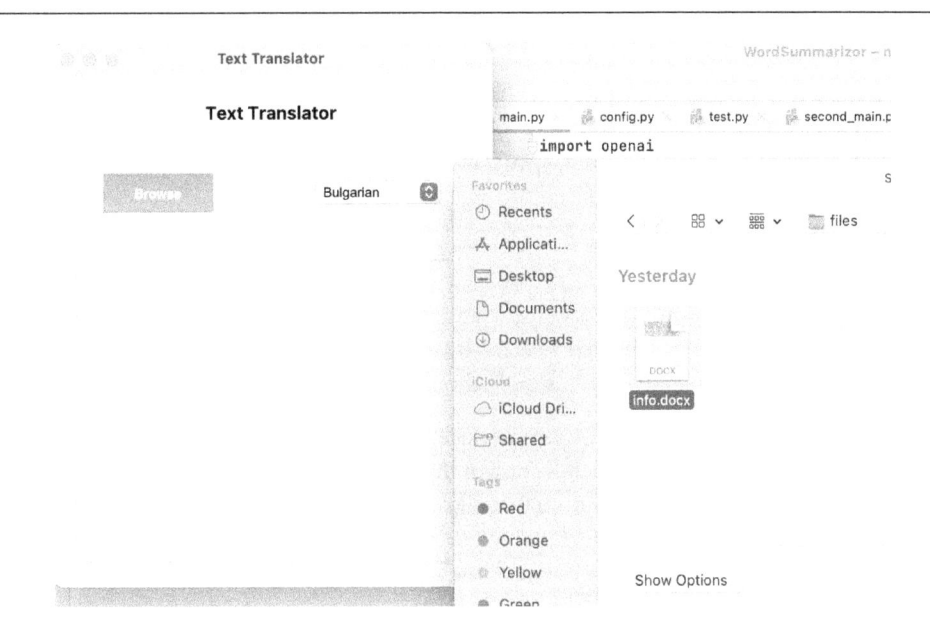

Figure 6.3: Browsing a Word File with the Text Translator App

Once the file is selected, the ChatGPT API will process your request, and the translated text will be displayed in the text field below the buttons, as shown in *Figure 6.4*.

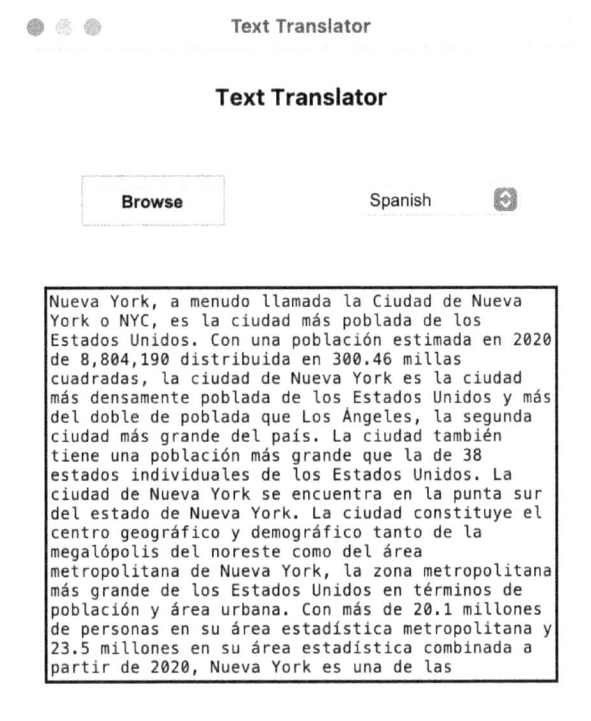

Figure 6.4: Text Translated Using the Text Translator App

In this section, you learned how to build the `translate_text()` function in Python using OpenAI's GPT-3.5 Turbo model, translating text in a Microsoft Word file into a language selected by the user through a GUI. We also discussed how to build the `browse_file()` function to get the path to the Word file using the **Browse** button, displaying the translated text to the user.

Summary

In this chapter, you learned how to develop a text translation application that can translate text from a Microsoft Word file into a target language selected by the user. The chapter covered the integration of Microsoft Word with the ChatGPT API using Python.

We learned how to use Tkinter to create a user interface for the text translation application. The user interface comprised a simple and user-friendly design that included a drop-down menu, with a list of languages to translate to, and a **Browse** button that allowed users to select a Word file. Once the user selected a file, the contents of the file were translated using the ChatGPT API, and the translated text was displayed in the large text field in the center of the window.

We also saw how to set up a `docx` Python library to extract text from Word documents. The `docx` library provided an interface to access information stored in Word files.

In the next chapter, *Building an Outlook Email Reply Generator*, you will learn how to build an **Outlook** Email Reply Generator application using the most advanced ChatGPT model – **GPT-4**. You will learn how to pass email data from Outlook to the ChatGPT API and use it to generate an original reply to a specific email. You will also learn how to automate the ChatGPT API prompt to get relevant email replies.

7
Building an Outlook Email Reply Generator

Email communication is an essential part of our personal and professional lives. However, crafting the perfect email response can be a time-consuming and challenging task. This is where **artificial intelligence** (**AI**) can come in handy. Using the **ChatGPT API**, you will learn how to generate automatic email replies that are both relevant and personalized to the sender's message.

Many companies have already started using AI to generate email replies to save time and increase productivity. For example, Google's Smart Reply feature uses machine learning algorithms to generate short, concise email responses that are contextually relevant to the message at hand. Similarly, we can use OpenAI's most powerful natural language processing model, GPT-4, to generate more complex replies compared to GPT-3, helping us to develop personalized email replies.

In this chapter, you'll learn how to build an **Outlook email reply generator** using OpenAI's GPT-4 language model. You will be able to build an app that automatically generates original replies to specific emails integrating the **Outlook API** and OpenAI's GPT-4. This will help you to save time and increase your productivity by automating the process of crafting well-written email responses. You will also learn how to use the Outlook API to send data to the ChatGPT API, and how to automate ChatGPT API prompts to get relevant email replies.

For this project, in addition to the `tkinter` and `openai` libraries, we'll use the `win32com` library in Python to interact with **Microsoft Outlook** and retrieve email data. This library provides us with a powerful set of tools to access the **Outlook's APIs** and retrieve email messages. By using `win32com`, we can easily retrieve the subject and body of an email message and use it as input for OpenAI's GPT-4 language model. Together with `tkinter` and `openai`, `win32com` provides us with a comprehensive set of tools to build a powerful and user-friendly email reply generator.

In this chapter, we will cover the following topics:

- Using the `win32com` library to interact with Microsoft Outlook
- Using the Outlook API to send data to the ChatGPT API

- Designing effective prompts for automatic email replies
- Using `tkinter` to build a simple GUI desktop app for the email reply generator

By the end of this chapter, you will be able to generate and send original email replies using **natural language processing** (**NLP**) techniques and a user-friendly graphical interface.

Technical Requirements

To complete this chapter, we assume that you have installed Microsoft Office and Outlook on your device. You can learn how to install Microsoft Office here: `https://learn.microsoft.com/en-us/microsoft-365/admin/setup/install-applications?view=o365-worldwide`.

However, we will walk through the complete installation of the Outlook API.

You will require the following:

- Python 3.7 or later installed on your computer
- An OpenAI API key
- A code editor, such as PyCharm (recommended)
- A **Windows** operating system
- The latest Microsoft Office 365 apps (Outlook) installed on your device.

In the next section, you will learn how to install Microsoft Outlook and the `win32com` library. You will also learn how to pass email data from Outlook to the ChatGPT API for automatic email reply generation.

The code for the Outlook Email Reply Generator project can be found on GitHub at `https://github.com/PacktPublishing/Building-AI-Applications-with-ChatGPT-APIs/tree/main/Chapter07%20ReplyTool`

Passing Outlook Data to the ChatGPT API

To get started, we will first cover the essential steps to set up your development environment for building the Outlook email reply generator. Here, you will start by installing Microsoft Outlook on your computer and setting up an email account. Once you have all the libraries installed, we will show you how to use the `win32com` library to extract email data from Outlook and pass it to the ChatGPT API, to generate an automatic email reply.

Let's set up your **PyCharm** project to build the Outlook email reply generator. To do this, open PyCharm and click on **Create New Project**. In the **New Project** dialog box, give your project the name `EmailReplyGenerator`. Keep the default location, and click on **Create** to create the new project. Once the project is created, you can create a new Python file called `app.py` and start writing the code to extract email data from Outlook, passing it to the ChatGPT API.

To complete the project setup, you will also need to install two Python libraries. You can install these libraries using the `pip` package manager. To get started, open Command Prompt or Terminal on your machine and type the following command to install both the libraries:

```
$pip install openai
$pip install pywin32
```

After installing these libraries, we can now proceed to the secure handling of the ChatGPT API key, which will enable us to authenticate ourselves when connecting to the AI. To do that, let's create a new file in our project called `config.py`. As demonstrated in the previous projects, this file will securely store all API keys utilized for the project. You can now include an API token and the necessary libraries in the appropriate files, as shown here:

config.py

```
API_KEY = "<YOUR_CHATGPT_API_KEY>"
```

app.py

```
import openai
import win32com.client
import tkinter as tk
import config

openai.api_key = config.API_KEY
```

The `config.py` file securely stores the ChatGPT API key, which is imported into the `app.py` file. The API key is then used to establish a secure connection with the ChatGPT API through the `openai` library. Additionally, the `win32com.client` and `tkinter` libraries are imported to work with Outlook email data and create the graphical user interface, respectively.

With these steps, you can ensure that your project is properly set up, allowing you to proceed with launching the installed Outlook application on your device smoothly.

Setting Up the Outlook Email

In this section, we will guide you through the process of setting up your Microsoft Outlook app. Microsoft Outlook is a widely used email client and personal information manager developed by Microsoft. It is part of the Microsoft Office suite of applications, which includes popular productivity tools such as Word, Excel, and PowerPoint. While Microsoft Outlook is commonly associated with Microsoft email services, it is important to note that Outlook can be used with any email account, regardless of the email provider. This means that users can leverage the power and features of Outlook even if they have an email account from providers such as Gmail, Yahoo, or any other email service.

To open and log in to your email account using Outlook installed on your computer, follow these steps:

1. **Launch Microsoft Outlook**: Look for the Outlook application icon on your computer and double-click it to open the program.
2. **Set up a new account**: Upon opening Outlook for the first time, you will be able to log in to your email address. Simply type your email address and click on the **Connect** button to begin the setup process (see *Figure 7.1*).

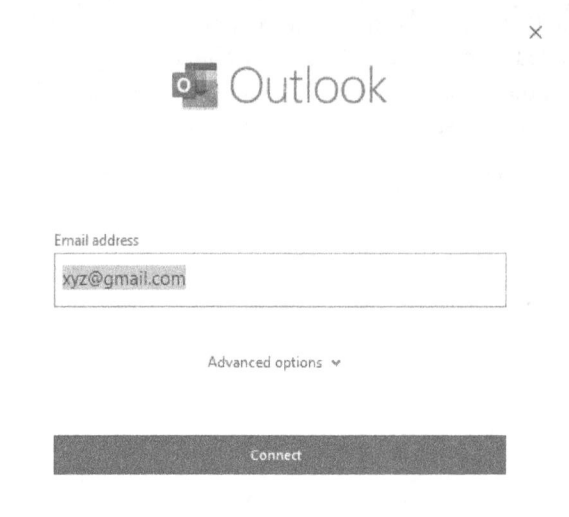

Figure 7.1: The Outlook Email Setup Window

3. **Follow the onscreen prompts**: Outlook will attempt to automatically configure the account settings based on your email address. You will see a confirmation message, and your email account will be added to Outlook.
4. **Access your email**: After the setup process is complete, you can access your email in the Outlook navigation pane. You will be able to view, send, receive, and manage your email messages within the Outlook application.

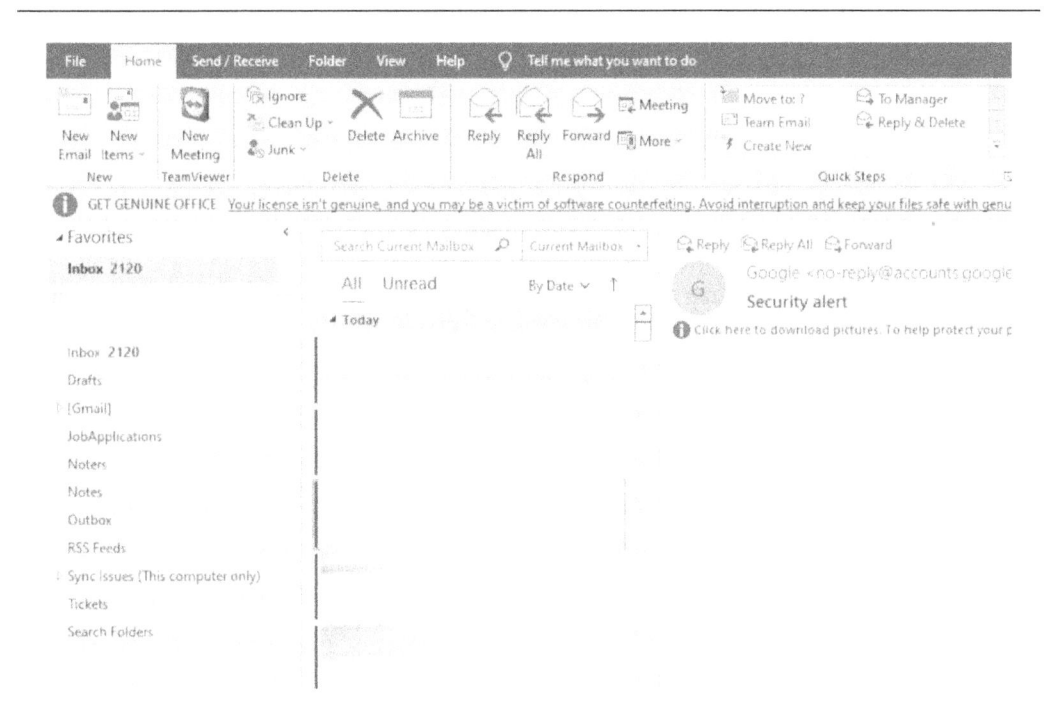

Figure 7.2: The Outlook Desktop Interface

Upon reaching the Outlook application interface, you can now use the Outlook API to access and use `win32com.client` to manage your email data.

Accessing Email Data with the win32com Client

In this section, we will guide you through the process of retrieving the last 10 email subjects from your **Outlook** account and displaying them in a user-friendly drop-down menu. You will learn how to use the `win32com` library to interact with **Outlook**, access email data, and populate the drop-down menu in a **graphical user interface** (**GUI**) created with Tkinter. This will allow users to conveniently select the email they want to generate a reply for.

To accomplish this, we will use the `last_10_emails()` function. Inside this function, we will utilize the `win32com.client` library. We will connect to the Outlook application and access the default email inbox folder. From there, we will retrieve the collection of email messages in the inbox:

```
def last_10_emails():
    outlook = win32com.client.Dispatch("Outlook.Application").GetNamespace("MAPI")
    inbox = outlook.GetDefaultFolder(6)
    messages = inbox.Items
    emails = [messages.GetLast().Subject]
    email_number = 10
```

```
    for i in range(email_number):
        emails.append(messages.GetPrevious().Subject)
return emails
```

First, we will use the `win32com.client.Dispatch()` function to create a connection to the Outlook application. This function takes a string argument, `Outlook.Application`, to specify the application we want to access. Then, we will use the `GetNamespace()` method with the `MAPI` argument to retrieve the messaging and collaboration services namespace within Outlook. This namespace provides access to various Outlook objects and folders.

By calling `GetDefaultFolder(6)`, we retrieve the default email `Inbox` folder. The 6 argument corresponds to the index of the `Inbox` folder within the Outlook namespace. This ensures that we access the correct folder. By assigning the result to the `inbox` variable, we now have a reference to the `Inbox` folder, which allows us to retrieve email messages and perform operations on them. `inbox.Items` retrieves the collection of items or email messages within the `Inbox` folder. This collection is assigned to the `messages` variable.

To retrieve the subject of the most recent email, `messages.GetLast().Subject` will be used. `GetLast()` returns the last email item in the collection, while `.Subject` retrieves the subject of that email. We can now wrap the email subject in a list to ensure it is a list containing a single subject. We can also define a variable called `email_number`. It represents the number of previous emails that we want to retrieve subjects for.

In addition to the `GetList` method, you can get specific email items using the following `win32com` methods:

- `FindNext`: This method is used to retrieve the next email item in a collection of emails that match the specified search criteria
- `GetFirst`: With this method, you can retrieve the first email item from a collection of emails, enabling access to its contents or properties
- `GetNext`: Used in conjunction with `GetFirst`, this method retrieves the next email item in a collection, facilitating sequential access to all the emails within the collection
- `GetPrevious`: This method complements `GetFirst` and allows you to retrieve the email item that comes before the currently accessed item in a collection of emails, enabling sequential backward access to the emails

We can now iterate over a range of the previous 10 subjects of the previous emails. Within the loop, we use `GetPrevious().Subject` to access the subject of the email preceding the current one in the iteration. This method moves the pointer to the previous email in the collection, and `.Subject` retrieves its subject.

For each iteration, we append the retrieved subject to the emails list using the `append()` method. This builds up a list of email subjects for the previous emails, starting from the most recent and going back in time.

Once the loop completes, we have a list of 10 email subjects stored in the emails list. We can then return this list of email subjects from the `last_10_emails()` function, allowing it to be used in our Outlook email reply generator.

Now, we can focus on creating the user interface to display the email subjects and allow the user to select one to generate a reply. Let's break down what each part of the following code does:

```
root = tk.Tk()
root.title("Outlook Emails")
root.geometry("300x300")

email_subjects = last_10_emails()
selected_subject = tk.StringVar()

dropdown = tk.OptionMenu(root, selected_subject, *email_subjects)
dropdown.pack()

label = tk.Label(root, text="")
label.pack()
root.mainloop()
```

Firstly, we will initialize and configure the main graphical window for the application using the `tkinter` library.

`root = tk.Tk()` creates the main window object, which is commonly referred to as the root or the top-level window. This object represents the main window that will contain the user interface elements of our application.

Then, we can set the title of the window to `Outlook Emails`. This title will be displayed in the title bar of the window. We will also set the dimensions of the window to `300` pixels wide and `300` pixels tall. This determines the initial size of the window when it is first displayed on the screen.

After the window template is completed, we can initialize the variables that will be used to manage the email subjects in the user interface. The `last_10_emails()` function is used here to retrieve the list of email subjects. The function returns a list of the last 10 email subjects from the Outlook application into the `email_subjects` variable.

The `selected_subject` variable creates a `StringVar` object from the `tkinter` library. This object is a special variable type that can be associated with various GUI widgets. By creating a `StringVar` object, we have a variable that can hold a string value and be easily associated with GUI elements, such as buttons or drop-down menus. This allows us to track and manipulate the selected email subject within our application.

Then, we create a drop-down menu in the user interface to display the list of email subjects. The `OpenMenu` widget represents a drop-down menu where the user can select an option from a list. The `root` argument specifies that the drop-down menu should be placed within the main window of our application, while the `selected_subject` argument specifies the variable that will be associated with the drop-down menu. It indicates the variable that will hold the currently selected email subject from the drop-down menu.

The `*email_subjects` argument uses the `*` operator to unpack the `email_subjects` list into individual items. This allows each email subject to be treated as a separate argument for the `OptionMenu` widget, providing the list of options for the drop-down menu.

We can then build a label widget and start the main event loop of the application. The `label` variable creates a label widget, used to display text or other information in the user interface. The text argument specifies the initial text to be displayed in the label, which is an empty string in this case. `label.pack()` packs the widgets within the main window.

Finally, `root.mainloop()` starts the main event loop. This method is responsible for handling user events, such as mouse clicks or button presses, and updating the GUI accordingly. The program will remain in this loop until the user closes the application window, ensuring that the application remains responsive and interactive.

To test the application, let's imagine that we are a software engineer that received 10 work emails from their colleagues.

Now, you can click on the **Run** button in **PyCharm** to execute the current version of your Outlook email reply generator. Once the code is running, a window titled **Outlook Emails** will appear. This window contains a drop-down menu listing the last 10 email subjects from the **Outlook** application, as shown in *Figure 7.3*:

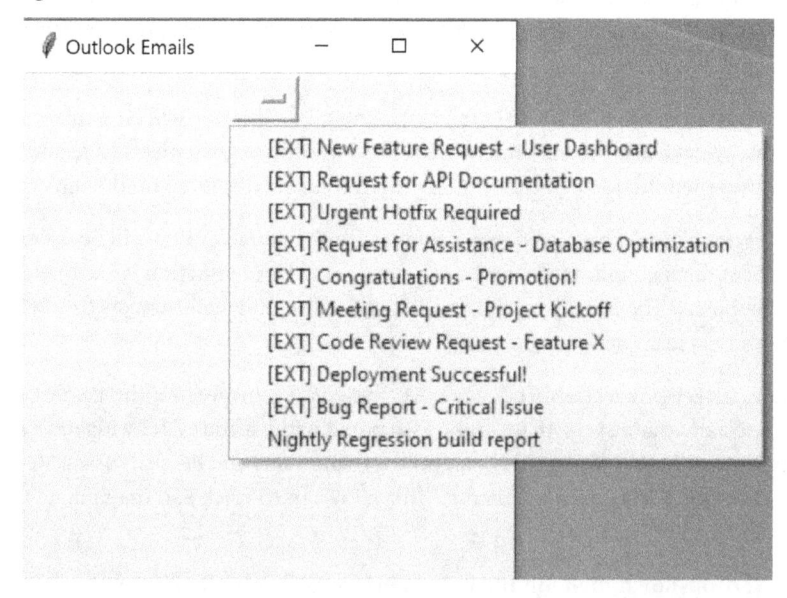

Figure 7.3: The Email Reply Generator Last 10 Emails Drop-Down Menu

You can now select an email subject from the drop-down menu. Upon selection, the text of the selected email subject will be stored in the `selected_subject` variable and displayed inside the drop-down menu button (see *Figure 7.4*).

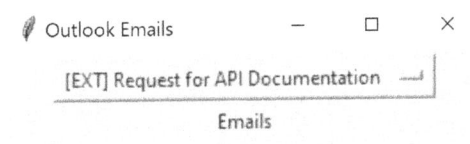

Figure 7.4: A Selected Email Subject Inside the Drop-Down Menu Button

Those are the essential steps to set up the development environment to build the Outlook email reply generator. We went through extracting email data from Outlook using the `win32com` library and passing it to the ChatGPT API. You also learned how to access and display email data using the `win32com` and `tkinter` libraries to create a GUI.

In the next section, you will complete your Outlook email reply generator by using the ChatGPT API to generate AI replies to a specific email selected by the user. We will also build the corresponding button for users to access that functionality from the desktop application.

Generating automatic email replies

Now, let's delve into the implementation of key functionality in our application to generate automatic replies to Outlook emails. We will go through the process of building the final portion of our app that utilizes the Outlook API to retrieve email data, leveraging the power of the ChatGPT API to generate original replies based on the data obtained in the previous section. Here, you will learn how to seamlessly integrate the ChatGPT API into your Outlook applications.

We will build the `reply()` function, which serves as the core component responsible for generating email replies. Within this function, you will retrieve the selected email subject from the user interface and use it to fetch the corresponding email content from Outlook. We will demonstrate how to leverage the ChatGPT API to generate AI-powered responses based on the email content. Through this process, you will gain hands-on experience in passing data between ChatGPT and Outlook.

You can include the `reply()` function just above the `root.mainloop()` inside your `app.py` file. Note that the `root.mainloop()` function call should always be the last line of the code in a `tkinter` application. This is because `root.mainloop()` initiates the main event loop, which is responsible for handling user events and updating the GUI:

```
def reply():
    email = win32com.client.Dispatch("Outlook.Application").\
        GetNamespace("MAPI").\
        GetDefaultFolder(6).Items.Item(selected_subject.get())
    response = openai.ChatCompletion.create(
```

```
            model="gpt-4",
            max_tokens=1024,
            n=1,
            messages=[
                {"role": "user", "content": "You are a professional email
                    writer"},
                {"role": "assistant", "content": "Ok"},
                {"role": "user", "content": f"Create a reply to this
                    email:\n {email.Body}"}
            ]
        )

        reply = email.Reply()
        reply.Body = response["choices"][0]["message"]["content"]

        reply.Display()
        return
```

Firstly, we can retrieve the selected email content from the Outlook application using the `win32com` library. We will access the Outlook application through the `Dispatch` method. From there, we retrieve the **Inbox** email folder using the `GetDefaultFolder(6)` and retrieve the specific email item, based on the subject obtained from `selected_subject`. The resulting `email` object represents the email with the subject specified by the user, and it can be further used to generate a reply or access other email properties.

Then, we can make use of the ChatGPT API to generate a response to an email. We will call the `openai.ChatCompletion.create()` method and provide several parameters to generate a response. The `max_tokens` parameter limits the length of the generated email reply to 1,024 tokens. By adjusting this parameter, you can increase or decrease the number of tokens to achieve the desired length for your email reply.

As you can see here, we are using the most advanced ChatGPT model **GPT-4**. This model is trained on significantly more data compared to the GPT-3 and is more accurate, factual, and relievable in solving complex tasks, which also include personalized email copywriting.

The `openai.ChatCompletion.create()` method is a crucial part of the implementation, as it leverages the ChatGPT API to generate automatic email replies. The `prompt` parameter is particularly significant, as it sets the initial input given to the language model. In this case, the prompt includes the email content obtained from Outlook, which serves as the context to generate the reply.

To improve the quality and diversity of responses, developers can experiment with different prompts. By crafting more specific or varied prompts, the model's output can be guided to meet specific criteria or generate replies tailored to different contexts. Here are a few alternatives:

- **Contextual prompt**: "You received an email from a colleague requesting your availability for a meeting. Compose a polite and concise reply confirming your attendance."

    In this prompt, the model is explicitly instructed to respond to a meeting request from a colleague. By providing a specific scenario and asking for a "polite and concise" reply, the generated response is more likely to align with the desired context and tone.

- **Emotion-infused prompt**: "You just received an email from a close friend sharing some exciting news. Draft a warm and enthusiastic reply to congratulate them and share your thoughts."

    By infusing the prompt with emotional keywords such as "exciting news," "warm," and "enthusiastic," the model is encouraged to produce a response that conveys a sense of joy and support, making it sound more authentic and human-like.

- **Formal business prompt**: "As a customer service representative, you received an email from a dissatisfied customer regarding a recent product issue. Craft a professional and empathetic response to address their concerns and offer a solution."

    Here, the prompt sets a formal business context, instructing the model to respond as a customer service representative dealing with a dissatisfied customer. Using the term "empathetic" emphasizes the importance of a compassionate and helpful reply, which can lead to a more realistic and considerate response.

- **Personalized prompt**: "Your colleague sent you an email with some exciting updates about their recent vacation. Reply with your genuine excitement, ask follow-up questions, and share a bit about what's been happening in your life too."

    This prompt encourages a more personalized response, as it specifies that the reply should express genuine excitement and involve asking follow-up questions. By emphasizing the reciprocity of sharing information about the sender's life, the generated reply is likely to feel more natural and akin to a real conversation.

- **Instructional prompt**: "You received an email from a colleague asking for detailed instructions on how to use a new software tool. Provide a step-by-step guide with clear explanations and visual aids where necessary."

    In this case, the prompt sets a clear instruction for the model to generate a reply containing detailed instructions. The use of terms such as "step-by-step guide" and "clear explanations" directs the model toward providing more informative and structured responses.

The subject and email content play vital roles in generating the reply. The selected email subject serves as a key identifier for the email that the user wants to respond to. Once the email is identified, its content body is used as the context to generate the reply. By utilizing both the subject and email content, the reply function ensures that the response generated by ChatGPT is relevant and contextual. The email content provides essential information about the sender's query or message, and the model uses this information to craft a coherent and appropriate reply.

Sharing mail content with ChatGPT, or any external API for that matter, raises valid security concerns. This can be prevented through appropriate privacy policies and user consent mechanisms. Furthermore, using secure communication protocols (for example, HTTPS) and working with reputable and trusted API providers, such as OpenAI, can help safeguard data during transmission and processing.

After the ChatGPT API response is obtained, we can prepare the email reply by creating a reply object using `email.Reply()`. The reply's body text is then assigned the extracted response text obtained from the ChatGPT JSON `response` parameter. This ensures that the AI-generated content is included in the reply.

The `reply.Display()` function is then called to display the reply in a separate window, allowing the user to review and potentially make any necessary edits before sending it. The return statement signifies the end of the `reply()` function and returns control to the main program, where we will build the **Reply** button:

```
button = tk.Button(root, text="Generate Reply",
                   command=reply)
button.pack()

root.mainloop()
```

The button is associated with the root window and displays the text `Generate Reply` as its label. The command parameter specifies that the previously build `reply()` function should be executed when the button is clicked. By calling `button.pack()`, the button is packed within the window, allowing it to be displayed to the user. This is how we can set up a user interface element that triggers the `reply()` function when clicked, enabling the generation of an email reply in response to user interaction.

You can now start your Outlook email reply generator app with a single click on the **Run** button in PyCharm. Once you do that, there will be a new button called **Generate Reply** displayed on your application window (see *Figure 7.5*).

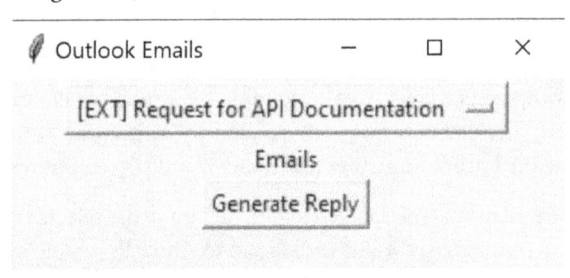

Figure 7.5: The Generate Reply Button

You can now select an email from the drop-down menu and click the **Generate Reply** button. The button will instantly activate the `reply()` function, passing the content of the email to the ChatGPT

API and asking it to generate a reply based on that content. This process will happen in the background, and within a few seconds, your app will launch the **Outlook reply window**. As you can see in *Figure 7.6*, the reply window will be populated with the generated ChatGPT reply to the selected email.

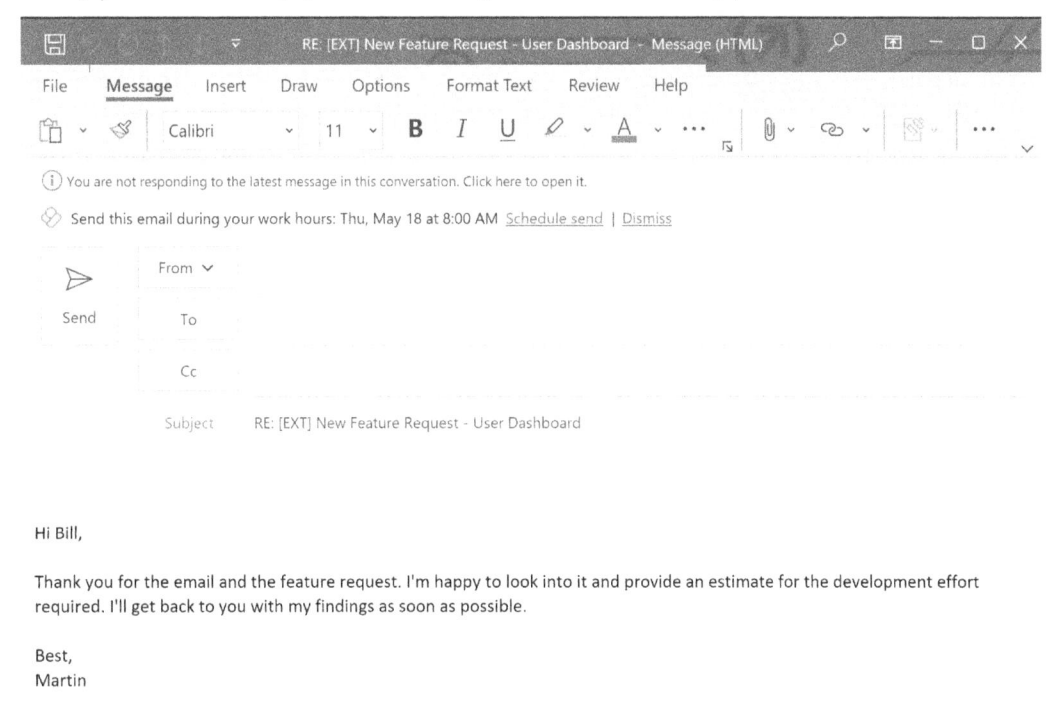

Figure 7.6: An Email Reply Generated by ChatGPT

To verify that the generated reply is relevant, you can check the content of the selected email and the ChatGPT reply, such as the following:

- **Selected email content**
- *Hi Martin,*

    I have an exciting new feature request for you. Our users have been asking for a personalized dashboard that provides an overview of their account activity and statistics.

    I would appreciate it if you could start working on this feature and provide an estimate for the development effort required.

    Regards,

    Bill

- **GPT-4 API reply**:

    Dear Bill,

Thank you for your email and for presenting such an exciting new feature request.

A personalized dashboard is indeed a wonderful addition that would significantly enhance the user experience. I understand the importance of a tool that could provide our users with a comprehensive overview of their account activity and statistics.

I will immediately commence with the preliminary work to evaluate the possibilities. This constitutes understanding user needs in depth, defining the necessary features, and analyzing the scope of work.

By considering the complexity and range of this feature, I anticipate the initial estimate to be concluded within a week's time. This will assist me in providing an accurate estimate of the development effort required.

I look forward to the potential positive impact this new feature could bring to our user experience. Thank you for entrusting this task to me.

Best regards,

Martin

In addition to generating a relevant reply, your application empowers the user to edit the AI-generated response before sending it. This functionality also allows them to address any minor imperfections or make adjustments to the reply, ensuring a polished final email. By providing the option to review and modify the AI-generated reply, the user has greater control over the content and can tailor it to their specific needs before sending the email.

This concludes our implementation of generating automatic email replies using Outlook and the ChatGPT API. You can now retrieve email data from Outlook, use the ChatGPT API to generate AI-powered responses, and integrate this functionality into an Outlook application, allowing users to review and modify the generated replies before sending them.

Summary

In this chapter, we covered the complete development of the Outlook email reply generator using Outlook and ChatGPT API with the state-of-the-art GPT-4 model. We learned how to retrieve email data from Outlook using the `win32com` library and display the email subjects in a drop-down menu using the `tkinter` library. We wrote the code to connect to the Outlook application, access the default email inbox folder, and retrieve the last 10 email subjects. We also covered the creation of the user interface, including the main window, the drop-down menu, and a label.

We also learned the process of building the `reply()` function, which retrieved email data from Outlook, generated AI-powered responses using the ChatGPT API, and displayed the generated reply in a separate window for reviewing and editing. The chapter also explained how to integrate the `reply()` function into the application and how to create a button in the user interface that triggers the `reply()` function. We also tested the application by selecting an email subject from the drop-down menu and generating an AI reply email, using the ChatGPT API.

In *Chapter 8*, you will learn how to integrate ChatGPT API with one of the most popular app development Python frameworks, **PyQT**. You will build an essay generation tool that will be able to create essays on any topic. Here, we will move one step further and show you how to control the API tokens directly from the application's frontend. This will allow you to specify the length of the responses and, consequently, the generated essay received from the ChatGPT API.

8

Essay Generation Tool with PyQt and the ChatGPT API

In this chapter, we will dive into the exciting world of integrating the ChatGPT API with one of the most popular Python frameworks for app development, **PyQt**. You will build a user-friendly desktop essay generation tool, powered by the integration of PyQt and the ChatGPT API, allowing users to effortlessly generate well-written essays on any topic. Here, you will gain valuable insights into the design stages involved in building a PyQt desktop application.

We'll guide you through the process of designing a desktop app using an object-oriented approach with PyQt, helping you to understand the fundamental concepts and components involved in that framework. With a solid foundation in place, we'll then shift our focus to leveraging the capabilities of the ChatGPT API. You will learn how to integrate the API into your PyQt application, enabling you to generate essays seamlessly.

By combining the strengths of PyQt and the ChatGPT API, you will be equipped to create an interactive and intelligent desktop app capable of generating well-written essays on various topics. Furthermore, we will demonstrate how to provide users with the ability to control API tokens directly from the frontend, giving them the power to specify the desired length of the essay responses obtained from the ChatGPT API. This level of customization empowers users to tailor their generated essays to meet specific requirements, whether they be concise summaries or in-depth analyses.

In this chapter, you will learn how to do the following:

- Use PyQt to design and build a desktop application
- Integrate the ChatGPT API into a PyQt application
- Generate essays using the ChatGPT API within the PyQt application
- Implement functionality that allows users to control the ChatGPT API tokens used
- Save generated essays in a Word document for future reference or further editing
- Build text fields, windows, and buttons for a fully functional PyQt desktop application

Essay Generation Tool with PyQt and the ChatGPT API

By the end of this chapter, you will be proficient in using PyQt to design and develop desktop applications, gaining a strong foundation in app development. Additionally, you will further develop the skills for integrating the ChatGPT API into your applications, having better control over the AI response parameters.

Technical Requirements

In this chapter, we will demonstrate the complete `PyQt6` installation. However, to successfully finish the Essay Generation Tool project, you should ensure that you also meet the following technical prerequisites:

- Python 3.7 or later installed on your machine
- A code editor, such as PyCharm (recommended)
- A Python virtual environment
- An OpenAI API key
- Familiarity with Python **Object-Oriented Programming** (**OOP**) concepts

The code snippets showcased in this chapter can be found on the GitHub platform. Access to the code can be obtained by visiting the following link: `https://github.com/PacktPublishing/Building-AI-Applications-with-ChatGPT-APIs/tree/main/Chapter08%20ArticleGenerator`

In the upcoming sections, you will embark on the journey of building a desktop application using PyQt. You will dive into the intricacies of GUI design and learn how to leverage PyQt's powerful features to develop a visually appealing and interactive desktop application.

Building a Desktop Application with PyQT

In this section, you will gain hands-on experience in creating various components of the PyQt application's user interface, such as windows, labels, buttons, text fields, and drop-down menus. Here, you will set up the PyCharm project, install the `PyQt6` and `docx` libraries, and build your desktop application frontend.

First, let's discuss what the PyQt library is, and how it differs from the rest of the Python application development tools, such as Tkinter (see *Table 8.1*). PyQt is a powerful Python framework widely used for creating desktop applications with rich **graphical user interfaces** (**GUIs**). It provides developers with a comprehensive set of tools, classes, and functionalities to design and build intuitive and visually appealing applications. PyQt is a wrapper around the popular **Qt** framework, offering seamless integration of Qt's extensive libraries and widgets into Python.

> **Important Note**
> PyQt is available under two licenses: GPL (GNU General Public License) and a commercial license. The GPL license allows you to use PyQt for free as long as you adhere to the terms and conditions of the GPL license, which include making your application's source code available if you distribute it. If you do not want to comply with the GPL requirements or need to use PyQt in a proprietary, closed source project, you can purchase a commercial license from Riverbank Computing, the company that develops PyQt. The commercial license allows you to use PyQt without the restrictions imposed by the GPL.

Framework	Based on Qt (powerful GUI toolkit)	Built-in Python GUI toolkit (Tkinter)
Cross-platform	Yes	Yes
License	GPL and commercial	Open-source (Python Software Foundation)
Widget Library	Extensive	Limited
Look and Feel	Native look on all platforms	Native look only on some platforms
Documentation	Comprehensive and well-documented	Basic but adequate
Popularity	Popular in both hobby and industry	Standard library, widely used in Python
Learning Curve	Moderate to steep	Beginner-friendly
Performance	Generally faster due to C++ backend	Generally slower due to Python backend
Community Support	Active community and third-party modules	Active community and ample resources

Table 8.1: Comparison between PyQt and Tkinter

PyQt is a Python framework, unlike `tkinter`, which is Python's standard library for creating GUIs using the Tk toolkit. PyQt offers a more extensive range of widgets and a highly customizable appearance. It also provides a more modern and aesthetically appealing look for GUIs. Now that you know what PyQt is, we can set up your PyCharm project and install this outstanding Python desktop app framework.

Setting Up the Essay Generation Tool Project

Let's first configure your PyCharm project by following the steps we are already familiar with. You can begin by launching PyCharm and selecting **Create New Project**. In the **New Project** dialog box, assign the name `EssayGenerationTool` to your project. You can maintain the default location and click on **Create** to establish the new project. Once the project is set up, you can create a Python file named `app.py` where the main code for the Essay Generation Tool is going to live.

To finalize the project setup, you will require the installation of several Python libraries. You can use the `pip` package manager to install these libraries. To commence, open a terminal in PyCharm and enter the following command to install all the necessary libraries:

```
pip install PyQt6
pip install openai
pip install python-docx
```

Additionally, let's set up the necessary API key from OpenAI by creating the `config.py` module. As we have seen in previous projects, this file will serve as a secure storage location for all the API keys used in our project. Make sure that you have the `config.py` file located in the same directory as the code. However, it is important to note that you should avoid pushing this file to a Git repository to maintain its confidentiality and prevent exposing the API key. With the API token securely stored, you can proceed to include it in the relevant files alongside the necessary libraries, as demonstrated in the following code snippet:

config.py

```
API_KEY = "<YOUR_CHATGPT_API_KEY>"
```

app.py

```
import sys
from PyQt6.QtWidgets import QApplication, QWidget, QLabel, QLineEdit, QPushButton, QTextEdit, QComboBox
import openai
import docx
import config
openai.api_key = config.API_KEY
```

Inside the `app.py` file, we can import several libraries to create our desktop application. The specific classes imported from `PyQt6` represent different GUI components such as the application window, labels, text fields, buttons, and drop-down menus. The `docx` module is also imported to handle the export of our AI-generated essays to a Microsoft Word document.

Building the Application GUI with PyQt

In this section, we will explore the process of creating a PyQt application. We will set up the foundation for the essay generation application using the PyQt6 library. The application user interface that you will build consists of various widgets such as labels, input fields, a text area, and buttons.

To begin our journey in creating a PyQt application for generating essays, we will start by creating the initial app window and setting up the application launch logic. As mentioned earlier, our application will use an **object-oriented design (OOP)** by encapsulating related data and functionality within the `EssayGenerator` class.

Using object-oriented design with PyQt is beneficial because PyQt is built upon the Qt framework, which itself is designed with object-oriented principles. By aligning our code with the underlying framework, we can leverage the full power and flexibility of PyQt. By encapsulating the app functionality in a class, we can easily manage and maintain our application. This promotes code reusability and extensibility, as classes can be inherited, modified, and extended as needed. The `EssayGenerator` class will be derived from the `QWidget` class, which is a base class for all user interface objects in PyQt:

```
class EssayGenerator(Qwidget):

    def __init__(self):
        super().__init__()
        self.initUI()

    def initUI(self):
        self.setWindowTitle("Essay Generator")
        self.setGeometry (300, 300, 1200, 800)

if __name__ == '__main__':
    app = Qapplication(sys.argv)
    ex = EssayGenerator()
    ex.show()
    sys.exit(app.exec())
```

The use of the `QWidget` class as a base class in the `EssayGenerator` class allows us to adopt all `QWidget` features in the GUI of our application. `QWidget` is a fundamental class in PyQt that provides functionality for creating windows, handling events, and managing layouts. While there are other alternative base classes available in PyQt, such as `QMainWindow` for more complex applications or `QDialog` for custom dialog boxes, `QWidget` is chosen here because it serves as a versatile foundation for most user interface elements and provides the necessary features for creating a basic window in our Essay Generation application.

The `EssayGenerator` class is a specialized type of widget that can be used to create a GUI element. Inside the class, we have the `__init__` method, which is a special method in Python known as a **Constructor**. It gets executed when an object of the class is created. Within the `__init__` method of the `EssayGenerator` class, we use the `super()` keyword to call the `__init__` method of the parent class, `QWidget`, and initialize it. This ensures that the necessary setup from the parent class is performed before any additional initialization specific to the `EssayGenerator` class.

Then the `initUI()` method is responsible for setting up the user interface and other elements of the application, such as the window title, size, and position. It sets the window title of the application to `Essay Generator` using the built-in `setWindowTitle` method and specifies the position and size of the window on the screen, where the numbers represent the x and y coordinates of the top-left corner of the window, followed by its width and height, respectively.

By calling `super().__init__()` and `self.initUI()`, we ensure that the application is properly initialized and the main application window is launched once we run it. This approach follows the principle of inheritance, where the `EssayGenerator` child class inherits and extends the functionality of the parent class, `QWidget`, resulting in a fully functional and customized widget for our application.

In Python, it is common to use the `__name__ == '__main__'` condition to ensure that the subsequent code is only executed when the script is run as the main module. If it is, the code proceeds to create an instance of the `QApplication` class, which manages the application's control flow.

The ex object is created from the `EssayGenerator` class to display the application window, and finally, `sys.exit(app.exec())` starts the event loop of the application, ensuring that the program remains active until the user closes the window or exits the application. This allows us to execute the application when the script is run directly. You can easily verify that a single click on the **Run** button in PyCharm results in the display of the main application window, as shown in *Figure 8.1*.

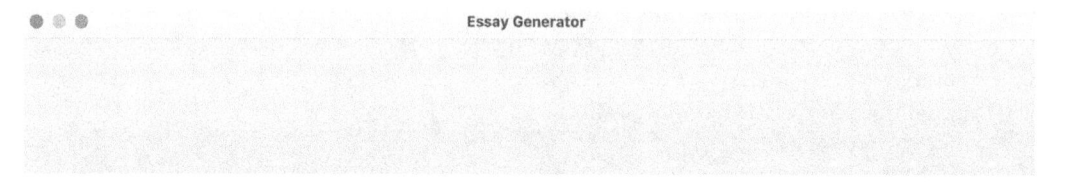

Figure 8.1: Essay Generator Tool Window

Now that we have built the application window, we can start adding the core elements of our essay generator tool. Those are as follows:

- **Topic Input**: The essay generator requires a mechanism for users to input the topic or subject of the essay. This can be done through a text input field.

- **Essay Output**: Once the generation algorithm produces the essay content, it needs to be displayed to the user. This can be achieved through a text area where the generated essay is presented.

- **Saving Functionality**: Providing an option for users to save the generated essay is often useful. This can involve saving the essay to a file, such as a Word document, or providing the ability to copy the text to the clipboard.

Those core elements can be easily included inside the `initUI()` function, which holds all elements shown in our application:

```
def initUI(self):
    self.setWindowTitle("Essay Generator")
    self.setGeometry(300, 300, 1200, 800)

    topic_label = QLabel('Enter the topic:', self)
    topic_label.move(20, 40)

    self.topic_input = QLineEdit(self)
    self.topic_input.move(20, 100)
    self.topic_input.resize(1000, 30)

    self.essay_output = QTextEdit(self)
    self.essay_output.move(20, 150)
    self.essay_output.resize(1100, 500)

    generate_button = QPushButton("Generate Essay", self)
    generate_button.move(1050, 100)
    generate_button.clicked.connect(self.generate_essay)

    save_button = QPushButton("Save", self)
    save_button.move(20, 665)
    save_button.clicked.connect(self.save_essay)
```

Before creating the essay topic input field, we can instantiate a `QLabel` object called `topic_label`. This label will be positioned above the `topic_input` field. The purpose of the label is to instruct the user on the purpose of the text field below. We then use the `move()` method to position the label at coordinates (20, 40) within the application window.

Next, we create a `QLineEdit` object named `topic_input` as the input field for the topic. Here, we can use the `move()` method again to position the input field below the label at coordinates (20, 100). Additionally, we use the `resize()` method to set the dimensions of the input field. This ensures that the input field has an appropriate size for user input.

Then we can define the `essay_output` attribute as an instance of the `QTextEdit` class, which represents a multi-line text editing widget. We again use the `move()` and `resize()` built-in methods to place the essay output filed under the topic input text field. The `essay_output` text area is used so that the generated essay text can be displayed. Users can now easily read and interact with the essay output, enhancing the usability and functionality of the application.

> **Important Note**
>
> In Python, the `self` keyword is a convention used to refer to the instance of a class within the class itself. It is not a reserved keyword but a commonly used name for the first parameter of instance methods in a class. When defining methods within a class, including the `self` parameter as the first parameter allows you to access and modify the instance variables and methods of that class.

Finally, we create two buttons for the essay generator application: the `Generate Essay` button and a `Save` button. For both buttons, we can use the `QPushButton` class, which provides a clickable button element that users can interact with by clicking or pressing it. Here, it is essential to use the `clicked.connect()` method, which connects the button's `clicked` signal to a method, allowing the method to be called when the button is clicked.

Once the user clicks the **Generate Essay** button, our app will automatically call the `generate_essay()` function. This method will be responsible for building a connection with the ChatGPT API and displaying the response, or the generated essay, inside our `essay_output` text field. Similarly, once the essay is generated, the user will be able to click on the **Save** button. This action will activate the `save_essay()` function, where we will later use the `docx` library to save our essay in a Word document.

Even though `save_essay()` and `generate_essay()` are not implemented yet, we can initialize them for the purpose of testing our application. Both methods should be placed inside the `EssayGeneration` class, but outside the `initUI()` method. It is also a good practice to place the function definitions above the main Python function to avoid any unexpected errors:

```
def initUI(self):
    ...
    ..
    .

def generate_essay(self):
    pass

def save_essay(self):
    pass
```

Currently, the method consists of a `pass` statement, which is a placeholder statement in Python that does nothing. This is used to indicate that the method does not have any implementation yet.

When you execute your application again, you will observe that all the text fields and buttons are presented within the application window (see *Figure 8.2*).

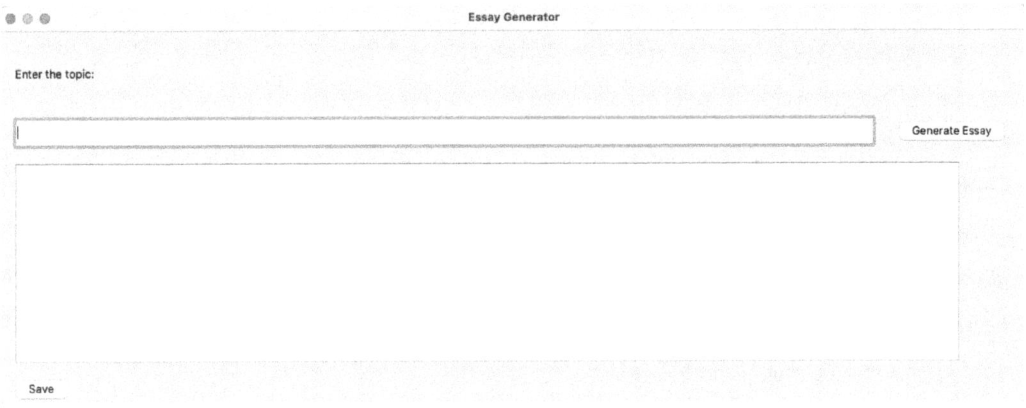

Figure 8.2: Essay Generator Text Fields and Buttons

This is how you can create a basic PyQt application. Now you know how to build the application window, initialize the user interface elements, and create the core elements of the essay generator tool, such as the topic input field, essay output text area, and buttons for generating and saving essays.

Since both the `save_essay()` and `generate_essay()` methods contain the placeholder `pass` keyword, clicking the buttons will not perform any substantial actions at this point. We would need to implement the necessary functionality within the respective methods to achieve the desired behavior when the buttons are clicked. You will learn how to build those methods in the upcoming section.

Creating Essay Generation Methods with the ChatGPT API

In this section, we will dive into the implementation of the key functions within the essay generator application. These functions are responsible for generating the essay based on user input and saving the generated essay to a file. By understanding the code, you will be able to grasp the inner workings of the application and gain insight into how the essay generation and saving processes are accomplished.

We will begin by exploring the `generate_essay()` function. This function will retrieve the topic entered by the user from the input field. It will then set the engine type for the OpenAI API, create a prompt using the topic, and make a request to the OpenAI API for essay generation. The response received from the API will contain the generated essay, which will be extracted and displayed in the essay output area of the application. To add that functionality, simply remove the `pass` placeholder and follow this code:

```
def generate_essay(self):
    topic = self.topic_input.text()
    tokens = 500

    engine = "gpt-4"
```

```python
        prompt = f"Write an {tokens/1.5} words essay on the following
            topic: {topic} \n\n"

        response = openai.ChatCompletion.create(
            model=model,
            messages=[
                {"role": "user", "content": "You are a professional
                    essay writer."},
                {"role": "assistant", "content": "Ok"},
                {"role": "user", "content": f"{prompt}"}
            ],
            max_tokens=tokens
        )
        essay = response["choices"][0]["message"]["content"]
```

Here, we retrieve the topic entered by the user from the `topic_input` QLineEdit widget and assign it to the topic variable using the `text()` method. This captures the user's chosen topic for the essay. For now, we can define the `tokens` variable and set it to `500`. This indicates the desired length of the generated essay. We will modify this value later by adding a drop-down menu with different token sizes to generate essays of different lengths.

We can also specify the engine used for the OpenAI API to be `text-davinci-003`, which will generate the essay. You can adjust this value to utilize different language models or versions based on your requirements. We can also create the `prompt` variable, which is a string containing the prompt for essay generation.

It is constructed by concatenating the `Write an {tokens/1.5} essay on the following topic:` text, where the `tokens/1.5` variable specifies how many words our essay should be. We need to divide the token number by 1.5, as 1 word in English represents about 1.5 tokens according to OpenAI. After specifying the instructions, we can pass the `topic` variable to the prompt. This prompt serves as the initial input for the essay generation process and provides context for the generated essay.

Once all variables are defined, we make a request to the ChatGPT API with the specified engine, prompt, and the maximum number of tokens (in this case, 500). The API processes the prompt and generates a response, which is stored in the `response` variable. From the response, we extract the generated essay by accessing the `text` attribute of the first choice. This represents the generated text of the essay. Finally, we can pass the AI response to the `essay_output()` function, displaying it in the user interface for the user to read and interact with.

Moving on, we will examine the `save_essay()` function. This function will retrieve the topic and the generated essay. It will utilize the `docx` library to create a new Word document and add the final essay to the document. The document will then be saved with the filename based on the provided topic, resulting in a Word document that contains the generated essay. After removing the `pass` keyword, you can implement the described functionality using the following code snippet:

```
def save_essay(self):
    topic = self.topic_input.text()
    final_text = self.essay_output.toPlainText()

    document = docx.Document()
    document.add_paragraph(final_text)
    document.save(topic + ".docx")
```

Here, we retrieve the text entered in the `topic_input` widget and assign it to the `topic` variable using the `text()` method. This captures the topic entered by the user, which will be used as the filename for the saved essay. Next, we use the `toPlainText()` method on the `essay_output` widget to retrieve the generated essay text and assign it to the `final_text` variable. This ensures that the user can edit the ChatGPT-generated essay before saving it. By capturing the topic and the final text, we are now equipped to proceed with the necessary steps to save the essay to a file.

We can now use the `docx` library to create a new Word document by calling `docx.Document()`, which initializes an empty document. We then add a paragraph to the document by using the `add_paragraph()` method and passing in the `final_text` variable, which contains the generated essay text. This adds the generated essay as a paragraph to the document. We can now save the document by calling `document.save()` and providing a filename constructed by concatenating the `topic` variable, which represents the topic entered by the user. This saves the document as a Word file with the specified filename.

You can now test your essay generator by running the code in PyCharm and generating an essay following these steps (see *Figure 8.3*):

1. Write an essay topic of your choice in the **Topic Input** field. For this example, I have chosen the topic `Ancient Egypt`.
2. Perform a single click on the **Generate Essay** button. The app will reach ChatGPT API and within a few seconds you will have your essay displayed inside the **Essay Output** field.
3. You can edit the essay generated by the artificial intelligence before saving it.
4. Perform a single click on the **Save** button. This action will save the edited essay to a Word document utilizing the `save_essay()` method. The Word document will be saved in the root directory of your project.

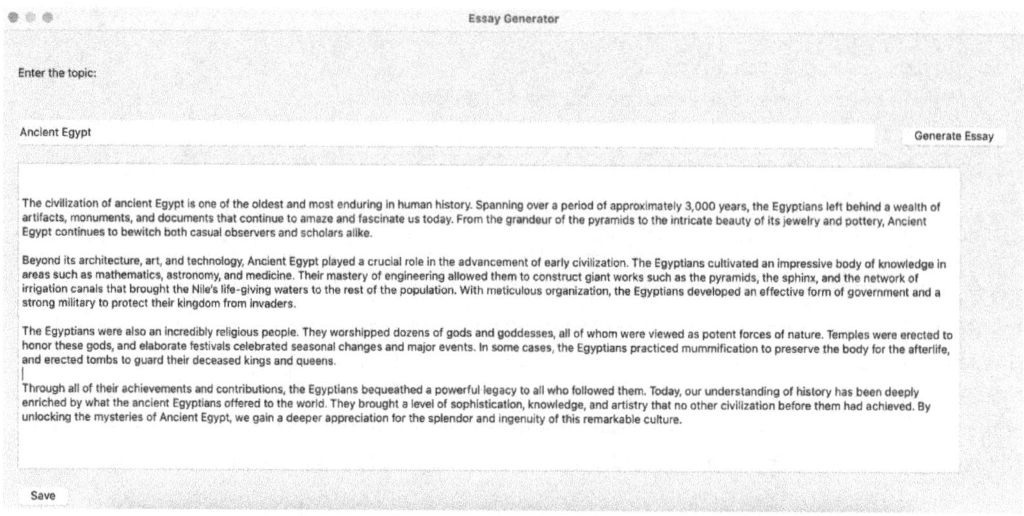

Figure 8.3: Essay Generator Creating an "Ancient Egypt" Essay

Once the essay has been saved to a Word document, you can reshare it with your peers, submit it as a school assignment or use any Word styling options on it.

This section discussed the implementation of key functions in our essay generator application using the ChatGPT API. We built the `generate_essay()` method, which retrieved the user's topic input and sent a request to the ChatGPT API to generate an AI essay. We also developed the `save_essay()` method, which saved the generated essay in a Word document.

In the next section, we will introduce additional functionality to the essay generator application. Specifically, we will allow the user to change the number of AI tokens used for generating the essay.

Controlling the ChatGPT API Tokens

In this section, we will explore how to enhance the functionality of the essay generator application by allowing users to have control over the number of tokens used when communicating with ChatGPT. By enabling this feature, users will be able to generate essays of different lengths, tailored to their specific needs or preferences. Currently, our application has a fixed value of 500 tokens, but we will modify it to include a drop-down menu that provides different options for token sizes.

To implement this functionality, we will make use of a drop-down menu that presents users with a selection of token length options. By selecting a specific value from the dropdown, users can indicate their desired length for the generated essay. We will integrate this feature seamlessly into the existing application, empowering users to customize their essay-generation experience.

Let's delve into the code snippet that will enable users to control the token length. You can add that code inside the `initUI()` methods, just under the `essay_output` resizing:

```
def initUI(self):
    self.setWindowTitle("Essay Generator")
    self.setGeometry(300, 300, 1200, 800)

    topic_label = QLabel('Enter the topic:', self)
    topic_label.move(20, 40)

    self.topic_input = QLineEdit(self)
    self.topic_input.move(20, 100)
    self.topic_input.resize(1000, 30)

    self.essay_output = QTextEdit(self)
    self.essay_output.move(20, 150)
    self.essay_output.resize(1100, 500)

    length_label = QLabel('Select Essay Length:', self)
    length_label.move(327, 40)

    self.length_dropdown = QComboBox(self)
    self.length_dropdown.move(320, 60)
    self.length_dropdown.addItems(["500", "1000", "2000", "3000",
        "4000"])

    generate_button = QPushButton("Generate Essay", self)
    generate_button.move(1050, 100)
    generate_button.clicked.connect(self.generate_essay)

    save_button = QPushButton("Save", self)
    save_button.move(20, 665)
    save_button.clicked.connect(self.save_essay)
```

The preceding code introduces `QLabel`, `length_label`, which serves as a visual indication of the purpose of the drop-down menu. It displays the text `Select Essay Length` to inform users about the functionality.

Next, we create `QcomboBox`, `length_dropdown`, which provides users with a drop-down menu to choose the desired token length. It is positioned below `length_label` using the `move()` method. The `addItems()` function is then used to populate the drop-down menu with a list of token length options, ranging from `500` to `4000` tokens. Users can select their preferred length from this list.

The final step is to implement the functionality that allows users to control the number of tokens used when generating the essay. We need to modify the `generate_essay()` function. The modified code should be the following:

```
def generate_essay(self):
    topic = self.topic_input.text()

    length = int(self.length_dropdown.currentText())

    engine = "gpt-4"

    prompt = f"Write an {tokens/1.5} words essay on the following
        topic: {topic} \n\n"

    response = openai.ChatCompletion.create(
        model=model,
        messages=[
            {"role": "user", "content": "You are a professional
                essay writer."},
            {"role": "assistant", "content": "Ok"},
            {"role": "user", "content": f"{prompt}"}
        ],
        max_tokens=tokens
    )
    essay = response["choices"][0]["message"]["content"]
```

In the modified code, the `length` variable is updated to retrieve the selected token length from the `length_dropdown` drop-down menu. The `currentText()` method is used to obtain the currently selected option as a string, which is then converted into an integer using the `int()` function. This allows the chosen token length to be assigned to the length variable dynamically.

By making this modification, the `generate_essay()` function will utilize the user-selected token length when making the request to the ChatGPT API for essay generation. This ensures that the generated essay will have the desired length specified by the user through the drop-down menu.

We can now click on the **Run** button in PyCharm and verify that drop-down menu works properly. As shown in *Figure 8.4*, a click on the drop-down menu will show users all options specified by the `addItems()` function.

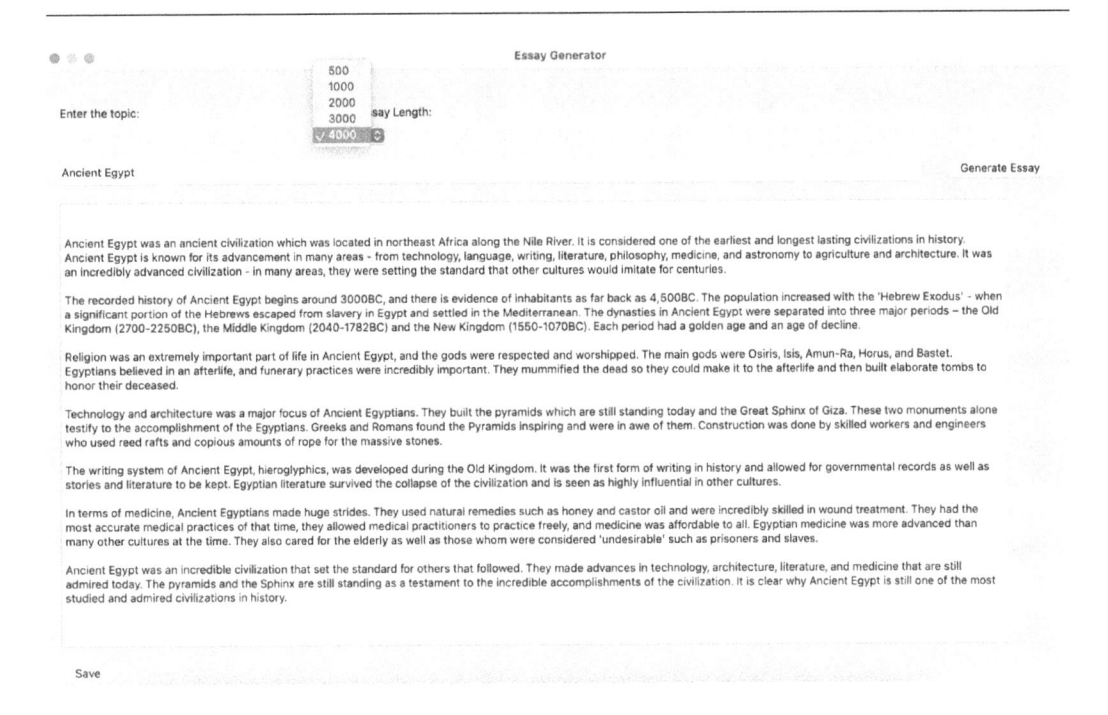

Figure 8.4: Controlling the Essay Length

The user will be able to choose a token amount between 500 and 4000. Now you can select the 4000 tokens option, resulting in a longer length for the generated essay. We can follow the steps from our previous example and verify that the ChatGPT API generates a longer essay for "**Ancient Egypt**" when the number of tokens is increased from 500 to 4000.

This is how you can enhance the functionality of an essay generator application by allowing users to control the number of tokens used when communicating with ChatGPT. By selecting a specific value from the drop-down menu, users can now indicate their desired length for the generated essay. We achieved that by using the QComboBox class to create the drop-down menu itself. The modified generate_essay() method retrieved the selected token length from the drop-down menu and dynamically assigned it to the length variable.

Summary

In this chapter, you learned how to build a desktop application with PyQt and enhance its functionality by integrating the ChatGPT API for essay generation. We discussed the basics of PyQt and its advantages over other Python GUI development tools. We used that framework to create the application's GUI components, such as windows, labels, input fields, text areas, and buttons.

The chapter also delved into the implementation of the essay generation functionality using the ChatGPT API. The main method discussed was generate_essay(), which took the user's chosen topic, set the engine type, created a prompt using the topic, and sent a request to the API to generate the essay. The generated essay was then displayed in the application's output area. You also learned how to build the `save_essay()` function, which used the `docx` library to save the generated essay as a Word document.

Furthermore, the chapter explored how to enhance the application by allowing users to control the length of the generated essay. It introduced a drop-down menu implemented with `QLabel` and `QComboBox` classes, allowing users to select different token sizes. The modified `generate_essay()` function retrieved the selected token length from the drop-down menu and adjusted the length of the generated essay accordingly.

In *Chapter 9*, called *Integrating ChatGPT and DALL-E API: Build End-to-End PowerPoint Presentation Generator*, you will learn how to integrate two AI APIs, **ChatGPT** and **DALL-E**, to build an end-to-end **PowerPoint** presentation generator. You will be introduced to the DALL-E API and learn about decoding JSON responses from the API. The chapter will also cover the PowerPoint Python framework and demonstrate how to generate AI art using the DALL-E API, enabling you to create PowerPoint slides and images.

9

Integrating ChatGPT and DALL-E API: Build End-to-End PowerPoint Presentation Generator

In this exciting chapter, we dive into the world of AI art and explore the incredible capabilities of **DALL-E**, an artificial intelligence model developed by OpenAI. We'll start by introducing you to DALL-E and its groundbreaking approach to generating images from textual descriptions. You'll learn how to access the power of DALL-E through the DALL-E API, allowing you to integrate this cutting-edge technology into your own Python applications. We will unleash your creativity as you discover the fascinating possibilities of generating AI art with DALL-E.

Presentations play a crucial role in conveying information effectively, and in this chapter, we'll show you how to automate the development of PowerPoint presentations using a Python framework and DALL-E image generation. You'll gain hands-on experience in leveraging the power of programming to streamline the creation process.

We will explore the integration of DALL-E and ChatGPT, two powerful AI models, to build an end-to-end PowerPoint presentation generator. This project will enable you to combine the abilities of DALL-E in generating captivating AI art with ChatGPT's expertise in generating human-like text. By integrating these APIs, you'll create an application that takes user-specified text and generates PowerPoint slides with accompanying images and text.

In this chapter, you will learn how to do the following:

- Use the DALL-E API to generate AI art from textual descriptions
- Utilize a PowerPoint Python framework to automate the development of PowerPoint presentations

- Leverage the DALL-E API to create images and integrate them into your own applications
- Integrate the DALL-E and ChatGPT APIs to build PowerPoint presentations
- Create presentation bullet points using the ChatGPT API

By the end of this chapter, you will boost your AI app development skills by integrating the DALL-E and ChatGPT APIs to build an end-to-end PowerPoint presentation generator. By combining the image generation capabilities of DALL-E with the text generation expertise of ChatGPT, you will learn how to automate the development of PowerPoint presentations that include both captivating AI-generated images and human-like text.

Technical Requirements

To make the most of this chapter, you'll need to have certain essential tools in place. We will provide detailed explanations and instructions for installations that were not covered in the previous chapter. Here's what you'll need:

- Python 3.7 or a later version installed on your computer
- An OpenAI API key, which you can obtain from your OpenAI account
- A code editor, such as PyCharm (recommended), to write and edit your code
- The Tkinter framework installed in your Python virtual environment
- PowerPoint software installed on your device

The code examples from this chapter can be found on GitHub at `https://github.com/PacktPublishing/Building-AI-Applications-with-ChatGPT-APIs/tree/main/Chapter09%20PowerPoint%20Generator`

In the next section, we will explore the DALL-E AI art generation AI model and cover the basics of the DALL-E API.

Using DALL-E and the DALL-E API

DALL-E is a remarkable AI model, that can generate stunning images from textual descriptions. In this section, you will gain an understanding of the concept behind DALL-E and its groundbreaking approach to image synthesis. You'll learn about the unique capabilities of DALL-E in translating text prompts into vibrant and imaginative visual representations. Additionally, we'll explore the practical application of DALL-E through the DALL-E API, empowering you to seamlessly integrate this powerful technology into your own applications and unlock a myriad of creative possibilities.

DALL-E is an advanced artificial intelligence model developed by OpenAI. It was introduced to the world in January 2021. DALL-E is a neural network-based model that combines elements of the ChatGPT language models with a generative adversarial network **GAN** architecture. The name DALL-E is a playful combination of the artist Salvador Dalí and the character WALL-E from the animated film. This unique model was designed to generate highly realistic and novel images based on textual descriptions, showcasing the incredible potential of AI in the field of visual creativity. By training on a massive dataset of images and textual prompts, DALL-E can create intricate and imaginative visual outputs, providing a glimpse into the groundbreaking advancements in AI-driven image synthesis.

Using DALL-E from the web provides an interactive and user-friendly approach to generating AI art. You can harness the capabilities of DALL-E through the web interface by following these steps:

1. Open your web browser and navigate to the DALL-E website at `https://labs.openai.com`. You can use your OpenAI credentials to access DALL-E.

2. On the DALL-E web page, you'll find a text input box where you can enter a textual description of the image you want to generate (see *Figure 9.1*). Be as specific or creative as you like in your description. For example, you can enter *a yellow banana wearing sunglasses on a beach*.

3. Once you've entered your text prompt, click the **Generate** button to trigger the image generation process. The DALL-E model will interpret your description and generate a corresponding image based on its understanding of the text.

4. After a moment, the generated image will be displayed on the web page. Take a moment to examine the output and observe how DALL-E has interpreted your text prompt. If necessary, you can iterate and refine your description to achieve the desired image.

5. Feel free to experiment with different text prompts, explore various concepts, and observe how DALL-E transforms your ideas into visual representations. This interactive process allows you to explore AI-generated art and encourages creative exploration.

Figure 9.1: DALL-E web interface

You can integrate DALL-E directly into your own application by using the DALL-E API. It provides a convenient interface to interact with DALL-E, enabling users to generate images based on custom textual prompts programmatically.

To use the DALL-E API, you can use the same API key from your OpenAI account. Once you have your API key, you can make requests to the API endpoint, specifying the text prompt for which you want to generate an image. You can create a single Python file and generate your first DALL-E image within a few lines of code. The API will process the request and return the generated image as a response, as shown in the following code example:

```
response = openai.Image.create(
    prompt="A cat sitting on a cloud",
    n=1,
    size="1024x1024"
)
image_url = response['data'][0]['url']
```

The provided code demonstrates how to use the `openai.Image.create()` function to generate an image using the DALL-E API and retrieve the URL of the generated image.

The `prompt` parameter serves as the textual description or instruction for the desired image. This prompt provides guidance to the DALL-E model on what the generated image should depict. The `size` parameter determines the dimensions of the generated image, indicating a square image with a resolution of 1024 pixels by 1024 pixels.

After making the API request, the response is stored in the `response` variable. The code then retrieves the URL of the generated image from the API response. The URL is obtained by accessing the appropriate keys in the response dictionary. By assigning `response` to `image_url`, the URL of the generated image is stored for further use in any application.

This is how you can use both the DALL-E user-friendly web interface to generate AI art and the DALL-E API to integrate that AI art into your own applications. In the next section, we will do that by launching our PowerPoint Presentation Generator app.

Building PowerPoint Apps with the PPTX Python Framework

In this section, we will guide you through the process of setting up your very own PowerPoint Presentation Generator app using the `pptx` Python library and the ChatGPT API. We'll explore how to leverage the power of the `pptx` library to automate the creation of PowerPoint presentations, allowing you to dynamically generate slides with customized content. Furthermore, we'll demonstrate how to integrate this PowerPoint generation functionality into a Tkinter application, enabling you to build a user-friendly interface for your slide generator.

For this project, we will use the PyCharm IDE, which is our preferred IDE when working with Python. Launch PyCharm and click on **Create New Project** or go to **File | New Project**. Choose the location where you want to create your project and name it **PowerPoint Generator**. Keep the default settings and click on the **Create** button.

Once your project is open, you can find the **Terminal** tab at the bottom of the PyCharm interface. It is in the tool window area, alongside other tabs such as **Project**, **Version Control**, and **Run**. Once the terminal tab is open, you can start using it just like a regular command-line interface to install the necessary libraries for our project:

```
$pip install python-pptx
$pip install openai
$pip install requests
```

Here is how we are going to use those libraries:

- python-pptx: The python-pptx package is used for working with PowerPoint files (.pptx) and provides functionalities to create, modify, and automate the development of PowerPoint presentations programmatically
- openai: The openai package provides access to the OpenAI API, which allows you to interact with AI models such as DALL-E and ChatGPT, enabling you to utilize their capabilities in your Python applications
- requests: The requests package is used for making HTTP requests and is used to communicate with the DALL-E API and retrieve the generated image URL after sending a request

We can continue developing our project structure by creating two files, app.py and config.py:

app.py

```
import collections.abc
import config
assert collections
import tkinter as tk
from pptx import Presentation
from pptx.util import Inches, Pt
import openai
from io import BytesIO
import requests

# API Token
openai.api_key = config.API_KEY
```

config.py

```
API_KEY = "YOUR_API_KEY"
```

Here, the `app.py` file is the core of the application and serves as the main entry point. It imports various libraries and modules to enable connection to the ChatGPT, DALL-E, and PowerPoint frameworks. Here's a breakdown of the imports and their purposes:

- `collections.abc` is imported to ensure compatibility with collections from the Python Standard Library
- `config` is imported to access the `API_KEY` variable, which holds the API key required for authentication with the OpenAI API
- `tkinter` is imported to utilize the Tkinter library for building the user interface of the application
- `pptx` and `pptx.util` are imported to work with PowerPoint files, allowing the application to create and modify PowerPoint presentations programmatically
- `openai` is imported to interact with the OpenAI API and access its services, such as language models and image generation
- `io` and `requests` are imported to handle input/output operations and make HTTP requests respectively

On the other hand, the `config.py` file serves as a configuration file for the project. It contains the API key, represented by the `API_KEY` variable, which is required for authentication with the OpenAI API. By separating the API key into a configuration file, it becomes easier to manage and update the key without modifying the main application code directly. This modular approach allows for better organization and flexibility in handling sensitive information.

Next, inside our `app.py` file, we will focus on building the Tkinter application window, which will serve as the **graphical user interface** (GUI) for our PowerPoint presentation generator:

```
app = tk.Tk()
app.title("Crate PPT Slides")
app.geometry("800x600")

# Create text field
text_field = tk.Text(app)
text_field.pack(fill="both", expand=True)
text_field.configure(wrap="word", font=("Arial", 12))
text_field.focus_set()

# Create the button to create slides
create_button = tk.Button(app, text="Create Slides", command=get_slides)
```

```
create_button.pack()

app.mainloop()
```

Here, we create the Tkinter application frame that will allow users to generate PowerPoint slides based on the input text.

Firstly, the code initializes a Tkinter application window using the `tk.Tk()` function. The `app` variable is assigned as the application instance. We set a title for the application window, which will be displayed in the window's title bar. Then we set the initial size of the application window to `800` pixels in width and `600` pixels in height.

We also create a text field using the `tk.Text()` function. This text field is used to accept user input for generating PowerPoint slides. The `pack()` method is called to place the text field within the application window. The `configure()` method is used to customize the text field's appearance. In this case, `wrap="word"` is set to wrap the text at word boundaries.

Lastly, we create a button using the `tk.Button()` function. The button is labeled `Create Slides` using the `text` parameter, and the `command` parameter is set to `get_slides`. This means that when the button is clicked, the `get_slides` function will be called.

Next, we will proceed to build the `get_slides()` function, which will be responsible for creating the PowerPoint presentation and slides. It is important to note that the `get_slides()` function should be defined above the lines that create the Tkinter application window and the associated widgets. This ensures that the function is defined and available for use when the application interacts with the user:

```
def get_slides():
    text = text_field.get("1.0", "end-1c")
    paragraphs = text.split("\n\n")
    prs = Presentation()
    width = Pt(1920)
    height = Pt(1080)
    prs.slide_width = width
    prs.slide_height = height
    for paragraph in paragraphs:
        slide_generator(paragraph, prs)

    prs.save("my_presentation.pptx")
app = tk.Tk()
app.title("Crate PPT Slides")
app.geometry("800x600")

# Create text field
text_field = tk.Text(app)
text_field.pack(fill="both", expand=True)
```

```
    text_field.configure(wrap="word", font=("Arial", 12))
    text_field.focus_set()

    # Create the button to create slides
    create_button = tk.Button(app, text="Create Slides",
        command=get_slides)
    create_button.pack()

    app.mainloop()
```

Here, the `text_field.get()` method is used to retrieve the contents of the text field. The `1.0` parameter indicates that the retrieval should start from the first character of the text field, and `end-1c` indicates that the retrieval should end at the last character excluding the newline character. This allows us to obtain the entire text entered by the user.

Next, the text string is split into paragraphs. The `\n\n` delimiter is used to identify the paragraphs, assuming that each paragraph is separated by two consecutive newline characters. This split operation will create a list of paragraphs stored in the `paragraphs` variable.

A new PowerPoint presentation object is created using `prs = Presentation()`. This initializes an empty presentation that will store the generated slides. Then we set the dimensions of the slides to `1920` points in width and the height is set to `1080` points.

A loop is then initiated to iterate over each paragraph in the `paragraphs` list. For each paragraph, the `slide_generator()` function is called, passing the paragraph and the presentation object as parameters. This function, which will be implemented separately, is responsible for creating individual slides based on the content of each paragraph.

Once the loop finishes, the generated presentation object is saved as a PowerPoint file. The resulting PowerPoint file will be named `my_presentation.pptx` and will contain the slides created from the user's input.

To test your application at this early stage, you can click the **Run** button in your PyCharm IDE. Once the app is running, you will see a Tkinter window titled **Create PPT Slides**, as shown in *Figure 9.2*, with a text field and a **Create Slides** button. The text field allows you to enter the content for your PowerPoint slides, and the button triggers the `get_slides()` function, which generates the slides based on the input text.

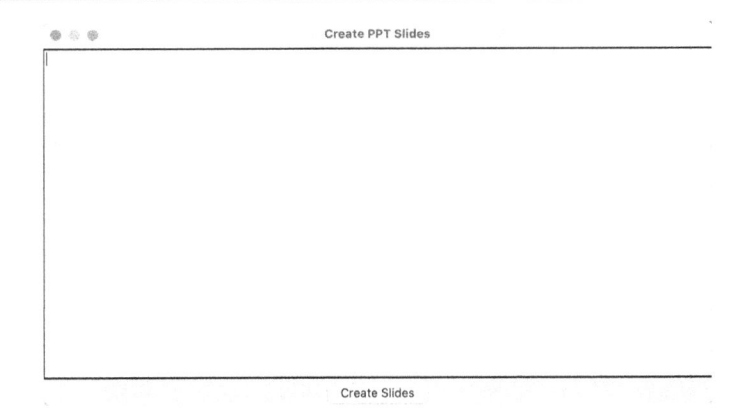

Figure 9.2: PowerPoint Presentation Generator GUI

However, at this point, if you try to generate the AI slides, you will encounter an error. This is because the `slide_generator()` function, which is responsible for creating the AI art and text for our slides, has not been defined yet.

In the upcoming section, we'll jump into building the `slide_generator()` function, where the text provided by the user will be transformed into AI art using the DALL-E API. This function will access the capabilities of the DALL-E API to generate images based on the text input, allowing for the creation of stunning slides with AI-generated artwork.

Generating Art with the DALL-E API

In this section, we will explore the exciting integration of the ChatGPT API and the DALL-E API. We will demonstrate how these two powerful artificial intelligence tools can be combined to create unique and visually stunning artwork. By leveraging the ChatGPT API, we will generate a DALL-E prompt based on user-provided paragraphs from our application. We will then utilize the DALL-E API to transform that prompt into a captivating image.

To begin, we can start building the `slide_generator()` function, which will play a crucial role in generating the PowerPoint slides based on the user's input. It is important to note that this function should be created right after the API key definition in the app.py file and above the `get_slides()` function. Placing it in this position ensures that it is defined and available for use when we invoke it within the `get_slides()` function. This approach allows for the structured organization of the code and ensures the smooth execution of the slide generation process:

```
def slide_generator(text, prs):
    prompt = f"Summarize the following text to a DALL-E image 
              generation " \
             f"prompt: \n {text}"
```

```python
        model_engine = "gpt-4"
        dlp = openai.ChatCompletion.create(
            model=model_engine,
            messages=[
                {"role": "user", "content": "I will ask you a question"},
                {"role": "assistant", "content": "Ok"},
                {"role": "user", "content": f"{prompt}"}
            ],
            max_tokens=250,
            n=1,
            stop=None,
            temperature=0.8
        )
        dalle_prompt = dlp["choices"][0]["message"]["content"]

        dalle_prompt = dlp.choices[0].text
        response = openai.Image.create(
            prompt=dalle_prompt + " Style: digital art",
            n=1,
            size="1024x1024"
        )
    image_url = response['data'][0]['url']
```

This is how we can define the `slide_generator()` function, responsible for generating a DALL-E image generation prompt based on the user-provided text and integrating it with the ChatGPT API. This function takes two parameters: `text`, which represents the user's input, and `prs`, which refers to the PowerPoint presentation object.

The `prompt` variable is defined by concatenating a static introductory text with the user-provided `text`. This prompt will be used to instruct the ChatGPT model to summarize the given text into a DALL-E image generation prompt.

The `create()` method is then called to make a request to the ChatGPT API for text completion. The JSON response from the ChatGPT API is stored in the `dlp` variable, which contains the completion result. The actual text from the ChatGPT completion result is extracted and assigned to the `dalle_prompt` variable. This `dalle_prompt` variable will serve as the input prompt for the DALL-E image generation API.

Now we can begin using the DALL-E API to generate an image based on the DALL-E prompt created in the `slide_generator` function. We call the `openai.Image.create()` method to make a request to the DALL-E API for image generation using the following parameters:

- `prompt`: The prompt for the image generation, which is constructed by appending `dalle_prompt` (generated by the ChatGPT API) with the desired style for the image, specified as `Style: digital art`. This prompts DALL-E to generate an image with a digital art style based on the text input. You can change this style according to your preferences.
- `n`: Specifies the number of images to generate. In this case, we request only one image.
- `size`: Sets the desired size of the generated image. Here, it is specified as `1024x1024` pixels, which is the highest-quality style.

The response from the DALL-E API is stored in the `response` variable. It contains information about the generated image, including its URL. The URL of the generated image is extracted from the response and assigned to the `image_url` variable. This URL can be used to retrieve and display the generated image in our PowerPoint slides.

In this section, we've built the `slide_generator()` function to generate a DALL-E prompt using the ChatGPT API based on user input, and then utilized the DALL-E API to generate an image with a desired style. This integration allows us to create visually stunning artwork and enhance the quality and impact of our PowerPoint slides.

In the next section, we will cover the creation of slide headers and bullet points in our PowerPoint presentation. We will demonstrate how to incorporate AI-generated images and text into slides.

Finalizing and Testing the AI Presentation Generator

In this final section, you will learn the process of creating slide content for our PowerPoint presentations using AI-generated images and text. We will explore how to seamlessly integrate AI-generated elements, including images from DALL-E and text from ChatGPT, into our slides. By following the steps outlined here, you will be able to pass AI-generated content to your PowerPoint slides, adding a touch of uniqueness and sophistication to your presentations.

You will learn how to retrieve an AI-generated image URL and apply it as a slide background or insert it into a specific slide element. Additionally, you will incorporate AI-generated text as bullet points in a slide. By combining the power of AI image generation with ChatGPT's text completion capabilities, users will be able to enrich their slides with visually appealing images and relevant text.

To begin, we will demonstrate how to create slide headers and bullet points using AI-generated images and text. To generate that content, you can include the following code snippet in your `slide_generator()` function:

```
prompt = f"Create a bullet point text for a Powerpoint" \
        f"slide from the following text: \n {text}"
ppt = openai.ChatCompletion.create(
    model=model_engine,
    messages=[
        {"role": "user", "content": "I will ask you a question"},
```

```
            {"role": "assistant", "content": "Ok"},
            {"role": "user", "content": f"{prompt}"}
        ],
        max_tokens=1024,
        n=1,
        stop=None,
        temperature=0.8
    )
    ppt_text = ppt["choices"][0]["message"]["content"]

    prompt = f"Create a title for a Powerpoint" \
            f"slide from the following text: \n {text}"
    ppt = openai.ChatCompletion.create(
        model=model_engine,
        messages=[
            {"role": "user", "content": "I will ask you a question"},
            {"role": "assistant", "content": "Ok"},
            {"role": "user", "content": f"{prompt}"}
        ],
        max_tokens=1024,
        n=1,
        stop=None,
        temperature=0.8
    )
    ppt_header = ppt["choices"][0]["message"]["content"]
```

In the first part of the code, a `prompt` string is constructed using a single paragraph entered by the user in the app. This prompt asks the AI model to generate a bullet-point text for a PowerPoint slide. The prompt is then passed to the ChatGPT `create()` method. The result of the completion is stored in the `ppt` variable, and the generated bullet point text is extracted from `ppt.choices[0].text` and assigned to the `ppt_text` variable.

Similarly, in the second part of the code, another `prompt` string is constructed to ask the AI model to generate a title for a PowerPoint slide based on the same user-provided text. The text result of the completion is extracted from `ppt.choices[0].text` and assigned to the `ppt_header` variable.

This generated bullet-point text and title will be used next to create the actual PowerPoint slides. You can include the following code, adding a new slide to the PowerPoint presentation and populating it with an image, bullet point text, and a title:

```
# Add a new slide to the presentation
slide = prs.slides.add_slide(prs.slide_layouts[1])

response = requests.get(image_url)
```

```
img_bytes = BytesIO(response.content)
slide.shapes.add_picture(img_bytes, Inches(1), Inches(1))

# Add text box
txBox = slide.shapes.add_textbox(Inches(3), Inches(1),
                                  Inches(4), Inches(1.5))
tf = txBox.text_frame
tf.text = ppt_text

title_shape = slide.shapes.title
title_shape.text = ppt_header
```

First, a new slide is added to the presentation using the `add_slide()` method. The method takes the desired slide layout as an argument, which in this case, represents the layout for a content slide.

Next, an HTTP request is made to retrieve the image from the image URL. The response is obtained, and its content is read into a `BytesIO` object named `img_bytes`. This allows the image data to be accessed and processed. To add the image to the slide, the `add_picture()` method is used. It takes the `img_bytes` object, along with the desired positioning parameters, as arguments. In this case, the image is positioned 1 inch from the left and 1 inch from the top of the slide.

A textbox is then added to the slide using the `slide.shapes.add_textbox()` method. The method takes the positioning parameters for the textbox as arguments. The text frame of the textbox is accessed using the `txBox.text_frame` attribute, and the `ppt_text` variable, which contains the generated bullet-point text, is assigned to `tf.text`. This sets the content of the textbox to the AI-generated text.

Finally, the title shape of the slide is accessed. The `ppt_header` variable, which contains the generated title text, is assigned to `title_shape.text`. This sets the title of the slide to the AI-generated title.

In that way, our presentation will be populated with the desired content, including images, bullet-point text, and titles.

Your PowerPoint Presentation Generator app is now complete and ready to be tested. To avoid any unexpected errors, you can verify that your lines of code are correct using the complete `app.py` file from Git: https://github.com/PacktPublishing/Building-AI-Applications-with-ChatGPT-APIs/blob/main/Chapter09%20PowerPoint%20Generator/app.py.

To run the app, simply execute the code or run the `app.py` file. This will launch the Tkinter application window, which serves as the user interface for your slide generator.

Once the app is running, you will see an application window with a text field where you can enter the content for your slides. Simply type or paste the desired text into the text field. For this example, we used an article about jellyfish (see *Figure 9.3*).

Jellyfish, also known as medusas or sea jellies, are fascinating creatures that inhabit the world's oceans. They belong to the phylum Cnidaria and are characterized by their gelatinous bodies and tentacles.

Jellyfish come in a wide variety of shapes, sizes, and colors, ranging from small and transparent to large and vibrant. They have a unique life cycle, starting as a polyp attached to the ocean floor before transforming into a free-swimming medusa.

One of the most intriguing aspects of jellyfish is their ability to sting. They possess specialized cells called cnidocytes, which contain nematocysts that deliver venomous toxins. These stinging cells allow jellyfish to capture prey and defend themselves from potential predators. While most jellyfish stings are harmless to humans, some species can cause painful or even dangerous reactions. It is advisable to exercise caution when swimming in waters known to have jellyfish populations.

Jellyfish play important roles in marine ecosystems. They are opportunistic feeders, consuming small planktonic organisms, fish eggs, and even other jellyfish. As predators, they help maintain a balance in the marine food web. Additionally, jellyfish have a unique ability to adapt to changing environmental conditions.

You can either use the text provided, or you can experiment with a text depending on your preferences.

> **Important Note**
> Ensure that you include a double line break between each paragraph to properly indicate the separation between paragraphs, allowing your application to accurately identify and distinguish them.

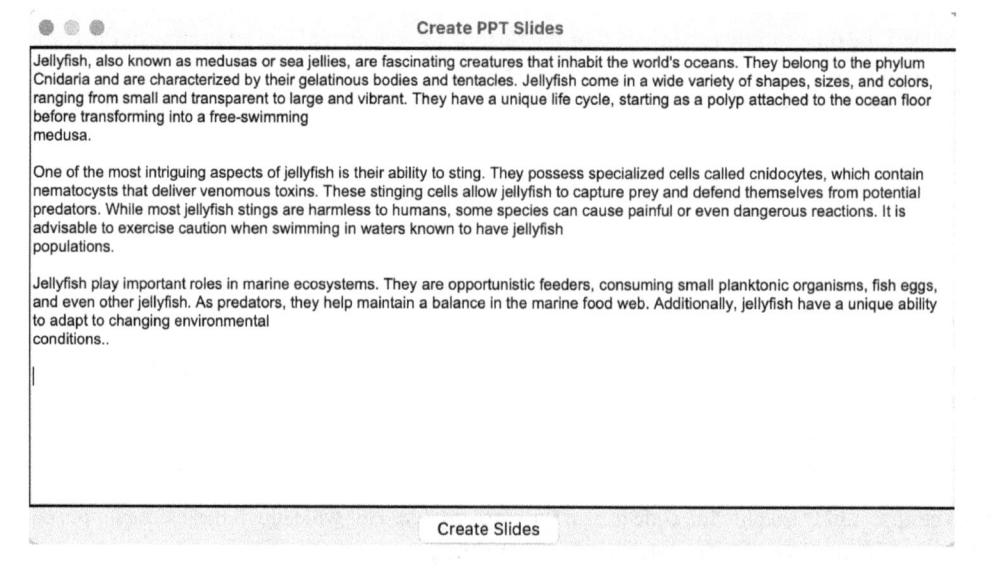

Figure 9.3: Populating the PowerPoint Presentation Generator with Text Input

Now you can click on the **Create Slides** button to generate the PowerPoint slides based on the entered text. Within a matter of seconds, your presentation will be swiftly generated and saved in the primary directory of your project.

Finalizing and Testing the AI Presentation Generator   181

> **Important Note**
> OpenAI has a rate limit that specifies the allowed number of tokens that can be used per minute. If you use the application extensively, it is possible that you will reach the free-trial rate limit, which is currently 40,000 tokens per minute.

Upon opening the presentation, you will be greeted with three slides, with each slide dedicated to a paragraph of the input text. These slides will showcase captivating AI art images created by DALL-E, accompanied by concise bullet points and a distinctive title for each slide (see *Figure 9.4*).

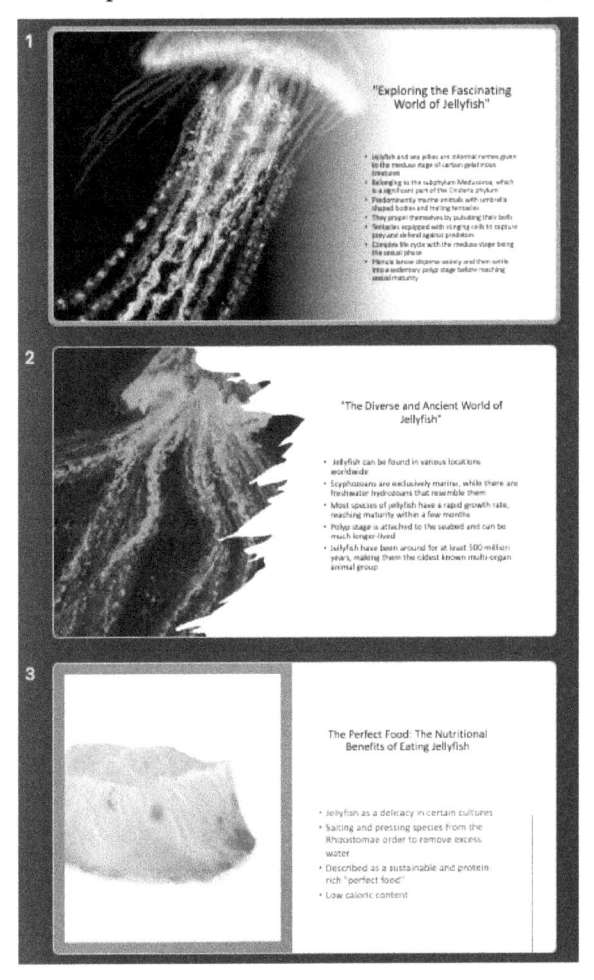

Figure 9.4: Slides Generated by the PowerPoint Presentation Generator App

To enhance the visual arrangement of elements on the slide, you have the flexibility to utilize the built-in **Designer** option within PowerPoint, conveniently located in the top-right corner.

That was the complete process of completing and testing the DALL-E AI presentation generator. You learned how to generate slide headers, bullet points, and AI-generated images. We covered the construction of AI prompts and retrieving the generated content. The section also outlined how to populate a PowerPoint presentation with generated content, including images, bullet points, and titles.

Summary

This chapter explored the capabilities of DALL-E, an advanced AI model, to generate realistic, novel images based on textual descriptions. You learned how to integrate DALL-E into your own applications using the DALL-E API. Additionally, we guided you in developing a PowerPoint Presentation Generator app using the `pptx` Python library and the ChatGPT API. We built the GUI using Tkinter, allowing users to generate slides with the `get_slides()` function, which retrieved user input and created a PowerPoint presentation.

We built the `slide_generator()` function, which played a key role in transforming the user input into AI-generated slides. The chapter also provided instructions for seamlessly incorporating AI-generated images and text, such as bullet points and slide headers, into the PowerPoint slides. We tested our AI Presentation Generator app, enabling you to run and evaluate your enhanced PowerPoint presentations.

In *Chapter 10*, titled *Speech Recognition and Text-to-Speech with the Whisper API*, you will learn how to utilize the Whisper API for audio transcription. We will focus on a practical project that involves transcribing various file types into text to create subtitles using human-level robustness and accuracy in English speech recognition.

10
Speech Recognition and Text-to-Speech with the Whisper API

Welcome to *Chapter 10* of our journey into the world of cutting-edge AI technologies. In this chapter, we embark on an exploration of the remarkable **Whisper API**. Harnessing the power of advanced speech recognition and translation, the Whisper API opens exciting possibilities for transforming audio into text. Imagine having the ability to transcribe conversations, interviews, podcasts, or any spoken content effortlessly. Whether you aim to extract valuable insights from multilingual audio files or create accessible content for a global audience, the Whisper API has you covered.

In this chapter, we will do a deep dive into the core functionalities of the Whisper API by developing a language transcription project using Python. We'll get acquainted with its essential endpoints, namely transcriptions and translations, which form the backbone of its speech-to-text capabilities. With its state-of-the-art open source model, Whisper equips developers with powerful tools to seamlessly transcribe audio files in multiple languages and even translate them into English. The Whisper API handles an extensive range of languages, ensuring compatibility with diverse speech requirements. It can be utilized in smart speakers, hands-free devices, and other voice-enabled technologies, enhancing user experiences by providing accurate and responsive speech synthesis capabilities.

In a world where global communication is more important than ever, the translations endpoint of the Whisper API plays a vital role. This endpoint not only transcribes audio files but also translates them into English, bridging the gap between languages and facilitating seamless understanding.

In this chapter, you will learn how to do the following:

- Code a speech-to-text conversion using the Whisper API
- Transcribe audio files from multiple languages
- Translate audio files into English
- Handle longer audio inputs and audio splitting using PyDub
- Explore the limitations and benchmarks of the Whisper model

By the end of this chapter, you will have gained a comprehensive understanding of the Whisper API and its remarkable capabilities, including speech-to-text conversion and language translation. You will also learn how to leverage the API to transcribe audio files accurately, translate them into English, handle longer inputs, and unlock the potential of spoken language in your applications.

Technical Requirements

To successfully undertake this project of developing a desktop application for language translation, you must meet the following technical prerequisites:

- Ensure that your machine has Python 3.7 or a newer version installed
- Have a code editor such as PyCharm (recommended) set up
- Create a Python virtual environment
- Obtain an OpenAI API key
- Install PyDub in your project

The code snippets showcased in this chapter are available on the GitHub platform. You can access them by following this link: https://github.com/PacktPublishing/Building-AI-Applications-with-ChatGPT-APIs/tree/main/Chapter10%20Whisper

Implementing Text Translation and Transcription with the Whisper API

In this section, we will explore the capabilities of the Whisper API to transcribe and translate audio files seamlessly using Python. With the advancements in speech recognition and translation technology, we now can effortlessly convert spoken language into text and bridge language barriers effectively. By following the step-by-step instructions provided, you will be equipped with the knowledge and skills necessary to integrate the Whisper API into your Python projects and unlock the potential of audio-based data.

Throughout this section, we will explore the different aspects of transcribing and translating audio files. Starting with the setup and installation requirements, we will ensure that you have the necessary tools, including Python, a code editor, a Python virtual environment, and an OpenAI API key.

To proceed with transcribing and translating audio files using the Whisper API in Python, it is recommended to create a new PyCharm project. PyCharm is a popular **integrated development environment** (**IDE**) that provides a convenient and efficient environment for Python development. Creating a new project in PyCharm will help organize your code and dependencies effectively.

To create a new PyCharm project, follow these steps:

1. Open PyCharm and select **Create New Project** from the welcome screen or go to **File | New Project** from the menu bar.
2. In the **New Project** dialog, keep the default location for where your project will be created.
3. Specify the project name as `WhisperAPI` and click **Create** to create the project.

Once the project is created, you will be presented with the PyCharm editor window, where you can start writing your Python code. You can create Python scripts, import libraries, and organize your project structure within the PyCharm project view.

Now that you have set up your PyCharm project, the next step is to install the necessary libraries, namely OpenAI and PyDub. To do that in PyCharm, open the terminal by going to **View | Tool Windows | Terminal**. From the terminal, type the following commands:

```
$pip install openai
$pip install pydub
$brew install ffmpeg
```

By executing these commands, PyCharm will automatically download and install the OpenAI and PyDub libraries, ensuring that they are readily available for your project.

Installing these libraries is crucial as OpenAI provides the necessary functionality to interact with the Whisper API, and PyDub allows for efficient handling of audio files, including splitting and exporting them.

Now, it's time to create a new file called `config.py` in your PyCharm project. This file will store your API key securely, allowing your code to access the Whisper API.

To create the `config.py` file and add your API key, follow these steps:

1. In PyCharm's project view, right-click on the root folder of your project.
2. Select **New** from the context menu and then choose **Python File**.
3. Name the file `config.py` and press *Enter*.

Now, you have created the `config.py` file. Open the file in the PyCharm editor and add the following line of code:

```
API_KEY = "YOUR_API_KEY"
```

To keep your audio files organized and easily accessible throughout this chapter, it is recommended to create a folder called `audio_files` within your PyCharm project. This folder will serve as a centralized location to store all the audio files that will be used in the various examples and demonstrations covered in the chapter.

To create the `audio_files` folder, follow these steps:

1. In PyCharm's project view, right-click on the root folder of your project.
2. Select **New** from the context menu and then choose **Directory**.
3. Name the directory as `audio_files` and press *Enter*.

Now that you have set up the necessary configurations and folder structure, it's time to create a new Python file called `transcribe.py`. This file will serve as the starting point for testing the transcription capabilities of the Whisper API. Open the file in the PyCharm editor, and this will be the space where you'll write the code to interact with the Whisper API and transcribe audio files.

Before writing any code, you can place an English speech audio file of your choice in our `audio_files` folder. For this example, I will use an audio file called `apple.mp3`. The file consists of a few sentences about Apple computers, and you can download it from our Git repository: https://github.com/PacktPublishing/Building-AI-Applications-with-ChatGPT-APIs/blob/main/Chapter10%20Whisper/audio_files/apple.mp3.

> **Important Note**
> When using the Whisper API for audio processing and transcription tasks, it is crucial to ensure that the audio files provided as input are in one of the supported file formats. The Whisper API currently accepts the following file types: `mp3`, `mp4`, `mpeg`, `mpga`, `m4a`, `wav`, and `webm`.

Once your audio file is in place, you can transcribe it by adding the following code to the `transcribe.py`:

```
import openai

import config

# API Token
openai.api_key = config.API_KEY

file= open("audio_files/apple.mp3", "rb")
result = openai.Audio.transcribe("whisper-1", file)

print(result)
```

Here, the `openai` library provides access to the OpenAI API, which allows developers to interact with various language models and AI capabilities. The API key is assigned to the `openai.api_key` variable, using the value stored in the API key.

Then, we open a file named `apple.mp3` located at the local file path `audio_files/apple.mp3` in read-binary mode, `rb`. This suggests that the code intends to read an audio file.

After that, the `openai.Audio.transcribe()` function is called with two arguments: `whisper-1` and the opened audio file. This function is part of the OpenAI library and is used to transcribe the audio file. The `whisper-1` parameter is the specific transcription model within the OpenAI system.

Finally, we see the result of the transcription in the console:

```
{
  "text": "Macbook laptops are known for their modern design and
  high-quality build, offering seamless experience. They are favored
  by many professionals and creators for their powerful performance and
  integration with Apple's ecosystem."
}
```

The result of the transcription, printed in the console, is a JSON object containing a single key-value pair. The key is `text`, and the corresponding value is the transcribed text.

This suggests that the transcription process has successfully converted the audio file into text, capturing the content related to the features and reputation of MacBook laptops.

If your audio file is in a language other than English, Whisper will handle that scenario too, by automatically transcribing and then translating the file in the background. Now, we will guide you on how to translate the transcribed text, using the Whisper API. For this example, we will use a German speech file called `german.mp3`. You can also use an mp3 file recorded in any language.

To utilize the Whisper API for translating audio files, you can create a new Python file called `translate.py` and add the following code:

```python
import openai
import config

# API Token
openai.api_key = config.API_KEY

whisper_file= open("audio_files/german.mp3", "rb")
result = openai.Audio.translate("whisper-1", whisper_file)

print(result)
```

Once the API key and the path to the audio file have been correctly set, the code calls the `openai.Audio.translate()` function, providing the model name or `whisper-1` configuration and the opened audio file, `whisper_file`. This function performs the translation using the Whisper API.

The translated result will be stored in the `result` variable, and it can be printed using `print(result)` to display the translated text in the console:

```
{
  "text": "The Germans are known for not liking to do small talk.
```

```
Today I'm going to try here in Berlin to see if I can do a little
small talk with the people here. Let's go!"
}
```

As you can see, the text was successfully transcribed and translated from German to English using the Whisper API in combination with less than 10 lines of Python code.

In this section, you learned about the capabilities of the Whisper API for transcribing and translating audio files seamlessly using Python. The step-by-step instructions guided you through the setup process to transcribe and translate audio files, along with the supported file formats. The section showcased successful transcription and translation examples, demonstrating the effectiveness of the Whisper API in converting audio to text and bridging language barriers with minimal code.

In the next section, you will learn how to integrate Tkinter and the Whisper API to develop a user-friendly language transcription application that can convert spoken language into text in real time.

Building a Voice Transcriber Application

In this section, we will explore the development of a language transcription application by integrating Tkinter, a popular Python GUI toolkit, with the powerful Whisper API. This integration will allow us to create a user-friendly interface that enables the real-time transcription of spoken language. By following the step-by-step instructions and harnessing the capabilities of Tkinter and the Whisper API, you will be empowered to develop your own GUI application, opening a myriad of possibilities in speech recognition and language processing.

Whether you aspire to create a tool for transcribing interviews, generating subtitles for videos, or simply exploring the potential of speech-to-text technology, this section will equip you with the knowledge and skills to bring your ideas to life. So, let's dive in and embark on this exciting journey of building a language transcription app with Tkinter and the Whisper API.

To continue with the language transcription application project, you can create a new Python file called `app.py` within the same project. This file will serve as the main code base for developing the application.

By creating the `app.py` file, you will have a dedicated space to write the necessary code to integrate Tkinter and the Whisper API, enabling real-time transcription functionality in your application.

In our pursuit of simplicity, our application will adopt a minimalist design featuring a text field and a button. The text field will serve as the dedicated space for displaying the transcribed text, while the button will provide the functionality to effortlessly browse through our file system and locate the desired audio file for transcription.

To convert our language translation code into an actual application, we will need to create the `transcribe_audio()` function and use it from the Tkinter graphics:

```
import tkinter as tk
```

```python
from tkinter import filedialog
import openai
import config

# API Token
openai.api_key = config.API_KEY

def transcribe_audio():
    file_path = filedialog.askopenfilename(
        filetypes=[("Audio Files", "*.mp3")])
    if file_path:
        try:
            audio_file = open(file_path, "rb")
            transcript = openai.Audio.transcribe(
                "whisper-1", audio_file)
            text_window.insert(tk.END, transcript.text)
        except Exception as e:
            text_window.insert(tk.END, f"Error: {str(e)}")
    else:
        text_window.insert(tk.END, "No file selected.")

# Create the Tkinter window
window = tk.Tk()
window.title("Whisper Transcription App")

# Create a text window
text_window = tk.Text(window, height=50, width=200)
text_window.pack()

# Create a button to select the audio file
button = tk.Button(window, text="Select Audio File",
command=transcribe_audio)
button.pack()

# Start the Tkinter event loop
window.mainloop()
```

Upon execution of the function, it first opens a file dialog window using the `filedialog.askopenfilename()` method, allowing the user to select an audio file for transcription. The file dialog is restricted to display only files with the `.mp3` extension, as specified by the `filetypes` parameter.

If a valid file path is obtained from the file dialog, indicating that the user has selected an audio file, the code proceeds to transcribe the audio. Inside a `try` block, the selected audio file is opened in read-binary mode using `open()` and assigned to the `audio_file` variable.

Using the `openai.Audio.transcribe()` function, the audio file is passed along with the specific transcription model to initiate the transcription process by the Whisper API. The resulting transcription is stored in the `transcript` variable.

Finally, the transcribed text is inserted into a text window. The `tk.END` argument ensures that the text is inserted at the end of the text window. In case of any exceptions or errors during the process, an error message is displayed in the text window.

If no file path is obtained from the file dialog, indicating that the user did not select an audio file, a `No file selected` message is inserted into the text window.

Under the `transcribe_audio()` function, we have created the Tkinter app that is using it. First, a Tkinter window is created using `tk.Tk()`. The window's title is set as `Whisper Transcription App`.

Next, a text window is created using `tk.Text()`, where the Whisper API transcription will be displayed. A button is also added to the Tkinter window using `tk.Button()`. The button's label is set as `Select Audio File`, and the command parameter is set to `transcribe_audio`. This means that when the button is clicked, the `transcribe_audio()` function (previously defined) will be executed.

To run the Whisper transcription app from PyCharm, follow these steps:

1. In PyCharm, locate the `app.py` file within your project structure.
2. Right-click on the `app.py` file and select **Run app**.
3. Once the application is running, a Tkinter window titled **Whisper Transcription App** will appear.
4. The window will display a text area where the transcribed text will be shown.
5. Click on the **Select Audio File** button. A file dialog window will open, allowing you to navigate your file system.
6. Find and select an MP3 audio file that you want to transcribe.

After selecting the file, the code will attempt to transcribe the audio. If successful, the transcribed text will be displayed in the text area within the Tkinter window (see *Figure 10.1*). If there are any errors during the transcription process, an error message will be displayed instead.

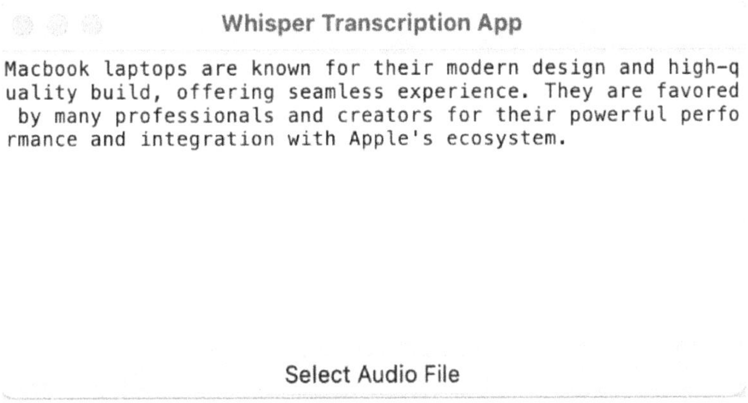

[Figure: Screenshot of "Whisper Transcription App" window showing transcribed text "Macbook laptops are known for their modern design and high-quality build, offering seamless experience. They are favored by many professionals and creators for their powerful performance and integration with Apple's ecosystem." and a "Select Audio File" button]

Figure 10.1 – Whisper transcription application

> **Important Note**
> Please be aware that in certain screen resolutions, the **Select Audio File** button might be concealed. To ensure its visibility, maximize the application window.

By running the app and selecting an MP3 file, you will be able to witness the Whisper API's transcription capabilities in action. The app will leverage the selected audio file, initiate the transcription process using the Whisper API, and display the transcribed text within the Tkinter window. This allows you to convert spoken language into written text, opening possibilities for various applications and use cases.

In this section, we embarked on the development of a language transcription application, integrating Tkinter and the Whisper API. With a minimalist design featuring a text field and a button, the application allows users to select an MP3 audio file for transcription. Upon selecting the file, the code initiates the transcription process using the Whisper API and displays the transcribed text in the Tkinter window.

In the next section, you will learn how to integrate PyDub with the Whisper API to overcome the file size limitation and efficiently split large audio files for seamless transcription.

Using PyDub for Longer Audio Inputs

In this section, we will explore the integration of **PyDub**, a powerful audio processing library for Python, with the Whisper API to overcome the file size limitation of 25 MB imposed by the API. With PyDub, we can efficiently split large audio files into smaller segments, enabling the seamless transcription of lengthy recordings. By following the instructions and leveraging PyDub's capabilities, you will be able to harness the full potential of the Whisper API for transcribing audio files of any size.

Leveraging the power of PyDub to enhance your language transcription workflow is a straightforward process. By utilizing this library, you can effortlessly divide lengthy audio files into smaller segments.

For instance, if you have a 10-minute audio file, you can easily split it into two separate files, each with a duration of 5 minutes. These smaller files can then be submitted to the Whisper API for transcription, ensuring that your files are not rejected due to their size limitations. With PyDub, you can seamlessly overcome the file size constraint and streamline your transcription process.

In this exercise, we utilized an approximately eleven-minute-long audio file from an iPhone review. Now, you can create a new Python file within your project, specifically named `longer_files.py`. This file will serve as a dedicated space to implement the necessary code for handling larger audio files in your language transcription workflow:

```python
import openai
from pydub import AudioSegment
import config

# API Token
openai.api_key = config.API_KEY

song = AudioSegment.from_mp3("audio_files/phone.mp3")

# 5 minute portion
five_minutes = 5 * 60 * 1000
first_min_5 = song[:five_minutes]
first_min_5.export("audio_files/phone_first_5.mp3", format="mp3")

last_min_5 = song[five_minutes:]
last_min_5.export("audio_files/phone_last_5.mp3", format="mp3")

file= open("audio_files/phone_first_5.mp3", "rb")
result = openai.Audio.transcribe("whisper-1", file)
print(result)

file= open("audio_files/phone_last_5.mp3", "rb")
result = openai.Audio.transcribe("whisper-1", file)
print(result)
```

The provided code demonstrates the usage of the `PyDub` library and the Whisper API for processing larger audio files in the language transcription workflow.

You can download the `phone.mp3` file from here: `https://github.com/PacktPublishing/Building-AI-Applications-with-ChatGPT-APIs/blob/main/Chapter10%20Whisper/audio_files/phone.mp3`.

First, the necessary imports are made, including the `openai` and `AudioSegment` modules from the respective libraries. We load an audio file named `phone.mp3` using PyDub's `AudioSegment.from_mp3()` method and assign it to the `song` variable.

To break down the audio file into smaller segments, the code defines a five-minute portion using the `five_minutes` variable, which represents the desired duration in milliseconds. The `song` variable is then sliced using the specified duration to obtain the first five minutes of the audio, which is stored in the `first_min_5` variable. This segment is then exported as a separate MP3 file named `phone_first_5.mp3` using the `export()` method.

Similarly, the code obtains the remaining portion of the audio file, starting from the five-minute mark until the end, using the slicing operation, and assigns it to the `last_min_5` variable. This segment is also exported as a separate MP3 file named `phone_last_5.mp3`.

The code proceeds to open the `phone_first_5.mp3` file with the `openai.Audio.transcribe()` method invoked. The resulting transcription is stored in the `result` variable, which is then printed to the console. Following the same procedure, the code repeats the transcription process for the `phone_last_5.mp3` file, opening it, transcribing it, and printing the result.

You can see the unique transcriptions for each file printed in the console as follows:

```
{
  "text": "It's finally here, the most wanted phone this year, the
most amazing camera set ever built in a phone. Here is the iPhone 13
Pro……..reduced the front camera module, now the phone will look good."
}
{
  "text": "weights about 10 grams more which is something you can't
really feel. However, while everybody is trying to reduce the weight
on the phones, Apple actually increased it……... Now thanks for
watching and I will see you in the next one."
}
```

By breaking down the larger audio file into smaller segments using PyDub, the code enables the processing of these segments within the size limits of the Whisper API. This approach allows for the efficient handling of larger audio files while leveraging the transcription capabilities provided by the Whisper API.

This is how we can integrate PyDub with the Whisper API to overcome the file size limitation, enabling the seamless transcription of longer audio files.

Summary

In this chapter, we explored the Whisper API, a powerful tool for converting audio into text through advanced speech recognition and translation. The chapter provided step-by-step instructions on developing a language transcription project using Python, covering essential aspects such as handling audio files, installing necessary libraries, and setting up the API key. You learned how to transcribe and translate audio files using the Whisper API. The chapter also introduced a voice transcription application, integrating Tkinter and the Whisper API for real-time transcription.

You also learned how to use PyDub, a powerful audio processing library for Python, with the Whisper API to overcome the file size limitation of 25 MB. By leveraging PyDub's capabilities, we can efficiently split large audio files into smaller segments, enabling the seamless transcription of lengthy recordings. You saw how to use PyDub and the Whisper API to process larger audio files in the language transcription workflow. By breaking down the audio file into smaller segments and transcribing each segment individually, we can handle larger audio files while benefiting from the transcription capabilities of the Whisper API.

In *Chapter 11*, you will learn about the different API models available in the ChatGPT API and gain insights into how to choose the most suitable model for your specific projects. We will explore the various parameters that can be utilized in API requests to achieve more efficient, improved prompt completions. You will also understand the limitations associated with different AI models.

Part 4: Advanced Concepts for Powering ChatGPT Apps

In this final part, you will explore AI models and their unique attributes, allowing you to develop a comprehensive grasp of their cost, quality, and prompt-length considerations. Armed with this knowledge, you will be empowered to select whichever optimal model aligns with the requirements of your specific applications. Moreover, you will unlock the ability to construct your very own ChatGPT model and enhance its functionalities through fine-tuning, thereby tailoring it to perfectly cater to your individual needs.

This part has the following chapters:

- *Chapter 11, Choosing the Right ChatGPT API Model*
- *Chapter 12, Fine-Tuning ChatGPT to Create Unique API Models*

11
Choosing the Right ChatGPT API Model

In the ever-evolving landscape of AI, it is crucial for developers to stay up to date with the latest advancements to maximize the potential of their projects. In this chapter, we talk about ChatGPT API models, explore the possibilities offered by GPT-3 and GPT-4, and even look beyond the horizon to future models. By gaining a comprehensive understanding of these models, you will be equipped with the knowledge to choose the most suitable one for your specific application. We will dive into the intricacies of each model, highlighting their strengths and unique characteristics to enable you to make informed decisions that align with your project requirements.

One of the key aspects of utilizing the ChatGPT API effectively is understanding how to optimize chat completions. We will guide you through the process of creating chat completion contexts and provide valuable insights into modifying API parameters to enhance the quality of responses. Through practical examples and explanations, you will gain the skillset necessary to harness the power of chat completions and leverage them to your advantage.

Furthermore, it is important to be aware of the limitations that exist within different AI models. We will outline the boundaries and constraints associated with each model, equipping you with the knowledge to navigate these limitations effectively. By understanding the boundaries of the models, you can set realistic expectations, make informed decisions, and explore workarounds to overcome any challenges you may encounter.

In this chapter, you will learn about the following:

- The differences between the GPT-3, GPT-3.5, and GPT-4 models
- How to choose the appropriate model for your application
- How to create chat completion contexts for optimal results
- How to modify API parameters to improve response quality

- The rate limits associated with the ChatGPT API
- The limitations and boundaries of different AI models

By the end of this chapter, you will have gained knowledge on choosing the right ChatGPT API model for your project, understanding the process of creating chat completion contexts, optimizing API parameters, and navigating the limitations of different AI models to create transformative AI applications.

Technical Requirements

To fully benefit from this chapter, it is essential to have the necessary tools in place for working with Python code and the ChatGPT APIs. This chapter will provide step-by-step guidance on installing the required software and completing the necessary registrations.

You will need to have the following:

- Python 3.7 or a later version installed on your computer
- An OpenAI API key, which you can obtain by signing up for an OpenAI account
- A code editor, such as PyCharm (recommended), to write and execute Python code

The code examples referenced in this chapter can be accessed on GitHub at `https://github.com/PacktPublishing/Building-AI-Applications-with-ChatGPT-APIs/tree/main/Chapter11%20Models`

In the next section, you will learn about various AI models, including GPT-3 and GPT-4, and develop the ability to select the most suitable model for your specific application.

ChatGPT API Models – GPT-3, GPT-4, and Beyond

In this section, we will understand and appreciate the intricacies of GPT-3 and GPT-4 and peer beyond the horizon at future models. By delving into these AI models, you will gain invaluable insights and knowledge that will empower you to choose the most appropriate model for your unique application.

Throughout this section, we will unravel the distinct features and capabilities of each model, equipping you with the necessary understanding to make informed decisions.

In *Table 11.1*, you can see an overview of all the ChatGPT language models currently supported by OpenAI, with valuable information about each model, including their unique features. Take a moment to explore the table and familiarize yourself with the diverse range of ChatGPT models at your disposal.

MODEL	AVERAGE COST	Info	Prompt Length
gpt-4	$0.03/1K tokens	Most advanced chat-oriented model surpasses the capabilities of GPT-3.5.	8,192 tokens
gpt-4-32k	$0.06/1K tokens	Has the same qualities as gpt-4 but 400% more context	32,768 tokens
gpt-4-32k-0314	$0.06/1K tokens	Presents a snapshot of the gpt-4 model with the newest information curently for 14rd March 2023	32,768 tokens
gpt-3.5-turbo	$0.002 / 1K tokens	More advanced chat-oriented model surpasses the capabilities of GPT-3	4,096 tokens
gpt-3.5-turbo-0301	$0.002 / 1K tokens	Presents a snapshot of the gpt-3.5-turbo model with the newest information curently for 1st March 2023	4,096 tokens
text-davinci-003	$0.02 / 1K tokens	This model surpasses the curie, babbage, and ada models in terms of quality.	4,096 tokens
text-davinci-002	$0.02 / 1K tokens	Reinforcement learning capabilities included.	4,096 tokens
davinci	$0.02 / 1K tokens	As capable as the rest of the davinci models, but data limited to Oct 2019	2,049 tokens
text-curie-001	$0.002 / 1K tokens	Not as capable as davinci, but faster and lower cost than Davinci.	2,049 tokens
text-babbage-001	$0.005 / 1K tokens	Faster, and very low cost but less capable that davinci and curie.	2,049 tokens

Table 11.1 – ChatGPT model information

The table provides an overview of various ChatGPT language models supported by OpenAI as of June 2023. The gpt-4 model stands out as the most advanced, surpassing the capabilities of GPT-3.5, while the gpt-4-32k version offers **400%** more context. The **gpt-3.5-turbo** model exceeds GPT-3's capabilities, and the **text-davinci-003** model outperforms the curie, babbage, and ada models in terms of quality. Different models have varying costs and prompt lengths, allowing developers to choose the most suitable option for their specific language tasks.

The `davinci` model, though as capable as others, has data limitations, while the `text-curie-001` and `text-babbage-001` models offer faster response times and lower costs but may have reduced capabilities. These models provide a range of choices, enabling developers to consider factors such as cost, quality, and prompt length when selecting the most appropriate ChatGPT model for their applications.

While it may seem logical to opt for the most advanced and capable model for your application, it is important to consider that sometimes a cheaper, less capable model can adequately fulfill your task requirements. In certain scenarios, a less sophisticated model may provide sufficient performance while being more cost-effective. By carefully evaluating the specific needs of your application, you can make an informed decision and potentially save resources by selecting a model that strikes the right balance between capability and cost. Remember, it is not always about using the most powerful tool, but rather about using the right tool for the job at hand.

As you can see, OpenAI provides an extensive selection of models, making it challenging to decide on the most suitable one. To simplify this process, a Python script can be utilized for easy comparison, empowering you to identify the optimal model that aligns with your specific task:

```
import openai
import config

# Define the prompt and test questions
prompt = "Estimate the square root of 121 and type a 'orange' after every digit of the square root"

# Set up OpenAI API credentials
openai.api_key = config.API_KEY

# Define the model names and their corresponding IDs
model_ids = {
    "DAVINCI 003": {"model": "text-davinci-003", "cost": 0.02},
    "DAVINCI 002": {"model": "text-davinci-002", "cost": 0.02},
    "DAVINCI": {"model": "davinci", "cost": 0.02},
    "GPT3.5 TURBO": {"model": "gpt-3.5-turbo", "cost": 0.002},
    "GPT3.5 TURBO 0301": {"model": "gpt-3.5-turbo-0301",
        "cost": 0.002},
    "GPT4": {"model": "gpt-4", "cost": 0.0045},
    "CURIE": {"model": "text-curie-001", "cost": 0.002},
    "BABBAGE": {"model": "text-babbage-001", "cost": 0.005},
}

# Make API calls to the models and store the responses
responses = {}
for model_name, model_id in model_ids.items():
    if "GPT" not in model_name:
        response = openai.Completion.create(
            engine=model_id["model"],
            prompt=prompt,
            max_tokens=50,
            n=1,
            stop=None,
            temperature=0.7
```

```
            )
            responses[model_name] = [response.choices[0].text.strip(),
                                     response['usage']['total_tokens']
                                     /1000*model_id["cost"]]

        else:
            response = openai.ChatCompletion.create(
                model=model_id["model"],
                messages=[
                    {"role": "user", "content": "I will ask you a
                        question"},
                    {"role": "assistant", "content": "Ok"},
                    {"role": "user", "content": f"{prompt}"}
                ]
            )
            responses[model_name] = [response["choices"][0]["message"]
                                     ["content"],
                                     response['usage']['total_tokens']
                                     /1000*model_id["cost"]]


for model, response in responses.items():
    print(f"{model}: {response[0]}")
    print(f"{model} COST: {response[1]}")
```

The purpose of the script is to compare the responses from different OpenAI models using the OpenAI Python library and make API calls to generate responses.

By effortlessly adjusting the `prompt` variable, you can ask the same question of multiple ChatGPT models and evaluate their respective responses and the associated cost. This approach empowers you to select the most suitable model that aligns with the requirements of your specific tasks.

Firstly, ChatGPT API credentials are set up by assigning the API key to the `openai.api_key` variable. This allows the code to authenticate and access the ChatGPT API. Additionally, a dictionary named `model_ids` is defined to store the names and corresponding model IDs of various ChatGPT models, along with their associated costs. The model names serve as keys, and each key is paired with a dictionary containing the model ID and cost as of June 2023. This enables easy referencing and the selection of specific models based on their names in the subsequent code execution. You can add and remove models to be tested from this dictionary.

Then we make the API calls to the ChatGPT models specified in the `model_ids` dictionary and store their respective responses.

The code initializes an empty dictionary called `responses` to store the responses from the models. It then iterates over each item in the `model_ids` dictionary, where `model_name` represents the name of the model and `model_id` contains the corresponding model information.

Inside the loop, an `if-else` condition is used to differentiate between the GPT-3.5 models and others. For models other than GPT-3.5, the `openai.Completion.create()` method is called to generate a completion based on the provided prompt. The response from the API call is stored in the `response` variable, and the total tokens used for the completion are printed. The generated text and the calculated `cost` based on token usage and the model's cost are then added to the responses dictionary using `model_name` as the key.

For the GPT-3.5 and GPT-4 models, the `openai.ChatCompletion.create()` method is employed instead. It simulates a conversation by providing a list of messages as input. The user, assistant, and prompt messages are included in the `messages` parameter, and the response from the API call is stored in the `response` variable.

Finally, we print the responses and associated costs for each model, enabling us to compare them and make an informed decision on selecting the most suitable option.

The answer to the question we asked in the preceding script, `"Estimate the square root of 121 and type a 'orange' after every digit of the square root"`, is `"1orange1orange"`. You can see the answers of the different models here:

```
DAVINCI 003: 11 orange 1 orange
DAVINCI 003 COST: 0.00052
DAVINCI 002: 10.5 orange
DAVINCI 002 COST: 0.00052
DAVINCI: .
Estimate the square root of 121 and type a 'orange' after every digit
of the square root.
Show transcribed image text Estimate the square root of 121 and type a
'orange' after every digit of the square
DAVINCI COST: 0.0014000000000000002
```
**GPT3.5 TURBO: The square root of 121 is 11. After every digit
in the square root, I'll type 'orange'. So the final answer is:
1orange1orange.
GPT3.5 TURBO COST: 0.000164
GPT3.5 TURBO 0301: The square root of 121 is 11, so the estimated
square root with 'orange' added after every digit is:
1orange1orange
GPT3.5 TURBO 0301 COST: 0.00015
GPT4: The square root of 121 is 11. So, typing 'orange' after every
digit of the square root, it becomes:
1orange1orange.
GPT4 COST: 0.00033749999999999996
CURIE: The square root of 121 is approximately 9.29.
CURIE COST: 6.6e-05
BABBAGE: 2, 3, 5, 7, 11, 13, 17, 19, 23, 29, 31, 37, 41, 43, 47, 53,
59, 61, 67, 71, 73, 79, 83, 89
BABBAGE COST: 0.00035000000000000005**

As this was a rather complex question, ChatGPT-3.5 Turbo and GPT-4 were the only models that answered correctly in this case. Since GPT 3.5 Turbo is two times cheaper compared to GPT-4, we can confidently use GPT-3.5 for this specific task.

That was a complete overview of the ChatGPT API models and the importance of selecting the right model for specific language tasks. We developed a Python script that compares the responses and costs of different models, allowing users to make informed decisions.

Having gained insights into ChatGPT API models and their comparisons, we will now proceed to the next section, where we will delve into the exploration of ChatGPT API parameters.

Using Chat Completion Parameters

In this section, we will be using ChatGPT API parameters and will look at their profound impact on the quality of responses generated by models. By understanding and harnessing the power of these parameters, you will gain the ability to optimize your interactions with the ChatGPT API, unlocking its true potential. Some of the key parameters to control the API response are as follows:

- `model`: Specifies the specific ChatGPT model to use for generating responses.
- `messages`: Provides the conversation history as a list of message objects, including user and assistant messages.
- `temperature`: Controls the randomness of the generated responses. Higher values (for example, `0.8`) make the responses more random, while lower values (for example, `0.2`) make them more focused and deterministic.
- `max_tokens`: Sets the maximum number of tokens in the generated response. Limiting this parameter can control the length of the response.
- `stop`: Allows you to specify a custom string or list of strings to indicate when the model should stop generating the response.
- `n`: Determines the number of alternative completions to generate. Setting a higher value increases the diversity of responses.

The `temperature` parameter is a key aspect of the OpenAI ChatGPT API that allows you to control the randomness and creativity of the generated responses. It influences the diversity and randomness of the text produced by the model.

When making a request to the API, you can specify the `temperature` parameter, which takes a value between 0 and 1. A lower temperature value (for example, `0.2`) produces more focused and deterministic responses with less diversity, while a higher temperature value (for example, `1`) leads to more random and diverse responses that can be more inaccurate and irrelevant.

The following example demonstrates the effect of modifying the `temperature` parameter:

```
import openai
```

```python
import config

# Set up OpenAI API credentials
openai.api_key = config.API_KEY

# Define a function to generate a response from ChatGPT
def generate_response(prompt, temperature):
    response = openai.Completion.create(
        engine='text-davinci-003',
        prompt=prompt,
        temperature=temperature,
        max_tokens=50,
        n=1,
        stop=None,
    )
    return response.choices[0].text.strip()

# Prompt for the conversation
prompt = "Suggest 4 names for a cat."

# Generate a response with low temperature (more focused and deterministic)
for i in range(3):
    low_temp_response = generate_response(prompt, 0)
    print(f"Response with low temperature (0) {i}:\n", low_temp_response)

for i in range(3):
    # Generate a response with default temperature (balanced and creative)
    default_temp_response = generate_response(prompt, 1)
    print(f"Response with default temperature (1) {i}:\n",
          default_temp_response)
```

In this example, we use the `generate_response` function to generate responses for a given prompt with two different temperature values: low (0) and high (1). We run the response generation at each temperature three times in a row, in order to compare the diversity of the responses.

By adjusting the `temperature` parameter, you can fine-tune the level of creativity and randomness in the responses generated by the ChatGPT API. You can experiment with different temperature values to achieve the desired output for your specific use case.

After the preceding code has been executed, we get the following output:

```
Response with low temperature (0) 0:
1. Fluffy
```

```
2. Simba
3. Tiger
4. Misty
Response with low temperature (0) 1:
 1. Fluffy
 2. Simba
 3. Tiger
 4. Misty
Response with low temperature (0) 2:
 1. Fluffy
 2. Simba
 3. Tiger
 4. Misty
Response with default temperature (1) 0:
 1. Max
 2. Sasha
 3. Tiger
 4. Shadow
Response with default temperature (1) 1:
 1. Mochi
 2. Milo
 3. Luna
 4. Misty
Response with default temperature (1) 2:
 1. Fluffy
 2. Simba
 3. Midnight
 4. Tigress
```

Let's look at the outputs:

- Response with low temperature (0): The response tends to be more focused and deterministic. It provides a specific and concise answer to the prompt. There is no variation between the three responses.

- Response with high temperature (1): The response is more random and diverse. It may introduce unexpected and imaginative elements into the generated text, but it might also veer off-topic or produce less coherent answers.

Increasing the n parameter in the ChatGPT API can also be beneficial in certain cases. When you increase the value of n, it determines the number of alternative completions generated by the model. This can be useful when you want to explore a wider range of possible responses or generate diverse variations of the same prompt.

You can try increasing the size of n following the example shown here:

```python
import openai
import config

# Set up OpenAI API credentials
openai.api_key = config.API_KEY

# Define a function to generate a response from ChatGPT
def generate_response(prompt, n):
    response = openai.Completion.create(
        engine='text-davinci-003',
        prompt=prompt,
        temperature=.8,
        max_tokens=50,
        n=n,
        stop=None,
    )
    return response

# Prompt for the conversation
prompt = "Suggest 4 names for a cat."


n_prompt = generate_response(prompt, 4)
print(n_prompt)
```

Here, we ask the ChatGPT API to create four alternative completions for our cat's name-generation prompt. The result is stored in the n_prompt variable and displayed in JSON format in the console:

```
{
  "choices": [
    {
      "finish_reason": "stop",
      "index": 0,
      "logprobs": null,
      "text": "\n\n1. Fluffy\n2. Simba\n3. Tigger\n4. Smokey"
    },
    {
      "finish_reason": "stop",
      "index": 1,
      "logprobs": null,
      "text": "\n\n1. Muffin\n2. Tigger\n3. Felix\n4. Gizmo"
    },
```

```
    {
      "finish_reason": "stop",
      "index": 2,
      "logprobs": null,
      "text": "\n\n1. Mittens \n2. Simba \n3. Merlin \n4. Daisy"
    },
    {
      "finish_reason": "stop",
      "index": 3,
      "logprobs": null,
      "text": "\n\n1. Sirius \n2. Loki \n3. Pumpkin \n4. Gizmo"
    }
  ],
  "created": 1685919169,
  "id": "cmpl-7NqsbkCoehG4LGT1Cj1Qus0j85pLg",
  "model": "text-davinci-003",
  "object": "text_completion",
  "usage": {
    "completion_tokens": 87,
    "prompt_tokens": 7,
    "total_tokens": 94
  }
}
```

As you can see, our choices list size has increased to four elements. This will provide four alternative names for a cat, showcasing the increased diversity of responses obtained by increasing the n parameter. By modifying the value of n in the generate_response function, you can experiment with different numbers to explore a broader range of suggestions or generate more creative and varied responses from the ChatGPT model.

By increasing n, you increase the diversity of the generated responses, allowing you to explore different perspectives, creative ideas, or alternative solutions to a given problem. However, it's important to note that increasing n also increases the API cost and response time, so it's a trade-off between diversity and efficiency. Therefore, if you're looking for a more varied set of responses or seeking creative inspiration, increasing the n parameter can be a valuable approach.

The messages parameter plays a vital role in the GPT-3.5 Turbo chat completion and allows for interactive and dynamic conversations with the model. This parameter enables you to simulate a conversation by providing a list of messages as input, where each message consists of a role (either "user" or "assistant") and the content of the message.

When utilizing the messages parameter, it is important to structure the conversation appropriately. The model uses the preceding messages to generate context-aware responses, considering the history of the conversation. This means that you can build upon previous messages to create engaging and interactive exchanges.

Here is an example code snippet demonstrating the usage of the `messages` parameter in GPT-3.5 Turbo chat completion:

```python
import openai
import config

# Set up OpenAI API credentials
openai.api_key = config.API_KEY

# Define a function for chat completion
def chat_with_model(messages):
    response = openai.ChatCompletion.create(
        model="gpt-3.5-turbo",
        messages=messages
    )
    return response.choices[0].message.content

# Define the conversation messages
messages = [
    {"role": "user", "content": "Hello, could you recommend a good
        book to read?"},
    {"role": "assistant", "content": "Of course! What genre are you
        interested in?"},
    {"role": "user", "content": "I enjoy fantasy novels."},
    {"role": "assistant", "content": "Great! I recommend 'The Name of
        the Wind' by Patrick Rothfuss."},
    {"role": "user", "content": "Thank you! Can you tell me a bit
        about the plot?"},
]

# Chat with the model
response = chat_with_model(messages)
print(response)
```

In the preceding code, we define the `chat_with_model` function, which takes the `messages` list as input. This function uses the `openai.ChatCompletion.create` method to send a request to the GPT-3.5 Turbo model. The model parameter specifies the model to be used, in this case, `gpt-3.5-turbo`. The `messages` parameter is set to the defined list of conversation messages.

We create a conversation by providing a series of messages from both the user and the assistant. Each message includes the role ("user" or "assistant") and the content of the message. The messages are structured in the order they occur in the conversation.

By utilizing the `messages` parameter, you can have dynamic and interactive conversations with the GPT-3.5 Turbo model, making it suitable for applications such as chatbots, virtual assistants, and more.

This section provided an overview of the parameters used in the ChatGPT API and their impact on response quality. It discussed the `temperature` parameter, and the `n` parameter, which determines the number of alternative completions to generate for increased response diversity. We also learned about the `messages` parameter and how it enables dynamic and interactive conversations with the model, allowing for context-aware responses based on the conversation history.

In the next section, you will learn about the rate limits imposed on the ChatGPT API. You will also come to understand the limitations and restrictions associated with different AI models when making requests to the API.

ChatGPT API Rate Limits

Rate limits play a crucial role in maintaining the stability and fairness of the ChatGPT API. They are restrictions placed on the number of requests and tokens that a user or client can access within a specific time frame. OpenAI implements rate limits for several reasons:

- **Protection against abuse and misuse**: Rate limits help safeguard the API from malicious actors who may attempt to overload the system by flooding it with excessive requests. By setting rate limits, OpenAI can mitigate such activities and maintain the quality of service for all users.

- **Ensuring fair access**: By throttling the number of requests a single user or organization can make, rate limits ensure that everyone has an equal opportunity to utilize the API. This prevents a few users from monopolizing the resources and causing slowdowns for others.

- **Managing server load**: With rate limits, OpenAI can effectively manage the overall load on its infrastructure. By controlling the rate of incoming requests, the servers can handle the traffic more efficiently, minimizing performance issues and ensuring a consistent experience for all users.

The rate limits can be measured as **Requests Per Minute** (**RPM**) and **Tokens Per Minute** (**TPM**). The default rate limits for the ChatGPT API vary depending on the model and account type. However, OpenAI offers the possibility of increasing the rate limits by submitting a rate limit increase request form.

Here are the default rate limits for the ChatGPT API as of June 2023.

Free trial users:

- Chat: 3 RPM, 150,000 TPM
- Codex: 3 RPM, 40,000 TPM
- Edit: 3 RPM, 40,000 TPM
- Image: 3 RPM, 150,000 TPM, 5 images per minute

Pay-as-you-go users:

- Chat: 3,500 RPM, 350,000 TPM
- Codex: 3,500 RPM, 90,000 TPM
- Edit: 20 RPM, 40,000 TPM
- Image: 20 RPM, 150,000 TPM, 50 images per minute

You will get a rate limit warning either when you reach the maximum number of tokens or by reaching the maximum requests per minute. For example, if the max requests per minute is 60, you can send 1 request per second. If you attempt to send requests more frequently, you will need to introduce a short sleep time to avoid hitting the rate limit.

When a rate limit error occurs, it means that you have exceeded the allowed number of requests within the specified time frame. The error message will indicate the specific rate limit that has been reached and provide information on the limit and your current usage.

To mitigate rate limit errors and optimize your API usage, there are several steps you can take:

- Retrying with exponential backoff: Implementing exponential backoff is a reliable strategy to handle rate limit errors. When a rate limit error occurs, you can automatically retry the request after a short delay. If the request fails again, you increase the delay exponentially before each subsequent retry. This approach allows for efficient retries without overwhelming the system.
- Modify the `max_tokens` parameter to align with the desired response length: The rate limit for your requests depends on the higher value between `max_tokens` and the estimated number of tokens calculated from the character count of your input. By setting the `max_tokens` variable close to your anticipated response size, you can reduce the token usage and respectively your cost.
- Batching requests: Occasionally, you may encounter a situation where you have reached the maximum RPM, but still have a considerable number of unused tokens remaining. In such instances, you have the option to enhance the efficiency of your requests by consolidating multiple tasks into a single request. To implement this approach, you can refer to the following example as a guideline:

```
import openai # for making OpenAI API requests

import config

# Set up OpenAI API credentials
openai.api_key = config.API_KEY

num_stories = 10
prompts = ["I was walking down the street and"] * num_stories
```

```
# Perform batched completions with 10 stories per request
response = openai.Completion.create(
            model="curie",
            prompt=prompts,
            max_tokens=20,
            )

# Match completions to prompts by index
stories = [""] * len(prompts)
for choice in response.choices:
    stories[choice.index] = prompts[choice.index] + choice.text

# Print the generated stories
for story in stories:
    print(story)
```

Here, we are using the ChatGPT API to generate stories based on a given prompt. Instead of performing the 10 requests to the ChatGPT API separately, we place all prompts into a list and send them at the same time. That way, multiple responses are generated with a single request.

Instead of making individual requests, you can send a list of prompts as input to the API. This allows you to process more tokens per minute, especially with smaller models.

Rate limits are important for maintaining the stability, fairness, and performance of the ChatGPT API, protecting against abuse, and ensuring fair access, while default rate limits vary based on account type, and techniques such as exponential backoff, optimizing `max_tokens`, and batching requests can help mitigate rate limit errors and optimize API usage.

Summary

In the section titled *ChatGPT API Models – GPT-3, GPT-4, and Beyond*, we explored the different ChatGPT API models. Then we provided you with a deeper understanding of these AI models and their features, enabling you to choose the most suitable model for your specific applications. The chapter emphasized the importance of considering factors such as cost, quality, and prompt length when selecting a model, as the most advanced and capable model may not always be the best choice. Additionally, we used Python to allow you to compare the responses and costs of different models, aiding in the decision-making process.

We also focused on the various parameters of the ChatGPT API and their impact on response quality. We highlighted key parameters such as `model`, `messages`, `temperature`, `max_tokens`, `stop`, and `n`, and explained how they can be manipulated to optimize interactions with the ChatGPT API. You learned about the importance of rate limits in maintaining the stability and fairness of the ChatGPT API. We explored how to implement appropriate strategies that can enhance the efficiency and cost-effectiveness of using the ChatGPT API.

In *Chapter 12, ChatGPT Fine-Tuning and Integrations*, we will dive into the process of fine-tuning ChatGPT API models. This chapter aims to equip you with the skills necessary to teach ChatGPT additional information tailored to a specific project or application. Through a series of case studies, you will gain insights into real-world applications of fine-tuning and be encouraged to think creatively. Additionally, we will emphasize the cost-saving potential of fine-tuning in the development of AI applications.

12
Fine-Tuning ChatGPT to Create Unique API Models

In this chapter, we will explore fine-tuning the ChatGPT API. This transformative process grants developers the power to mold the behavior of ChatGPT API responses to align with their distinct needs. We will immerse ourselves in the art of fine-tuning, exploring the intricate techniques and critical factors at play. By mastering the craft of building and deploying our very own fine-tuned model, we unlock the potential to enhance our AI applications in unprecedented ways.

ChatGPT fine-tuning is a process that involves training a pre-trained language model, such as `davinci`, on a specific dataset to improve its performance and adapt it to a particular task or domain. The fine-tuning process typically begins with a dataset that is carefully curated and labeled, and it involves training the model on this dataset using techniques such as transfer learning. The model's parameters are adjusted during fine-tuning to make it more accurate and contextually appropriate to generate responses in the target domain. By fine-tuning, the model can acquire domain-specific knowledge, language patterns, and nuances, enabling it to generate more relevant and coherent responses for specific applications or use cases.

We will demonstrate how to fine-tune ChatGPT to generate concise book summaries using JSON prompts and completions data.

In this chapter, we will cover the following topics:

- The API models that can be fine-tuned
- The cost involved in fine-tuning an AI model
- Using JSON to prepare the training data
- Creating a fine-tuned model with the OpenAI **command-line interface** (**CLI**)
- Listing all available fine-tuned models and their information
- Using fine-tuned models with the ChatGPT API completions

- Deleting a fine-tuned model

Technical Requirements

The technical requirements for this chapter are listed as follows:

- Python 3.7 or later installed on your machine
- An OpenAI API key
- The OpenAI Python library installed

In the forthcoming section, we shall commence our journey into ChatGPT fine-tuning by examining the array of available models, establishing our development environment, and acquainting ourselves with the book summary fine-tuned model that we are about to construct.

You can find all code examples from this chapter on GitHub at `https://github.com/PacktPublishing/Building-AI-Applications-with-ChatGPT-APIs/tree/main/Chapter12%20FineTuning`

Fine-Tuning ChatGPT

In this section, you will learn about the process of fine-tuning ChatGPT models. We will talk about the ChatGPT models available for fine-tuning and provide information on their training and usage costs. We will also cover the installation of the `openai` library and set up the API key as an environmental variable in the terminal session. This section will serve as an overview of fine-tuning, its benefits, and the necessary setup to train a fine-tuned model.

Fine-tuning enhances the capabilities of API models in several ways. Firstly, it yields higher-quality outcomes compared to designing prompts alone. By incorporating more training examples than can be accommodated in a prompt, fine-tuning enables models to grasp a wider range of patterns and nuances. Secondly, it reduces token usage by utilizing shorter prompts, resulting in more efficient processing. Additionally, fine-tuning facilitates lower-latency requests, enabling faster and more responsive interactions.

GPT-3 has undergone extensive pre-training on a vast corpus of text sourced from the internet. When given a prompt with limited examples, it often demonstrates the ability to understand the intended task and generate plausible completions – a concept referred to as **few-shot learning**. However, fine-tuning takes few-shot learning a step further by utilizing a larger set of examples, surpassing the prompt's capacity. This comprehensive training enables superior performance across a wide array of tasks.

If a model has undergone fine-tuning, we can use the resultant model without the need to pass any further training data. On *Table 12.1*, taken from the official OpenAI pricing page at `https://openai.com/pricing`, you can see all the ChatGPT models that are available for fine-tuning, each accompanied by detailed information about their training and usage costs per 1,000 tokens, as of June 2023.

MODEL	TRAINING	USAGE
Ada	$0.0004 / 1K tokens	$0.0016 / 1K tokens
Babbage	$0.0006 / 1K tokens	$0.0024 / 1K tokens
Curie	$0.0030 / 1K tokens	$0.0120 / 1K tokens
Davinci	$0.0300 / 1K tokens	$0.1200 / 1K tokens

Table 12.1: The Pricing for ChatGPT Model Fine-Tuning

During the fine-tuning process, it is necessary to provide the training data in the form of a JSON file, and the training token count specifically refers to those used within the prompt and completion fields contained within that file.

Each line of the JSON document should consist of a prompt and completion field that corresponds to our desired training data, as shown here:

```
{"prompt": "Book Summary: The Adventure Begins", "completion": "A
thrilling tale of courage and discovery."}
{"prompt": "Book Summary: Secrets Unveiled", "completion": "An
intriguing mystery that will keep you guessing until the end."}
```

This snippet is an example of how two of the training lines should be displayed in the JSON file. In the next sections, we will build the complete JSON file, using a considerably larger dataset and with the help of the **OpenAI CLI data preparations tool**.

Our objective is to develop a fine-tuned model that specializes in generating concise, one-sentence summaries for books provided by the user. To accomplish this, we will construct a new JSON training file that includes the book titles in the prompt field and their corresponding summaries in the completion field. This training process will equip our model with the necessary skills to effectively generate book summaries based on user-provided input, once it has completed its training phase.

Upon the completion of the training phase, OpenAI will provide us with a distinct and exclusive name for our fine-tuned model. This unique name can then be utilized within the ChatGPT completion prompt to effectively engage with the model.

Before jumping into the preparation of our dataset, we need to ensure that we have the openai library installed on our device. To do that, open a new terminal or Command Prompt and type the following:

```
$ pip install --upgrade openai
```

This line will ensure that the last version of the openai package has been installed on your device.

To fine-tune a model from your local terminal, you will need to also provide the ChatGPT API key as an environmental variable:

- Mac users:

  ```
  $ export OPENAI_API_KEY="<OPENAI_API_KEY>"
  ```

- Windows users:

  ```
  set OPENAI_API_KEY=<your_api_key>
  ```

In this line, the `export` command is used to create an environment variable named `OPENAI_API_KEY`. The `<OPENAI_API_KEY>` value is a placeholder that you should replace with the API key obtained from your OpenAI account. By setting this environment variable, we ensure that the API key is securely stored and can be accessed by the rest of the commands we execute in the terminal session.

This section provided an overview of fine-tuning ChatGPT models. It discussed how fine-tuning enhances few-shot learning and the necessity of providing training data in a JSON file. We discussed the fine-tuned model that we will build to generate concise book summaries based on user-provided input. We also covered the environment setup, which included the installation of the `openai` library and setting the API key as an environmental variable in our terminal session.

Fine-Tuned Model Dataset Preparation

To effectively fine-tune our model, we need to prepare the training data in a specific format. In this section, we will walk you through the process of data preparation using a JSON file and the OpenAI CLI data preparations tool.

When preparing data for a fine-tuned model such as OpenAI's, it's essential to follow a structured process to ensure optimal performance and accurate results. The first step is to gather the relevant data that will be used to train the model. This data can come from a variety of sources, such as books, articles, or even specialized datasets.

To begin, create a new folder called `Fine_Tune_Data` on your desktop, and inside the folder, create a new file called `train_data.json`. For our book summary fine-tuned model, we will use one-sentence summaries for 30 different books. Those summaries will be written inside the file we just created in a JSON format:

```
[
{"prompt": "Book Summary: The Adventure Begins", "completion": "A thrilling tale of courage and discovery."},
{"prompt": "Book Summary: Secrets Unveiled", "completion": "An intriguing mystery that will keep you guessing until the end."},
{"prompt": "Book Summary: Love and Betrayal", "completion": "A heart-wrenching story of love, trust, and deception."},
{"prompt": "Book Summary: The Quest for Freedom", "completion": "A captivating journey of self-discovery and liberation."},
{"prompt": "Book Summary: Beyond the Stars", "completion": "An epic science fiction adventure that pushes the boundaries of
```

imagination."},
{"prompt": "Book Summary: The Power Within", "completion": "A gripping exploration of inner strength and resilience."},
{"prompt": "Book Summary: Shadows of the Past", "completion": "A haunting tale of redemption and confronting the ghosts of the past."},
{"prompt": "Book Summary: A World Apart", "completion": "A mesmerizing exploration of parallel universes and the power of choices."},
{"prompt": "Book Summary: Into the Unknown", "completion": "A suspenseful journey into uncharted territories and the pursuit of truth."},
{"prompt": "Book Summary: The Lost Artifact", "completion": "A thrilling archaeological adventure that unravels ancient mysteries."},
{"prompt": "Book Summary: Broken Pieces", "completion": "A poignant story of healing, forgiveness, and the beauty of imperfection."},
{"prompt": "Book Summary: Echoes of Silence", "completion": "A tale of loss and resilience, where words hold the power to heal."},
{"prompt": "Book Summary: The Forgotten Realm", "completion": "An enchanting fantasy world brimming with magic and destiny."},
{"prompt": "Book Summary: Life's Unexpected Turns", "completion": "A captivating narrative of life's twists and the resilience to overcome."},
{"prompt": "Book Summary: From Ashes to Glory", "completion": "A triumphant story of rising from adversity and finding one's purpose."},
{"prompt": "Book Summary: The Last Stand", "completion": "A gripping account of courage, sacrifice, and the fight for justice."},
{"prompt": "Book Summary: In the Shadows of Time", "completion": "A mesmerizing blend of past and present, weaving a tale of love and destiny."},
{"prompt": "Book Summary: A Journey of Discovery", "completion": "An introspective expedition that uncovers the mysteries of the self."},
{"prompt": "Book Summary: Torn Between Worlds", "completion": "A captivating exploration of identity and the search for belonging."},
{"prompt": "Book Summary: The Art of Letting Go", "completion": "A transformative journey of releasing the past and embracing the future."},
{"prompt": "Book Summary: Whispers in the Wind", "completion": "A lyrical narrative that captures the ephemeral beauty of fleeting moments."},
{"prompt": "Book Summary: The Hidden Truths", "completion": "A riveting exposé of secrets, lies, and the quest for truth."},
{"prompt": "Book Summary: Beyond the Veil", "completion": "A spellbinding adventure that blurs the boundaries between reality and the supernatural."},
{"prompt": "Book Summary: Unbreakable Bonds", "completion": "A tale of friendship, loyalty, and the unyielding strength of human connections."},
{"prompt": "Book Summary: The Songbird's Melody", "completion": "A melodic tale of passion, dreams, and the pursuit of artistic expression."},

```
{"prompt": "Book Summary: Shattered Reflections", "completion": "A
psychological thriller that delves into the darkest corners of the
human mind."},
{"prompt": "Book Summary: A Patchwork of Memories", "completion": "A
nostalgic journey through fragments of the past, weaving a tapestry of
remembrance."},
{"prompt": "Book Summary: Embers of Hope", "completion": "A tale
of resilience and hope, where even the smallest spark can ignite
change."},
{"prompt": "Book Summary: Beneath the Surface", "completion": "A
suspenseful exploration of hidden truths lurking beneath seemingly
ordinary lives."},
{"prompt": "Book Summary: The Road Less Traveled", "completion":
"A transformative odyssey that challenges conventions and embraces
individuality."}
]
```

The given JSON file contains a collection of book summaries represented as prompt-completion pairs. Each entry consists of a `prompt` field that introduces the book with a summary title, followed by a `completion` field that provides a brief description of the book. The prompts highlight different genres, themes, and emotions associated with the books, while the completions capture the essence of each story. The summaries encompass a variety of genres, including adventure, mystery, romance, science fiction, and fantasy. This JSON file data will serve as a dataset to train a fine-tuned model to generate concise book summaries, based on user-provided input.

Once the JSON file has been created, we can now prepare the data using the default `prepare_data` function part of the `openai` library. This versatile tool can accept various file formats if they have a `prompt` and `completion` column or key. Whether you have a JSON, JSONL, CSV, TSV, or XLSX file, this tool can handle it. Once you provide the input file, the tool will guide you through any necessary adjustments and save the output in the JSONL format, which is specifically designed for fine-tuning purposes.

Unlike using base models where prompts can include detailed instructions or multiple examples, for fine-tuning, each prompt should conclude with a specific separator (such as `\n\n###\n\n`) to signal to the model when the prompt ends and the completion begins. Those separators can be added either by you or the ChatGPT data preparation tool.

To achieve superior performance through fine-tuning, it is advisable to include a substantial number of high-quality examples. Even though our project includes only 30 examples, for optimal results surpassing base models, you should aim to provide a few hundred or more high-quality examples, preferably vetted by human experts. Typically, as the number of examples doubles, performance shows a linear increase. Increasing the number of examples is usually the most effective and reliable approach to enhance performance.

To activate the data preparation tool for our project type, execute the following commands by using our `train_data.json`:

```
$ cd Fine_Tune_Data
$ openai tools fine_tunes.prepare_data -f train_data.json
```

After executing the command, the data preparation tool will meticulously examine the contents of our JSON file. Considering that our JSON data may not be flawlessly formatted and lacks appropriate separators, with each example beginning with the prefix Book Summary:, the data preparation tool will generate a helpful suggestion to rectify the training data, which will be displayed in the terminal output:

```
Analyzing...

- Your file contains 30 prompt-completion pairs. In general, we
recommend having at least a few hundred examples. We've found that
performance tends to linearly increase for every doubling of the
number of examples
- Your data does not contain a common separator at the end of your
prompts. Having a separator string appended to the end of the prompt
makes it clearer to the fine-tuned model where the completion should
begin. See https://platform.openai.com/docs/guides/fine-tuning/
preparing-your-dataset for more detail and examples. If you intend to
do open-ended generation, then you should leave the prompts empty
- All prompts start with prefix `Book Summary: `. Fine-tuning doesn't
require the instruction specifying the task, or a few-shot example
scenario. Most of the time you should only add the input data into the
prompt, and the desired output into the completion
- All completions end with suffix `.`
- The completion should start with a whitespace character (` `). This
tends to produce better results due to the tokenization we use. See
https://platform.openai.com/docs/guides/fine-tuning/preparing-your-
dataset for more details
```

Furthermore, as part of the data preparation process, the tool will inquire whether you would like to incorporate the suggested modifications into your data before proceeding with the creation of the JSONL output file. **JSONL** stands for the **JSON Lines** format, which is a text-based data interchange format where each line in the file represents a single JSON object. This format is commonly used to store and exchange structured data, making it easy to read, write, and process data in a streaming fashion. This interactive feature ensures that you can review and consider the proposed adjustments, enabling you to refine your dataset and generate a more refined JSONL file:

```
Based on the analysis we will perform the following actions:
- [Recommended] Add a suffix separator ` ->` to all prompts [Y/n]: Y
- [Recommended] Remove prefix `Book Summary: ` from all prompts [Y/n]:
Y
- [Recommended] Add a whitespace character to the beginning of the
completion [Y/n]: Y


Your data will be written to a new JSONL file. Proceed [Y/n]: Y
```

```
Wrote modified file to `train_data_prepared.jsonl`
Feel free to take a look!

Now use that file when fine-tuning:
> openai api fine_tunes.create -t "train_data_prepared.jsonl"
```

By offering this option, the tool empowers you to exercise greater control and make informed decisions regarding the preparation of your data to fine-tune the model.

Once the task has been completed, you will find a new file, `train_data_prepared.jsonl`, inside the `Fine_Tune_Data` directory. If you accepted all recommendations from the data preparation tool, your JSONL file should look as follows:

```
{"prompt":"The Adventure Begins ->","completion":" A thrilling tale of courage and discovery."}
{"prompt":"Secrets Unveiled ->","completion":" An intriguing mystery that will keep you guessing until the end."}
{"prompt":"Love and Betrayal ->","completion":" A heart-wrenching story of love, trust, and deception."}
{"prompt":"The Quest for Freedom ->","completion":" A captivating journey of self-discovery and liberation."}
{"prompt":"Beyond the Stars ->","completion":" An epic science fiction adventure that pushes the boundaries of imagination."}
.......
```

You can find the full JSOL file in our Git repository: https://github.com/PacktPublishing/Building-AI-Applications-with-ChatGPT-APIs/blob/main/Chapter12%20FineTuning/train_data_prepared.jsonl.

To prepare the dataset to fine-tune the model, the JSON file was modified by adding a separator at the end of each prompt, removing the prefix `Book Summary:` from the prompts, starting the completions with a whitespace character, and saving the data in the JSONL format. These modifications enhance the model's understanding and generate concise book summaries based on user input.

With our dataset prepared and optimized, we have laid the foundation to construct the fine-tuned model, a crucial step that will be explored in detail in the next section.

Building and Using the Fine-Tuned Model

In this section, we will explore the process of creating and utilizing a fine-tuned model using OpenAI's CLI. OpenAI offers newcomers the opportunity to avail of a $5 credit to access the ChatGPT API and its fine-tuning services.

Fine-tuning involves building a specialized model based on an existing base model, and in our example, we will use the most advanced ChatGPT model available for fine-tuning called **davinci**. We will improve the performance of that model for book summarization tasks.

We will learn how to start a fine-tuning job, which uploads and processes the training data, and then we'll monitor its progress until completion. Once the fine-tuning job is done, we will use the newly created fine-tuned model to generate text. We'll learn how to make requests to the fine-tuned model using the completions API, and we'll cover how to manage and delete fine-tuned models if needed.

We will begin by using our newly created JSONL file to create the fine-tuned model with the following command:

```
openai api fine_tunes.create -t train_data_prepared.jsonl  -m davinci
```

The preceding command is used to create a fine-tuning job for a text dataset. The command starts the process of fine-tuning a model by specifying the training data file and the base model to start from. In this case, we will use our training data file called `train_data_prepared.jsonl`. By executing this command, the training data will be uploaded and processed, and a fine-tuning job will be created using the specified base model:

```
Upload progress: 100%|██| 3.68k/3.68k [00:00<00:00, 2.95Mit/s]
Uploaded file from train_data_prepared.jsonl: file-QzFonh5QTZKu2IVc4lBKdwp1
Created fine-tune: ft-GrpW4DOXtWkXIgznJrSB9kOD
Streaming events until fine-tuning is complete...

(Ctrl-C will interrupt the stream, but not cancel the fine-tune)
[2023-06-26 18:01:23] Created fine-tune: ft-GrpW4DOXtWkXIgznJrSB9kOD
```

In the provided output, you can find the ID of your fine-tuned model, `ft-GrpW4DOXtWkXIgznJrSB9kOD`. It's important to note that the process of creating the model may vary in duration, taking anywhere from a few minutes to hours. If you accidentally interrupt the data stream by pressing *Ctrl + C*, rest assured that your job will not be canceled. The OpenAI servers will continue processing your fine-tuned model until it reaches completion. To ensure you stay informed about the progress of the fine-tuning job, OpenAI offers you the option to monitor its status using the provided model ID. This way, you can keep track of the creation process and be notified once your fine-tuned model is ready.

To find that information, you can type the following:

```
$ openai api fine_tunes.follow -i ft-GrpW4DOXtWkXIgznJrSB9kOD
```

To consistently monitor our fine-tuning job, we will utilize the `follow` function. It is important to note that your specific ID will be unique and distinct from the one demonstrated in the previous example. If you happen to misplace your ID, there's no need to worry, as you can effortlessly retrieve the details of all completed and pending fine-tuned models associated with your account by entering the following command:

```
$ openai api fine_tunes.list
```

You can also find the information about a specific model by referring to its ID:

```
$ openai api fine_tunes.get -i ft-GrpW4DOXtWkXIgznJrSB9kOD
```

As there is currently only one fine-tuning job in progress, the output from both prompts will yield identical results:

```
{
  "object": "fine-tune",
  "id": "ft-GrpW4DOXtWkXIgznJrSB9kOD",
  "hyperparams": {
    "n_epochs": 4,
    "batch_size": null,
    "prompt_loss_weight": 0.01,
    "learning_rate_multiplier": null
  },
  "organization_id": "org-yBpXCfCEnXErZ6PUZZE3VKZx",
  "model": "davinci",
  "training_files": [
    {
      "object": "file",
      "id": "file-QzFonh5QTZKu2IVc4lBKdwp1",
      "purpose": "fine-tune",
      "filename": "train_data_prepared.jsonl",
      "bytes": 3679,
      "created_at": 1687816883,
      "status": "processed",
      "status_details": null
    }
  ],
  "validation_files": [],
  "result_files": [],
  "created_at": 1687816883,
  "updated_at": 1687816883,
  "status": "pending",
  "fine_tuned_model": null,
  "events": [
    {
      "object": "fine-tune-event",
      "level": "info",
```

```
      "message": "Created fine-tune: ft-GrpW4DOXtWkXIgznJrSB9kOD",
      "created_at": 1687816883
    }
  ]
}
```

The provided output represents the details of a fine-tuning job. It includes information such as the object type, job ID, hyperparameters, organization ID, base model, training files, validation files, result files, timestamps of creation and update, current status, fine-tuned model, and a list of events. The `hyperparameters` section specifies the settings for the fine-tuning process. The `training_files` section contains details about the training data file used for the fine-tuning job. The most important parameter to consider is `status` of the fine-tuning job. It is currently `pending`, indicating that the fine-tuning process is still in progress.

By utilizing the provided commands, you can continually track and monitor the progress of your fine-tuned model until its creation is finalized. Throughout this period, you can regularly check the status field to remain informed about the current state of the job.

If you wish to cancel the job for any reason, you can initiate the cancellation process by inputting the following command:

```
$ openai api fine_tunes.cancel -i ft-GrpW4DOXtWkXIgznJrSB9kOD
```

Once the fine-tuning process is successfully completed, the status field returned from the `.get` or `.list` functions will be updated, and it will also reveal the name of the newly generated model:

```
      "status": "succeeded",
      "fine_tuned_model": "davinci:ft-personal-2023-06-26-06-55-07"
```

The `fine_tuned_model` field corresponds to the distinctive name assigned to the recently generated model. This name holds significant value, as it can be seamlessly incorporated into any ChatGPT API `completion` function by assigning it to the `model` parameter. By doing so, you can leverage the capabilities of the fine-tuned model and harness its enhanced text generation abilities.

After the successful creation of your fine-tuned model, you can conduct easy and quick tests directly from the terminal using the `curl` command. This allows you to seamlessly interact with your fine-tuned model and assess its performance without any complications:

```
$ curl https://api.openai.com/v1/completions \
  -H "Content-Type: application/json" \
  -H "Authorization: Bearer $OPENAI_API_KEY" \
  -d '{
    "prompt": "Secrets Unveiled ->",
    "max_tokens": 30,
    "model": "davinci:ft-personal-2023-06-26-01-42-07"}'
```

The given example includes several parameters and headers to specify the details of the request.

The URL specified in the command is `https://api.openai.com/v1/completions`, indicating the endpoint for the ChatGPT completion API.

The `-H` flag is used to set headers for the request. In this case, two headers are included:

- The `Content-Type` header: `application/json` specifies that the content type of the request is JSON
- The `Authorization` header: `Bearer $OPENAI_API_KEY` is an authentication header, where the `$OPENAI_API_KEY` variable should be replaced with the actual API key if we previously set it as an environmental variable

The `-d` flag is used to pass data or payload in the request. In this example, the data being passed is a JSON object enclosed in single quotes. The JSON object contains the following fields:

- `prompt`: This is the text prompt used to start the completion. In this case, it is set to `Secrets Unveiled ->`, which is the header and the separator of one of the books with which we trained our book summary fine-tuned model.
- `max_tokens`: This is the maximum number of tokens expected in the completion response. Here, it is set to 30.
- `model`: This is the name of the model to be used for completion. The example shows a fine-tuned model named `davinci:ft-personal-2023-06-26-01-42-07` being used. Here, you should place the unique name of your ChatGPT fine-tuned model.

Once the `curl` command is executed, you will receive the following response in the JSON format.

```
{
  "id": "cmpl-7Vpp9P3vv6JKZwjYbrmjSPeasxiDH",
  "object": "text_completion",
  "created": 1687821735,
  "model": "davinci:ft-personal-2023-06-26-23-07-29",
  "choices": [
    {
      "text": " An intriguing mystery that will keep you guessing until the end. A hidden truth, an unsolved puzzle, and the pursuit of truth. A gripping tale of",
      "index": 0,
      "logprobs": null,
      "finish_reason": "length"
    }
  ],
  "usage": {
    "prompt_tokens": 6,
```

```
    "completion_tokens": 30,
    "total_tokens": 36
  }
}
```

The preceding output is a standard ChatGPT response, except that here we used our fine-tuned book summary model. To verify that the model worked properly, you can compare the `text` field with the training data provided in our JSONL file for the corresponding book header prompt:

```
{"prompt":"Secrets Unveiled ->","completion":" An intriguing mystery
that will keep you guessing until the end."}
```

Comparing the two preceding code snippers, you can clearly see that our fine-tuned model has worked properly and the `completion` field from our training data is part of our ChatGPT API response in its entirety. This means that the trained model shows an improved performance incorporating the training data.

Finally, if you decide to remove or delete a fine-tuned model that you created, OpenAI provides a straightforward command that you can use. Execute the following command in your command-line interface:

```
$ openai api models.delete -i davinci:ft-personal-2023-06-26-06-55-07
```

It is important to note that deleting a fine-tuned model should be done judiciously, as it permanently removes the model and its associated data. Therefore, it is advisable to carefully consider your decision and ensure that you no longer need the fine-tuned model before proceeding with the deletion command.

In this section, we have explored the entire life cycle of fine-tuning models. Armed with this knowledge, you are now equipped to continue your journey of experimentation by constructing fine-tuned models that specialize in various tasks and incorporate a larger volume of training data entries. This opens a realm of possibilities to refine and enhance the performance of your models, enabling you to achieve even more impressive results.

Summary

In this chapter, we discussed the concept of fine-tuning within the ChatGPT API, exploring how it can help us to tailor ChatGPT API responses to our specific needs. By training a pre-existing language model on a diverse dataset, we enhanced the `davinci` model performance and adapted it to a particular task and domain. Fine-tuning enriched the model's capacity to generate accurate and contextually fitting responses by incorporating domain-specific knowledge and language patterns. Throughout the chapter, we covered several key aspects of fine-tuning, including the available models for customization, the associated costs, data preparation using JSON files, the creation of fine-tuned models via the OpenAI CLI, and the utilization of these models with the ChatGPT API. We underscored the significance of fine-tuning to achieve superior outcomes, reduce token consumption, and enable faster and more responsive interactions.

Additionally, the chapter offered a comprehensive step-by-step guide on dataset preparation for fine-tuning. It dived into the process of data organization using a JSON file and the OpenAI CLI data preparation tool. The dataset comprised prompt-completion pairs representing book summaries. The tool analyzed the data and proposed modifications, such as adding separators to prompts, eliminating unnecessary prefixes, and initiating completions with whitespace characters. These modifications enhanced the model's comprehension. Once the dataset was prepared and optimized, the chapter detailed the process of constructing and utilizing the fine-tuned model. It provided insights on initiating a fine-tuning job, monitoring its progress, and harnessing the fine-tuned model for text generation through the ChatGPT API. We emphasized the importance of fine-tuning in improving model performance and learned how to manage and delete fine-tuned models as necessary.

In this book, you embarked on a comprehensive journey into the world of ChatGPT and its API, gaining knowledge and skills to build a variety of powerful applications. You gradually built a ChatGPT clone, developed a SaaS application, integrated payment services, and explored frameworks such as Django and PyQt for web and desktop app development. You also discovered the possibilities of integration with Microsoft Word, Outlook, and PowerPoint, as well as transcribing audio files. You gained insights into selecting the right model and optimizing completions, and you even explored the realm of ChatGPT fine-tuning. With these skills, you are now well equipped to create innovative AI applications and leverage the full potential of the ChatGPT API.

Index

A

AI Presentation Generator
  finalizing 177-182
  testing 177-182
API Key
  obtaining 8-10
  URL 8
API usage
  reference link 11
application GUI
  building, with PyQt 154-159
artificial intelligence (AI) 135
artwork
  generating, with DALL-E API 175-177
automatic email replies
  contextual prompt 145
  emotion-infused prompt 145
  formal business prompt 145
  instructional prompt 145
  personalized prompt 145
auto-reloading 99
Azure Cloud
  ChatGPT App, deploying to 54-59

B

Bootstrap 28, 29
Bulma CSS framework 74

C

ChatGPT 3, 85
  advancements 5
  integrating, for quiz generation 100
  URL 5
  using, from web 5
ChatGPT 3.5 Turbo
  used, for translating Word Text 129-134
ChatGPT API Endpoints
  intercepting 33-36
ChatGPT API, models
  GPT-3 199-203
  GPT-4 198-203
ChatGPT API Response 16-20
ChatGPT APIs 8, 135
  API Key, obtaining 8-10
  integrating, with Microsoft Office 122-124
  Outlook Data, passing 136, 137
  multiple requests, performing 40, 41

parameters, using 203-208
pricing 10-12
rate limits 209-211
tokens 10-12
tokens, controlling 162-165
used, for creating essay generation methods 159-162
used, for integrating Microsoft Word Text 128
views, creating with Django 102-107
working with 8

ChatGPT Application
deploying, to Azure Cloud 54-59
payments, adding 74
payments page, building 74-80
User Payments, confirming 80-83

ChatGPT Clone
creating, with Flask 24-28

ChatGPT Clone Design
enhancing 31, 33

ChatGPT models
fine-tuning 214, 215

ChatGPT Revolution 4, 5

ChatGPT web interface 7, 8

Code Bug Fixer App
testing 51-54

Code Bug Fixer Back-End
implementing 44-46

Code Bug Fixer Project
setting up 41-43

command-line interface (CLI) 55

constructor 155

Content Delivery Network (CDN) 34

D

DALL-E 167, 168
URL 169

DALL-E API 167
art, generating with 175-177
using 168-170

Dashboard template
reference link 94

dataset preparation
for fine-tuned model 216-220

davinci 221

davinci model 199

desktop application
building, with PyQT 152, 153

Django 85
integrating, for quiz generation 100
used, for creating ChatGPT API views 102-107

Django application
connecting, views and URLs 91-93
running 98, 99
templates, developing 93-98
views, creating 91

Django Project
building 86-91

docx library 122

download quiz views
building 110-112

E

essay generation methods
creating, with ChatGPT APIs 159-162

essay generation tool project
setting up 153, 154

Exam App Frame
creating 91

F

few-shot learning 214
fine-tuned model
  building 221-225
  dataset, preparing for 216-220
  using 221-225
Flask 23
  used, for creating ChatGPT Clone 24-28
Front-End HTML Generation 28-31
f-strings 44

G

generative adversarial network (GAN) architecture 168
Generative Pre-trained Transformer (GPT) 8
Git repository 27
Google Chrome 94
gpt-3.5-turbo model 199
GPT-4 144
graphical user interface (GUI) 139

I

integrated development environment (IDE) 12, 184

J

Jinja2 template 28
jQuery 28, 74
JSON Lines format (JSON) 219
JSON object 18

L

large language models (LLMs) 4

M

messages variable 130
Microsoft Office
  ChatGPT APIs, integrating with 122-124
Microsoft Outlook 135
Microsoft Word Text
  integrating, with ChatGPT APIs 128

N

natural language processing (NLP) 3, 4, 136

O

object-relational mapping (ORM) 88
OpenAI 3
OpenAI Account
  creating 5, 6
openai package 171
OpenAI platform
  URL 8
Outlook API 135
Outlook Data
  automatic email replies, generating 143-148
  passing, to ChatGPT API 136, 137
Outlook Email
  data, accessing with win32com Client 139-143
  setting up 137-139
Outlook reply window 147

Index

P

Payments
   integrating, with Stripe 62-64
pip Package Installer 15
PowerPoint apps
   building, with PPTX Python Framework 170-175
PPTX Python Framework
   PowerPoint apps, building with 170-175
publishable keys 64
PyCharm IDE
   download link 13
   installing 12, 13
PyCharm project 136
PyDub
   using, for large audio files 191-193
PyQt
   used, for building application GUI 154-159
   used, for building desktop application 152, 153
Python
   development environment, setting up 12
   download link 12
   installing 12, 13
python-pptx package 171
Python virtual environment
   building, from Terminal 16
   setting up 13-15

Q

Qt framework 152
quiz generation
   ChatGPT, integrating 100
   Django, integrating 100
   download quiz view, building 110-112
   download template, designing 112-116
   generated quizzes, saving in SQLite database 107-110
   generated quizzes, storing and downloading 107
   submit button, building 100-102
   text area, building 100-102

R

requests package 171
Requests Per Minute (RPM) 209

S

secret key 64
secure payment form 79
SHA-256 algorithm 69
slide_generator() function 175
software-as-a-service (SaaS) 65
SQLite database
   generated quizzes, saving 107-110
SQL User Database
   Application Users, tracking 69-71
   Browser Fingerprint ID, obtaining 68, 69
   initializing 67
   one-time payment plan 65
   setting up 65, 66
   SQL Database, initializing 66
   subscription plan 65
   usage-based plan 65
   Usage Counters, implementing 71-73
Stripe API 61, 64
   used, for integrating Payments 62-64

T

Terminal
 Python virtual environment,
  building from 16
test API keys 64
 publishable keys 64
 secret key 64
 test key 64
test key 64
Text Areas and Containers
 using 46-51
text transcription
 implementing, with Whisper API 184-188
text translation
 implementing, with Whisper API 184-188
Tkinter library 123
 using, to build User Interface 125-128
tokenizer 10
 reference link 10
Tokens Per Minute (TPM) 209

U

User Interface
 building, with Tkinter library 125-128

V

voice transcriber application
 building 188-191

W

web
 ChatGPT, using from 5
Web Server Gateway Interface (WSIG) 88
Whisper API
 used, for implementing text
  transcription 184-188
 used, for implementing text
  translation 184-188
Word Text
 translating, with
  ChatGPT 3.5 Turbo 129-134

‹packt›

www.packtpub.com

Subscribe to our online digital library for full access to over 7,000 books and videos, as well as industry leading tools to help you plan your personal development and advance your career. For more information, please visit our website.

Why subscribe?

- Spend less time learning and more time coding with practical eBooks and Videos from over 4,000 industry professionals
- Improve your learning with Skill Plans built especially for you
- Get a free eBook or video every month
- Fully searchable for easy access to vital information
- Copy and paste, print, and bookmark content

Did you know that Packt offers eBook versions of every book published, with PDF and ePub files available? You can upgrade to the eBook version at packtpub.com and as a print book customer, you are entitled to a discount on the eBook copy. Get in touch with us at customercare@packtpub.com for more details.

At www.packtpub.com, you can also read a collection of free technical articles, sign up for a range of free newsletters, and receive exclusive discounts and offers on Packt books and eBooks.

Other Books You May Enjoy

If you enjoyed this book, you may be interested in these other books by Packt:

Exploring GPT-3

Steve Tingiris

ISBN: 978-1-80056-319-3

- Understand what GPT-3 is and how it can be used for various NLP tasks
- Get a high-level introduction to GPT-3 and the OpenAI API
- Implement JavaScript and Python code examples that call the OpenAI API
- Structure GPT-3 prompts and options to get the best possible results
- Select the right GPT-3 engine or model to optimize for speed and cost-efficiency
- Find out which use cases would not be suitable for GPT-3
- Create a GPT-3-powered knowledge base application that follows OpenAI guidelines

Building Data Science Applications with FastAPI - Second Edition

François Voron

ISBN: 978-1-83763-274-9

- Explore the basics of modern Python and async I/O programming
- Get to grips with basic and advanced concepts of the FastAPI framework
- Deploy a performant and reliable web backend for a data science application
- Integrate common Python data science libraries into a web backend
- Integrate an object detection algorithm into a FastAPI backend
- Build a distributed text-to-image AI system with Stable Diffusion
- Add metrics and logging and learn how to monitor them

Packt is searching for authors like you

If you're interested in becoming an author for Packt, please visit `authors.packtpub.com` and apply today. We have worked with thousands of developers and tech professionals, just like you, to help them share their insight with the global tech community. You can make a general application, apply for a specific hot topic that we are recruiting an author for, or submit your own idea.

Hi!

I am Martin Yanev, author of *Building AI Applications with ChatGPT APIs*. I really hope you enjoyed reading this book and found it useful for increasing your productivity and efficiency using ChatGPT API.

It would really help me (and other potential readers!) if you could leave a review on Amazon sharing your thoughts on this book.

Go to the link below or scan the QR code to leave your review:

`https://packt.link/r/180512756X`

Your review will help me to understand what's worked well in this book, and what could be improved upon for future editions, so it really is appreciated.

Best Wishes,

Martin Yanev

Download a free PDF copy of this book

Thanks for purchasing this book!

Do you like to read on the go but are unable to carry your print books everywhere? Is your eBook purchase not compatible with the device of your choice?

Don't worry, now with every Packt book you get a DRM-free PDF version of that book at no cost.

Read anywhere, any place, on any device. Search, copy, and paste code from your favorite technical books directly into your application.

The perks don't stop there, you can get exclusive access to discounts, newsletters, and great free content in your inbox daily

Follow these simple steps to get the benefits:

1. Scan the QR code or visit the link below

`https://packt.link/free-ebook/9781805127567`

1. Submit your proof of purchase
2. That's it! We'll send your free PDF and other benefits to your email directly